FOUNDING MYTHS

FOUNDING MYTHS

Stories That Hide Our Patriotic Past

RAY RAPHAEL

THE NEW PRESS

NEW YORK
LONDON

Published in the United States by The New Press, New York, 2004
Distributed by W. W. Norton & Company, Inc., New York

ISBN-13 978-1-56584-921-1 (hc) 978-1-59558-073-3 (pbk)
ISBN-10 1-56584-921-3 (hc) 1-59558-073-5 (pbk)
CIP data available.

The New Press was established in 1990 as a not-for-profit alternative to the large, commercial publishing houses currently dominating the book publishing industry. The New Press operates in the public interest rather than for private gain, and is committed to publishing, in innovative ways, works of educational, cultural, and community value that are often deemed insufficiently profitable.

www.thenewpress.com

Composition by dix!

Printed in the United States of America

10   9   8   7   6   5   4   3   2   1

To my family—Marie, Neil, Kelli, Maia,
and a host of Guillemins, Raphaels, Ridley-McKennas, and
Evensons—and to Nick, who lives in our hearts.

"Who shall write the history of the American Revolution? Who can write it? Who will ever be able to write it?"

—John Adams to Thomas McKean,
July 30, 1815

CONTENTS

ACKNOWLEDGMENTS

As usual, I thank my wife, Marie Raphael, for sharing her ideas, conjuring key phrases, and editing portions of the manuscript. Gilles Carter gave the entire work a careful reading and offered many useful suggestions. Marc Favreau and Cathy Dexter gave excellent editorial assistance. Anthony Arnove, Jeff Pasley, Howard Zinn, and Hugh Van Dusen nurtured the idea in its formative stages, and Jeff Kleinman persuaded me to broaden the scope. Several scholars commented on portions of the manuscript pertaining to their fields of research: Al Young, Pauline Maier, Gary Nash, Colin Calloway, James Merrell, Andrew Burstein, and Cassandra Pybus. I hope I have done justice to their suggestions; my own views are not always the same as theirs. Others gave friendly words of advice or encouragement: Mike McDonnell, Eric Foner, David Hackett Fischer, and Gary Kornblith. David McCullough provided a key reference. Gilles Carter helped locate and identify pictures, as did Jessica Reed from the Granger Collection, while John Angus put the art work together. I thank Jack Bareilles, Gayle Olson-Raymer, and Delores McBroome for involving teachers in the project, and I thank those in the "Teaching American History" program who volunteered their time to prepare lesson plans. Once again, my research would not have been possible without assistance from Julia Graham and the Interlibrary Loan Department of Humboldt State University.

FOUNDING MYTHS

"Let the world admire our patriots and heroes."

Washington Crossing the Delaware.
Engraving based on painting by Emanuel Leutze, 1851.

INTRODUCTION:
INVENTING A PAST

W hen settlers from across the Atlantic arrived on the east coast of
North America, they felt they were on uncharted territory.
From the Old World they imported the traditions that defined them as
a people, since the New World, which they treated as a blank slate, appeared to have no history of its own.

Slowly, over more than a century and a half, colonists developed
local, homegrown histories. These remained separate and distinct
until suddenly, with one cataclysmic event, they merged. The Revolutionary War provided Americans with shared stories of a common
past. This past, ever since, has served the interest of nation building.
For more than two centuries, the oft-repeated story of how the United
States achieved its independence has bound Americans together.

All nations like to celebrate their origins, but the birth of our nation
makes a particularly compelling story. The United States has a clearly
defined "founding," the work of a single generation. Most nations are
not so fortunate. The story of Britain's founding would have to cover
centuries and include the Norman invasion (1066), the Magna Carta
(1215), the Glorious Revolution (1688), and the Act of Union (1707).
China's founding would include the rise of ancient dynasties, the
Nationalist Revolution in 1911, and the Communist Revolution in

1949—too much to tell in a simple story. Mexico has only two founding moments, independence in 1821 and revolution in the early twentieth century, but these were separated by ninety years. Canada eased into nationhood so gracefully that it hardly has a story to tell.

Our story, by contrast, is simple yet grand. Its plotline is easy to follow: American colonists resisted British oppression, fought a war, achieved independence, and established their own government. Within this straightforward structure we can embellish as we please, but the storyline itself is clean and efficient. It gets the job done. It establishes a separate identity for the American people.

How we choose to tell this story helps define our nation. Daily, politicians invoke "our founders" in support of some cause totally foreign to the American experience of the late eighteenth century. They place the past—more precisely, a past they imagine—in service of a political present.

Stories of the American Revolution were first communicated by word of mouth, and these folkloric renditions, infinitely malleable, provided fertile grounds for the invention of history. Before the Revolution, angry and animated colonists gathered in taverns and meeting houses to rail against acts of Parliament; after the fighting was done, this same crew downed pint after pint of hard cider while exchanging old war stories. For decades, men and women of the early republic told and retold what had happened, augmenting and enriching their skeletal memories of actual events, removing what was too painful to recall (no shortage there) while embellishing what could be seen as heroic (no shortage there either). At funerals or Fourth of July celebrations, orators used tales of the Revolution as grist for their rhetoric. While audiences applauded and critics ranked their performances, these civic preachers competed in the art and sport of patriotic expression. This vibrant oral tradition helped produce a history that was detailed but unfettered. Divested of any need for documentation, it went freely wherever it wanted.

The visual arts, like the oral tradition, gave the past a place in the present. During and after the Revolution, engravings and lithographs depicted the major events to popular audiences. More pliable than photography, these artistic forms allowed for leeway in interpretation. In the early nineteenth century, grandiose Romantic paintings offered indelible images of battles and key political proceedings. Subsequent generations, viewing reproductions in popular histories and textbooks, used these images to help shape a collective "memory" of the Revolution. Set to canvas long after the war had ended, they became national icons. Today, the two most dominant visual reflections of the American Revolution are John Trumbull's 1818 painting, *The Declaration of Independence, 4 July 1776*, and Emmanuel Leutze's 1851 masterpiece, *Washington Crossing the Delaware*—even though there was no ceremonial signing of the Declaration on July 4, and the flag displayed prominently in Washington's boat had not yet been created.

Oral tradition and artistic imagination filled in the blanks left by incomplete and selective documentation. Although a handful of exceptionally literate men bequeathed volume after volume of declarations, letters, diaries, and memoirs, these writings emanated from a very small segment of the population, unrepresentative of the whole. Many of these first-person accounts were set to paper decades after the fact. Because of skewed sampling, personal bias, and the effects of time on memory, they cannot always be accepted at face value.

Selective written sources, rich but loose oral and visual traditions, and the intrusion of politics and ideology—these have presented open invitations to the historical imagination. Creatively, if not accurately, we have fashioned a past we would like to have had.

Fiction parted from fact at the very beginning. Shortly after the Revolutionary War, Charles Thomson, secretary of the Continental Congress, embarked on writing a history of the conflict. Privy to insider information, Thomson had much to reveal—but then, surprisingly, he gave the history up. "I shall not undeceive future generations," he later explained. "I could not tell the truth without giving great offense. Let the world admire our patriots and heroes." [1]

Since people like Mr. Thomson chose not to tell the truth, what might they tell instead? In 1790 Noah Webster provided an answer:

"Every child in America," said the dean of the Anglo-American language, "as soon as he opens his lips, . . . should rehearse the history of his country; he should lisp the praise of Liberty and of those illustrious heroes and statesmen who have wrought a revolution in his favor."[2]

So the romance began. Starting in the decades following the Revolution and continuing through much of the nineteenth century, writers and orators concealed the naked truth of a bloody civil war behind glamorous tales conjured from mere shreds of evidence. We still tell these classics today—Paul Revere's ride, "Give me liberty or give me death," the shot heard 'round the world at Lexington and Concord—and we assume they are true representations of actual occurrences. Mere frequency of repetition appears to confirm their authenticity.

Our confidence is misplaced. In fact, most of the stories were created up to one hundred years after the events they supposedly depict. Paul Revere was known only in local circles until 1861, when Henry Wadsworth Longfellow made him immortal by distorting every detail of his now-famous ride. Patrick Henry's "liberty or death" speech first appeared in print, under mysterious circumstances, in 1817, forty-two years after he supposedly uttered those words. The "shot heard 'round the world" did not become known by that name until 1836, sixty-one years after it was fired.

The list goes on. Sam Adams, our most beloved rabble-rouser, languished in obscurity through the first half of the nineteenth century, only to be resurrected as the mastermind of the Revolution three-quarters of a century after the fact. Thomas Jefferson was not widely seen as the architect of American "equality" until Abraham Lincoln assigned him that role, four score and seven years later. The winter at Valley Forge remained uncelebrated for thirty years. Textbooks did not begin featuring "Do not fire until you see the whites of their eyes" until after the Civil War. Molly Pitcher, the Revolutionary heroine whose picture adorns most elementary and middle-school textbooks today, is a complete fabrication. Her legend did not settle on a specific, historic individual until the nation's centennial celebration in 1876.

These stories, invented long ago, persist in our textbooks and popular histories despite advances in recent scholarship that disprove their authenticity. One popular schoolbook includes all but two of the tales exposed in this book, and several of the stories, still taken as gospel, are featured in all modern texts.[3]

Why do we cling to these yarns? There are three reasons, thoroughly intertwined: they give us a collective identity, they make good stories, and we think they are patriotic.

We like to hear stories of our nation's beginnings because they help define us as a people. Americans have always used the word "we," highlighting a shared sense of the past. Likewise, this book uses the first person plural when referring to commonly held beliefs. This usage is more than just a linguistic convenience—it pinpoints actual cognitive habits. *We* are history's protagonists. Few Americans read about the Revolutionary War or World War II without identifying with *our* side. George Washington, we are told in myriad ways, is the father of *our* country, whether our forebears came from England, Poland, or Vietnam.[4]

Like rumors, the tales are too good *not* to be told. They are carefully crafted to fit a time-tested mold. Successful stories feature heroes or heroines, clear plotlines, and happy endings. Good does battle against evil, David beats Goliath, and wise men prevail over fools. Stories of our nation's founding mesh well with these narrative forms. American revolutionaries, they say, were better and wiser than decadent Europeans. Outnumbered colonists overcame a Goliath, the mightiest empire on earth. Good prevailed over evil, and the war ended happily with the birth of the United States. Even if they don't tell true history, these imaginings work as stories. Much of what we think of as "history" is driven not by facts but by these narrative demands.

This invented past, anointed as "patriotic," paints a flattering self-portrait of our nation. We pose before the mirror in our finest attire. By gazing upon the Revolution's gallant heroes, we celebrate what we think it means to be an American. We make our country perfect—if not now, at least in the mythic past—and through the comforting thought of an ideal America, we fix our bearings. We feel more secure in the confused and changing world of today if we can draw upon an honored tradition.

But is this really "patriotism"? Only from a narrow and outdated perspective can we see it that way. While it espouses good citizenship, our invented past leads in quite the opposite direction. Nominally, it encourages us to act heroically, but in fact, it takes away our power. It belittles popular sovereignty, the revolutionary spirit that propelled Americans to independence. It leaves us in awe of superhuman stars. It encourages us to follow leaders who ostensibly know more than we do. It discourages ordinary citizens from acting in their own behalf. It promotes a passive nostalgia for an irretrievable past. It touts militarism and glorifies war.

Perhaps if we examine more closely who we were, who we are, and who we want to be, we can do better than this. We do not have to be confined to such a limiting self-portrait. Our nation was a collaborative creation, the work of hundreds of thousands of dedicated patriots—yet we exclude most of these people from history by repeating the traditional tales.[5] Worse yet, we distort the very nature of their monumental project. The United States was founded not by isolated acts of individual heroism but by the concerted revolutionary activities of people who had learned the power of working together. This rich and very democratic heritage remains untapped precisely because its story is too big, not too small. It transcends the artificial constraints of traditional storytelling. Its heroes are too many to contain, and its patriotism is too strong, too real, to be reduced to simple morality tales. This sprawling story needs to be told—but our invented past, neat and tidy, has hidden it from view.

Our stories of national creation reflect the romantic individualism of the nineteenth century, and they sell our country short. They are strangely out of sync with both the communitarian ideals of Revolutionary America and the democratic values of today. The image of a perfect America in a mythic past hides our Revolutionary roots, and this we do not need.

The notion of popular sovereignty, by contrast, is more appropriate for the twenty-first century. People can seize control of their own political destinies—the American Revolution serves as a case in point, a model for all time. "Government has now devolved upon the people," wrote one disgruntled Tory in 1774, "and they seem to be for using it." [6] That's a story we do not have to conjure, and what an epic it is.

HEROES AND HEROINES

"The fate of a nation was riding that night."

Paul Revere's Ride. Drawing by Charles G. Bush,
Harper's Weekly, June 29, 1867.

1

PAUL REVERE'S RIDE

In 1860, with the approach of the Civil War, Americans who supported the preservation of the Union were in the market for a new Revolutionary hero. Earlier, at the turn of the nineteenth century, patriotic writers like Mason Weems had helped unify the nation by deifying George Washington (see conclusion), but with Americans deeply divided over the issue of slavery, Washington's credentials were suspect. True, he was the undisputed Father of the Country, but he had owned hundreds of slaves. Southern secessionists, even as they threatened to destroy the Union, could rightfully claim him as their own and gain from his prestige.[1] Washington's slave ownership threatened to divide the people further, not pull them together. Americans hoping to heal their nation through an appeal to tradition would have to look elsewhere.

On April 5, while walking past Boston's Old North Church, Henry Wadsworth Longfellow heard a folkloric rendition of Paul Revere's midnight ride from a friend, George Sumner. The story stirred him, and the next day, with America's destiny hanging in the balance, he began setting thoughts to paper.[2] Longfellow gained inspiration from the dramatic opening to the American Revolution, when "the fate of the nation" (as he would soon write) seemed to hinge on a single courageous act. For Longfellow, Revere was a timely hero: a lonely rider who issued a wake-up call. If Revere had roused the nation once, perhaps he could do it again, this time riding the rhythmic beat of Longfellow's verse:

> So through the night rode Paul Revere;
> And so through the night went his cry of alarm
> To every Middlesex village and farm,
> A voice in the darkness, a knock at the door,
> And a word that shall echo forevermore!
> For, borne on the night-wind of the Past,
> Through all our history, to the last,
> In the hour of darkness and peril and need,
> The people will waken and listen to hear
> The hurrying hoof-beats of that steed,
> And the midnight message of Paul Revere.[3]

In close replication of Revere's own effort, Longfellow passed word of the ride to every household on America's highways and byways, issuing his alarm, line by line, as he distorted every detail of the actual deed. In the process he made Paul Revere.

Longfellow himself made history in two ways: he conjured events that never happened, and he established a new patriotic ritual. For a century to follow, nearly every schoolchild in the United States would hear or recite "Paul Revere's Ride." In their history texts, students read pared-down prose renditions of Longfellow's tale, the meter gone but distortions still intact. Even today, one line remains in our popular lexicon, known to those who have never read or heard the entire piece: "One, if by land, and two, if by sea." These words, all by themselves, call forth the entire story, and Paul Revere's ride remains the best-known heroic exploit of the American Revolution.

THE EARLY YEARS

Before Longfellow, Paul Revere was not regarded as a central player in the Revolutionary saga. He was known for his engravings (especially his depiction of the Boston Massacre), for his work as a silversmith, and for his political activities in prewar Boston. John Singleton Copley painted his portrait, which showed Revere displaying his silver work—but that was several years *before* the midnight ride.[4] Locally, Revere was also remembered as a patriotic man who climbed on a horse and rode off with a warning—but similar feats had been performed by countless others during the Revolutionary War. Although Revere was certainly respected for the various roles he played, he wasn't exactly celebrated. Schoolbooks made no mention of Revere or his derring-do.

Shortly after the fact, Paul Revere offered his own rendition of the ride that would someday make him famous. Three days after British Regulars marched on Lexington and Concord, the Massachusetts Provincial Congress authorized the collection of firsthand reports from those who were participants or observers.[5] Paul Revere came forward to tell what he knew.

Revere's version—in simple prose, not verse—differed considerably from Longfellow's. At about 10 o'clock on the evening of April 18, 1775, Revere stated in his deposition, Dr. Joseph Warren requested that he ride to Lexington with a message for Samuel Adams and John Hancock: "a number of Soldiers" appeared to be headed their way. Revere set out immediately. He was "put across" the Charles River to Charlestown, where he "got a Horse." After being warned that nine British officers had been spotted along the road, he set off toward Lexington. Before he even left Charlestown, he caught sight of two, whom he was able to avoid. "I proceeded to Lexington, thro Mistick," Revere stated flatly, "and alarmed Mr. Adams and Col. Hancock."

That was it—Revere devoted only one short sentence to the ride that would later make him so famous. Additions were to come later. Nowhere in his statement did Revere mention the lantern signals from the Old North Church, a matter that seemed more trivial to him than it did to Longfellow. On the other hand, Revere did include much concrete information that Longfellow would later suppress, such as the fact that Dr. Warren sent a second messenger, a "Mr. Daws" (William Dawes), along an alternate route.

For Revere, the night featured a harrowing experience that Longfellow, for reasons of his own, saw fit to overlook. After giving his message to Adams and Hancock, Revere and two others set out toward Concord to warn the people there—but he did not get very far before being captured by British officers. For most of the deposition, Revere talked of this capture, of how the officers had threatened to kill him five times, three times promising to "blow your brains out." Though he had carried messages from town to town many times before, Revere had never encountered such serious danger.[6] For him, this was the main event of the story.

Revere's ordeal ended without personal calamity. After taking his horse, the officers released him. On foot, Revere retreated to Lexington, where he heard the first round of fire. Perhaps because he did not state point-blank that the British had fired first, the Provincial Congress thought Revere's testimony was of little consequence, and they chose not to include it in their official report, *A Narrative of the Excursion and Ravages of the King's Troops.*

Seeming to concur with the judgment of the Congress, others granted Revere no more than a place on history's sidelines. William Gordon, the early historian who conducted his own on-site interviews in the weeks to follow, did not feature Paul Revere's ride in his detailed account of the events of Lexington and Concord. "Expresses were forwarded to alarm the country, some of whom were secured by the officers on the road"—that was all he bothered to say.[7] Gordon expanded his treatment in the full-length history he published thirteen years later, but he still made no mention of any heroic exploits by Paul Revere:

Dr. Warren, by mere accident, had notice of it [the British mobilization] just in time to send messengers over the neck and across the ferry, on to Lexington, before the orders for preventing every person's quitting the town were executed. The officers intercepted several, but some being well mounted, escaped their vigilance; and the alarm, being once given, spread apace, by the ringing of bells, and the firing of signal guns and vollies.[8]

All the early historians of the Revolution agreed: Revere was not a major player in the outbreak of hostilities. David Ramsay, writing in 1789, said only that "intelligence" was "sent to the country militia, of what was going on."[9] John Marshall (1804) mentioned Warren but not Revere: "The country was alarmed by messengers sent out by Doctor Warren, some of whom eluded the vigilance of the patrols."[10] Mercy Otis Warren (1805) wrote simply that "a report reached the neighboring towns very early."[11] For the four most prominent contemporary historians, the transport of a message from Dr. Warren to Samuel Adams and John Hancock appeared of less lasting import than nearly everything else that happened during the historic events of April 18 and 19, 1775.

Although Paul Revere's ride was a nonstarter in the early histories, Revere's friends, neighbors, and fellow Freemasons knew of it and praised it. Joshua Fowle, who grew up near Revere in post-Revolutionary Boston, had heard of the signal lanterns and the midnight ride in his youth: "I have heard it told over many times and never doubted," he later recalled. "It was common talk."[12] Early on, though neglected by formal history, the tale was germinating in folklore, and in 1795, a poet who signed his name "Eb. Stiles" set forth a doggerel prototype:

> He raced his steed through field and wood
> Nor turned to ford the river,
> But faced his horse to the foaming flood
> They swam across together.
>
> He madly dashed o'er mountain and moor,
> Never slackened spur nor rein

Until with shout he stood by the door
Of the Church on Concord green.[13]

In Stiles's poem the story took on a life of its own, richly decorated by nonexistent mountains and moors and foaming flood. Finally, twenty years after the fact, Stiles enabled Revere to reach "the Church on Concord green"—a destination that eluded him on April 19, 1775.

Perhaps in response to this emerging folklore, Jeremy Belknap, corresponding secretary for the Massachusetts Historical Society, asked Revere to provide a detailed account of his ride. Revere obliged, but he signed his paper "A Son of Liberty of the year 1775," and then added "do not print my name." When Belknap published the piece in the society's *Collections,* dated January 1, 1798, he contradicted Revere's wish and set his name in print.

In this account, delivered nearly a quarter of a century after his initial deposition, Revere abridged the once traumatic saga of his capture but included the story of the signal lanterns, perhaps by popular request. Revere also wrote at length about Benjamin Church's alleged treachery, unknown at the time of his original deposition.[14] Since Revere's new account, like its predecessor, was undoubtedly less dramatic than folkloric renditions, it might actually have slowed the growth of the incipient legend.

When Revere died in 1818, his obituary in the *Boston Intelligencer and Weekly Gazette* made no mention of his midnight ride.[15] Still, local history enthusiasts kept the memory alive. Through midcentury, reports of his ride emerged and reemerged. On the fiftieth anniversary of the opening battles of the Revolutionary War, William Munroe, who had guarded the house where Adams and Hancock were staying, cited Paul Revere's role: "I told him the family had just retired, and had requested, that they might not be disturbed by any noise about the house. 'Noise!' said he, 'you'll have noise enough before long. The British are coming out.' "[16] In 1849 Richard Frothingham published the first comprehensive account of the warning of the countryside, and he included Paul Revere's role. Basing his report on depositions by Revere and other participants, Frothingham demonstrated that at least four different couriers had been sent to Lexington on the evening of April 18, including Paul Revere, and three of these had delivered their messages.[17]

With the facts laid out, Revere's story inched its way into the core narrative of the Revolution. In his 1851 *Pictorial Field-Book of the Revolution*, Benson Lossing mentioned both Paul Revere and William Dawes by name, and he included William Munroe's anecdote.[18] In 1854 George Bancroft gave a fairly accurate rendering of the story: both Revere and Dawes delivered their messages to Lexington, he said, but only Samuel Prescott was able to elude the British officers and deliver the warning to Concord.[19]

Although the story was beginning to receive attention beyond local boundaries, it was still only one of many. Three-quarters of a century after his ride, Paul Revere had not yet become a household name— and with good reason. Revere did not distinguish himself as a military hero. He was not a famous statesmen—in fact, he was not even one of the signers of the Declaration of Independence. He delivered no memorable speeches, he swayed no crowds, he made no public pronouncements of lasting significance. In the 1850s, there was no reason to suspect that Paul Revere was about to be initiated into the pantheon of Revolutionary heroes—one of the five or ten most celebrated figures of his generation.

Still, Revere had found an appropriate niche in the annals of history. Writers during this period treated history as a series of anecdotes—distinct moments that made the past come alive—and the story of the midnight ride fit right in.[20] Between them, Lossing and Bancroft relayed literally thousands of such tales, isolated moments featuring individual deeds in service of the Revolution.[21] That's where Paul Revere's ride might stand today—just one short scene in a giant epic—had Henry Wadsworth Longfellow not discovered the Revolutionary bit player and cast him in a leading role.

POETIC LICENSE

Longfellow's "Paul Revere's Ride" first appeared in the January 1861 issue of the *Atlantic*. The poem opened with an endearing invocation:

> Listen, my children, and you shall hear
> Of the midnight ride of Paul Revere. . . .

Then, in the galloping cadence of anapestic tetrameter—two slow beats followed by one long, repeated four times—Longfellow created an unforgettable tale that appealed to adults and children alike. Even in those days, nothing could thrill an audience more than an exciting chase:

> A hurry of hoofs in a village street,
> A shape in the moonlight, a bulk in the dark,
> And beneath, from the pebbles, in passing, a spark
> Struck out by a steed flying fearless and fleet;
> That was all! And yet, through the gloom and the light,
> The fate of a nation was riding that night;
> And the spark struck out by that steed, in his flight,
> Kindled the land into flame with its heat.

For Longfellow, one man alone held "the fate of the nation" in his hands. The notion that an individual hero could generate a "spark" that would "kindle the land into flame" was central to the worldview of nineteenth-century Romanticism. It also conformed to the formula for successful narratives. A storyteller par excellence, Longfellow naturally emphasized the motive force of individual action.[22]

Although "Paul Revere's Ride" has enjoyed more exposure than any other historic poem in American culture, it is riddled with distortions. These are not incidental—they are the very reasons the story has endured for almost a century and a half. Four historical misrepresentations are particularly significant:

(1) Strangely, in 130 lines, Longfellow says not a word about the detention by British officers, the major focus of Paul Revere's own tale. That would reveal a British presence in the vicinity of Lexington and Concord—what need then for a messenger? For the story to work, all British soldiers have to be stationed to the rear of Revere and his horse. "The Redcoats are coming" loses its dramatic effect if we know that some Redcoats have already arrived.

(2) To achieve maximum effect, Longfellow has Revere visit "every Middlesex village and farm." Although some allowance can be made for hyperbole, Longfellow certainly knew that his protagonist never reached Concord, the destination of the British troops and the town most in need of warning. The real Revere had tried and failed to get that far. Understandably, Longfellow did not wish to burden his story with the sober realization that the hero had been prevented from achieving his final objective.

(3) Longfellow's Revere works both ends of the signal lantern ploy, which accounts for more than half the poem. Before crossing the Charles River, Revere tells a "friend" how to work the signal; then, after arriving on the opposite shore, Revere waits to receive it, "impatient to mount and ride." For sixteen lines Revere pats his horse, gazes across the landscape, and stamps the earth, fretfully passing the time until he finally spots two lights. In reality this is not what happened. We do not know who waited to receive the signal on the opposite shore, but we do know it was not Paul Revere. After being dispatched by Joseph Warren, but before crossing the river, Revere himself arranged for two lanterns to be lit—so that someone else might see them in Charlestown and set off to warn other patriots. Someone *else?* Again, facts had to be altered to accommodate the story. There could be no other rider in "Paul Revere's Ride."

(4) Except for two bit players—his horse and the friend who lit

the lanterns—Longfellow's Revere acted alone. In fact, there were many others. In 1994 historian David Hackett Fischer reconstructed the event with a full cast of characters, including:

- A stable boy, a hostler, and at least two other Bostonians who sent word to Revere that British soldiers were readying for an offensive.
- Someone within General Gage's closest circle (possibly his own wife, Margaret Kemble Gage) who informed Dr. Joseph Warren of the offensive.
- Dr. Warren, who, on behalf of the Boston Committee, asked Revere to deliver a warning to Samuel Adams and John Hancock.
- William Dawes, who carried the same message by a different route, also at the request of Joseph Warren.
- Three different "friends" who engineered the clandestine lighting of the signal lanterns: John Pulling, Robert Newman, and Thomas Bernard.
- Two boatmen who rowed Revere across the Charles River.
- Colonel Conant and other patriots from Charlestown, who waited patiently to receive the lantern signal they had arranged with Revere two days earlier.
- An unidentified messenger who was dispatched from Charlestown as soon as the signal from the lanterns was received. (Since this messenger never reached either Lexington or Concord, the entire signal lantern subplot did not lead to a successful conclusion.)
- Richard Devens of Charlestown, who greeted Revere by the river's shore and warned him that British officers were patrolling the road to Lexington and Concord.
- Devens, Abraham Watson, Elbridge Gerry, Charles Lee, and Azor Orne, members of the Provincial Committee of Safety, who sent a note to Hancock in Lex-

ington, warning him that British officers were headed
his way.

- An anonymous courier who successfully delivered this
  message at about 8:00 in the evening, three hours before
  Revere would mount his horse.

- The innkeeper at the Black Horse Tavern in Menotomy
  (now Arlington), who later that night warned Gerry, Lee,
  and Orne that British troops had arrived, enabling them
  to escape out the back door.

- Solomon Brown of Lexington, who warned William
  Munroe, a sergeant in the town militia, that British officers were headed toward Lexington, and who later tried
  to alert the people of Concord to the presence of the officers, but was soon captured.

- Munroe and eight other militiamen, who stood guard
  through the night at the house of Jonas Clarke, the
  Lexington minister, where Adams and Hancock were
  staying.

- Thirty other Lexington militiamen, who gathered at
  Buckman's Tavern to deal with the crisis at 9:00 P.M., two
  hours prior to Revere's departure on his famous ride.

- Elijah Sanderson and Jonathan Loring of the Lexington
  militia, who volunteered to keep a watch on the British
  officers.

- Josiah Nelson, a farmer who resided on the road to Concord, who had his head slashed by the sword of one of the
  British officers, then alerted all his neighbors.

- John Larkin of Charlestown, who lent Revere a horse
  that belonged to his father, Samuel.

- Another unidentified messenger from Charlestown who
  set off at the same time as Revere, heading north. This
  rider reached Tewksbury, twenty-five miles from Boston,
  at about the time Revere himself was taken captive by the
  British officers.

- Captain John Trull of Tewksbury, who, upon receiving news from the Charlestown rider, fired three shots from his bedroom window—a signal that lacked the finesse of the lanterns in Old North Church but that had a greater impact. The militia commander in Dracut, on the New Hampshire boundary, heard the shots and mustered his militia—several hours before the bloody dawn at Lexington.
- Samuel Tufts of East Cambridge, who embarked on a ride of his own after his neighbor, Elizabeth Rand, told him she had spotted the British column.
- Solomon Bowman, lieutenant of the Menotomy militia, who immediately mustered his town's company after viewing the British soldiers.
- Isaac Hull, captain of the Medford militia, who received word from Revere, then mustered his company.
- Dr. Martin Herrick, who left Medford to alarm Stoneham, Reading, and Lynn. These towns, in turn, sent out their own riders; by dawn, the entire North Shore of Massachusetts Bay was aroused and in the process of mustering.
- Another messenger from Medford, who headed east to Malden, and from there to Chelsea.
- Yet another messenger from Medford, who journeyed to Woburn, and still another from Woburn to the parish above it, now Burlington, and so on, ad infinitum, until almost every "Middlesex village and farm" had been warned by a vast network of messengers and signals—all in the wee hours of the morning on April 19, 1775.
- Finally, Samuel Prescott, a doctor from Concord, who managed to get the message to the people of his hometown that hundreds of British troops were coming their way to seize their military stores. Although Revere, Dawes, and Prescott had all been captured on the road

between Lexington and Concord, Prescott alone staged a successful escape and completed the mission.[23]

Paul Revere was not so alone after all. When the main British column approached Lexington, bells and signal shots echoed from front and rear. The entire countryside was aroused and ready. This wasn't the work of one man but of an intricate web of patriotic activists who had been communicating with each other for years. Ever since the overthrow of British authority late in the summer of 1774 (see chapter 4), they had prepared for military confrontation. Anticipating just such an event as the battle at Lexington and Concord, they had rehearsed it. Each man within each town knew whom to contact and where to go once the time came—and now the time had come. Like Paul Revere, myriad patriots sounded their local alarms and readied themselves for action.

AN ENDURING TALE

Facts matter little when a good story is at stake. From the time of its first publication, "Paul Revere's Ride" was a national classic, and readers assumed it signified actual events. Schoolbooks confidently reiterated Longfellow's distortions. According to a 1888 text, *A History of the United States and Its People, for the Use of Schools,* Revere "waited at Charlestown until he saw a light hung in a church-steeple, which was a signal to him that the British were moving." It dutifully cited a source, referring students to "Longfellow's famous poem on the subject."[24] Although some texts noted that the poem was "not strictly historical," others blithely accepted Longfellow's altered plotline. A 1923 text, *History of Our Country, for Higher Grades,* stated fancifully, "On that night there was at Charlestown, across the river from Boston, an American of Huguenot descent holding a horse by the bridle, while he watched for a lantern signal from a church tower. His name was Paul Revere, and he is known as 'the courier of the Revolution.'"[25] Texts in 1935 and 1946 also had Revere waiting for the

lantern signal—accompanied for a change by William Dawes, who in
fact never went through Charlestown.[26]

Fiction, in conscientious hands, often follows history, but here history unquestionably followed fiction. Even serious scholars fell into
line behind the poet. In 1891 John Fiske, one of the most prominent
historians of his generation, told how Paul Revere crossed "the broad
river in a little boat," then waited "on the farther bank until he
learned, from a lantern suspended in the belfry of the North Church,
which way the troops had gone." [27]

Starting in the 1920s, iconoclastic "debunkers" poked fun at
Longfellow's Revere. William Dawes, one of the other riders, en-
joyed something of a renaissance when his descendent, Charles
Dawes, became vice president of the United States under Calvin
Coolidge. Traditionalists fought back: in 1922 an army captain, E. B.
Lyon, dropped patriotic pamphlets from a military aircraft, which fol-
lowed the trail of Paul Revere's ride.[28]

The most serious challenge came not from debunkers or Progressive historians, however, but from Progressive educators, who opposed rote memorization. But as recitations of Longfellow's poem
began to fade from the standard curricula, Esther Forbes breathed
new life into the Revere story with her Pulitzer Prize–winning *Paul
Revere and the World He Lived In*. Resuscitated, her Revere is a simple
artisan who leads an everyday life. Although Forbes used Revere to
celebrate the common man, she reiterated the traditional view that
Revere served as the "lone horseman" who saved the day for the
patriots.[29]

Not until 1994 were Longfellow's errors laid to rest in David Hackett Fischer's *Paul Revere's Ride*, a masterful work of historical detec-
tion that has influenced the writing of textbooks. No longer is Revere
portrayed as the lonely messenger who rowed himself across the
river, waited to receive the lantern signals, and alerted the countryside
all by himself. (One notable exception is Joy Hakim's *A History of
US*, which still follows Longfellow word for word.)[30] Others were involved, most texts now say—but they don't say it very forcefully.

"Paul Revere, a member of the Sons of Liberty, rode his horse to Lexington to warn Hancock and Adams," says one text—then, almost as an afterthought, it adds, "Revere was joined by William Dawes and Samuel Prescott." [31] The visual accompaniment, of course, features a statue of Revere, not Dawes or Prescott. According to another, "*Paul Revere*, a Boston silversmith, and a second messenger, William Dawes, were charged with spreading the news about British troop movements. . . . When the British moved, so did Revere and Dawes. They galloped over the countryside on their 'midnight ride,' spreading the news." [32] In these watered-down versions one rider has turned into two or three. The romance is gone, yet there is no hint of the elaborate web of communication that was activated on that momentous night.

Significantly, all current United States history textbooks at the elementary, middle school, and secondary levels still include the story of Paul Revere's ride. (This includes advanced texts that undertake no more than a cursory review of the American Revolution.)[33] The tale itself has become part of our heritage, and no history of our nation's beginnings would dare ignore it.

The story of "Paul Revere's ride" needs not only correction but perspective. One hundred twenty-two people lost their lives within hours of Revere's heroics, and almost twice that number were wounded.[34] Revere's ride was not the major event that day, nor was Revere's warning so critical in triggering the bloodbath. Patriotic farmers had been preparing to oppose the British for the better part of a year. Paul Revere himself had contributed to those preparations with other important rides. The previous September he traveled from Boston to Philadelphia, bearing news that the Massachusetts countryside had erupted in rebellion; the First Continental Congress, after hearing from Revere, offered its stamp of approval. The previous December, four months before the shots at Lexington, he instigated the first military offensive of the Revolution by riding to Portsmouth, New Hampshire. His ride to Lexington continued this tradition, but, as in the previous rides, it took on meaning only because numerous other political activists had, like Revere, dedicated themselves to the cause.

Paul Revere was one among tens of thousands of patriots from Massachusetts who rose to fight the British. Most of those people lived outside of Boston, and, contrary to the traditional telling, these people were not country cousins to their urban counterparts. They were rebels in their own right, although their story is rarely told. We have neglected them, in part, because Paul Revere's ride has achieved such fame; one man from Boston, the story goes, roused the sleeping farmers, and only then did farmers see the danger and fight back.

In truth, the country folk had aroused themselves, and they had even staged their own Revolution more than half a year before. (See chapter 4.) The story of Paul Revere's ride marks the end, not the beginning, of that inspiring tale. It bridges the gap between two momentous events: the political upheaval that unseated British authority in 1774 and the outbreak of formal hostilities on April 19, 1775. But ironically, in its romanticized form, the tale has helped obscure the revolution of the people that was going on both before and after. The true story of patriotic resistance is deeper and richer than Henry Wadsworth Longfellow, with his emphasis on individual heroics, ever dared to imagine.

2

MOLLY PITCHER

How nice it would be to discover a true heroine of the American Revolution. We have tried Betsy Ross, the woman who supposedly made the first American flag, but that story is now discredited.[1] We honor Abigail Adams, who cajoled her husband to "Remember the Ladies," but Abigail enters the story as the wife of a famous man, and she never went near a battlefield.[2] We would like to celebrate Deborah Sampson, who dressed as a man to enlist in the army, but if truth be told, some female soldiers were unjustly drummed out to the "whore's march" once their identity was uncovered.[3]

Our preferred heroine, if we could find her, would have braved enemy fire in a famous battle—dressed as a woman, not a man. This is not too much to imagine. Try to picture, for instance, the Battle of Monmouth, where men are suffering from the heat as well as from enemy fire. A woman passes through the thirsty and wounded troops with a pitcher of nice, cold water. Perhaps, when her husband falls while manning a cannon, our heroine takes his place and continues to fire his weapon. This, of course, inspires the rest of the soldiers to continue fighting in the face of mortal danger. In the end, after the battle is over, George Washington naturally bestows a medal on our lady warrior—perhaps even making her an officer.

"Her cannon must be fired!"

Molly Pitcher, Heroine at Monmouth.
Lithograph by Currier and Ives, 1876.

This is the heroine we would like to celebrate—and we do. We have not only dreamed up such a tale, but we have convinced ourselves it is true. Although it would have shocked all her contemporaries, a current middle-school textbook pronounces point-blank that Mary Ludwig Hays McCauly, a poor "camp follower" from Carlisle, Pennsylvania, was the "best known" woman to serve on Revolutionary War battlefields.[4] Another text tells her story: "Mary Ludwig Hays McCauly took her husband's place at a cannon when he was wounded at the Battle of Monmouth. Known for carrying pitchers of water to the soldiers, McCauly won the nickname 'Molly Pitcher.' Afterward, General Washington made her a noncommissioned officer for her brave deeds."[5] A third text shows a picture of two women soldiers, one wearing a long dress and the other clad in modern military fatigue. The captions read, "Past: Molly Pitcher" and "Present: Women marines served in the Gulf War."[6]

So eager we are for a Revolutionary heroine that we have made Molly Pitcher, a folk legend, into a real person. Out of six elementary and middle school texts, all published since 2002, five include the story of Molly Pitcher, and four feature vivid pictures, including one of Molly's dress flowing in the wind as she plunges a ramrod into a cannon.[7] These images were painted in the mid- to late-nineteenth century; now, thanks to high-quality color reproduction, they provide our textbooks with visual "evidence" of a female presence in the Revolutionary War. Because these paintings appear suitably old-fashioned and quaint, any differences between the Revolutionary and Victorian eras are easily overlooked. The key concept—what really excited the artists—is the juxtaposition of masculine and feminine imagery: a figure bearing prominent female features (in some of the paintings, Molly's breasts are partially exposed) braves the grit of the battlefield to master the ramrod and cannon. If a real woman can fight like this, these artists tell us, real men can hardly fail to follow suit.[8]

One volume of Macmillan's "Famous Americans Series," intended for a juvenile audience, reveals Molly Pitcher's perfect blend of mas-

culine and feminine virtues. Just as thirsty soldiers at Monmouth were
beginning to give up hope, they heard a woman speak:

> "Let me give you a drink," said a voice. "I'll hold up your
> head. Come, now, drink from my pitcher."
> They drank and lived. Then other fallen soldiers drank from
> that pitcher. And others and others until it was empty.
> "I will get more," the woman said. "The well is near. It is just
> across the road. Call me if you want another drink. Just say,
> 'Molly'—I will come to you."
> The sick men whispered her name to others. Before long
> many feeble voices were calling, "Molly! Molly! Pitcher!
> Pitcher!" Sometimes these calls were just "Molly Pitcher, Molly
> Pitcher." . . .
> A hundred fallen men were kept alive by that water. Some
> were able to fight again. All blessed the woman who saved them.

When her husband was also overcome by the heat, the story continues, Molly volunteered to fire his cannon in his place:

> The bullets fell around Molly. But she swabbed and loaded
> and fired. The hot sun blazed down on her, but she swabbed and
> loaded and fired.
> Her dress was black from gunpowder. There were smudges
> on her face and hands. She paid no attention. Her cannon must
> be fired!

Once the battle had ended, the commander-in-chief himself honored
the army's new heroine:

> General Washington took her powder-stained hand in his. He
> smiled at her and spoke kindly.
> "Mrs. Hays, the courage you showed yesterday has never
> been equaled by any woman. Your kindness has never been sur-

passed. You were an angel of mercy to suffering men. You were a pillar of strength at the cannon, with the skill of an experienced gunner. . . . Therefore, I make you a sergeant in this army. And I now pin this badge of honor upon you."

There was silence until this was over. Then a thousand soldiers began to cheer.

"Hooray for Sergeant Molly!" they cried. "Hooray for Molly Pitcher!" [9]

Here is the tale writ large. In this children's biography, Molly Pitcher takes her place beside Abraham Lincoln, Albert Einstein, Babe Ruth, and thirty other "famous Americans" featured in the same series of biographies. There is one significant difference, however, between Molly Pitcher and the others: all the rest were real people, while Molly is only a myth.

HOW TO CREATE A LEGEND

To begin, the facts:

At the Battle of Monmouth, amid scorching temperatures, thirty-seven soldiers died from heatstroke. This accounted for more than one-third of the battlefield fatalities. [10] Several hundred women were either on the battlefield or close at hand. These were "camp followers," women who followed the army and assisted in the logistics of everyday living. On normal days, they cooked, washed, and hauled things about; during battles, they nursed the wounded and carried supplies to and from the lines. Undoubtedly, some of these women tended to thirsty, sweltering soldiers. Very likely, some helped in the firing of cannons.

One of the women who might have been present at Monmouth was Mary Hays, of Carlisle, Pennsylvania, but we have no definite proof she was there, and we don't know very much about her life before and during the Revolutionary War. In fact, we don't even know the identity of the husband whom she supposedly accompanied into battle.

Some historians claim he was Casper Hays, who married Mary Ludwig in 1769; some say he was John Hays, who first enlisted in the army in 1775; others say he was William Hays, who enlisted as a gunner in the artillery in 1777. There is no record from that time that John Hays, Casper Hays, or William Hays fell during the Battle of Monmouth, or that a woman named Mary Hays took her husband's place firing a cannon.[11]

Tax records for 1783 show a William and Mary Hays living in Carlisle with their three-year-old son, John. After William Hays died in 1786, Mary Hays married a laborer named John McCalla, spelled variously in contemporary records and later accounts as McKolly, McKelly, McCauly, McCauley, McAuley, McCawley, McCaley, and McCalley.[12] By 1810 John had either died or disappeared, and Mary, by then at least fifty-five years old, supported herself by whitewashing public buildings, cleaning, and laundering. In 1822, forty-four years after Monmouth, she was awarded a small pension from the government.[13]

Mary Hays McCauly was never "made a noncommissioned officer for her brave deeds." She received neither riches nor fame in the wake of the Revolutionary War. Years later, a contemporary described her as "a very masculine person, alike rough in appearance and character; small and heavy with bristles in her nose, and could both drink and swear." She "drank grog and used language not the most polite," said another. One woman recalled that Mary was "a vulgar, profane, drunken old woman . . . I was afraid of her."[14]

There is no record that anybody called Mary Hays "Molly Pitcher" during her lifetime. When she died in 1832, her obituaries failed to mention "Molly Pitcher," the name she would assume decades later. One stated that "to the sick and wounded she was an efficient aid," but none told about her presence at Monmouth or her firing a cannon. The legend of "Molly Pitcher" had yet to attach to this unsuspecting woman, who died with a modest pension but no other recognition.[15]

We have no firsthand descriptions, recorded at the time, of women at Monmouth. We do have one secondhand account, written five days after the battle. Albigence Waldo, an army surgeon, stated that a wounded officer had told him that he had seen a woman take up the "gun and cartridges" of her fallen "gallant"; then, "like a Spartan heroine," she had "fought with astonishing bravery, discharging the piece with as much regularity as any soldier present." This woman fired a musket, not a cannon, for cannons do did not use "cartridges." [16]

There is one firsthand account of a woman at Monmouth firing a cannon, but it wasn't recorded at the time. In 1830, fifty-two years after the fact, Joseph Plumb Martin recalled seeing a women and her husband firing artillery at Monmouth: "A cannon shot from the enemy passed directly between her legs without doing any other damage than carrying away all the lower part of her petticoat,—looking at it with apparent unconcern, she observed, that it was lucky it did not pass a little higher, for in that case it might have carried away something else, and ended her and her occupation." But Martin's protagonist does not match the "Molly Pitcher" description: she did not carry water to thirsty soldiers, and she did not spring to action because her husband had fallen—she had been helping all along. [17]

We do have direct evidence of a woman taking the place of her fallen husband at a cannon—but not at Monmouth. At Fort Washington on November 16, 1776, Margaret Corbin stood in for her husband John, who had just been killed. Margaret herself was wounded by three grapeshot during the battle, and she lost the use of one arm for the rest of her life. She later became part of the "Invalid Regiment" at West Point, and on July 6, 1779, the Supreme Council of Pennsylvania awarded a lifetime pension, "one-half of the monthly pay drawn by a soldier," to the woman who had been "wounded and disabled in the attack on Fort Washington, while she heroically filled the post of her husband who was killed by her side serving a piece of artillery." [18] Although this conforms to parts of the "Molly Pitcher" story, the location and timing are off, and there is nothing about quenching the thirst of soldiers with heatstroke.

That's all there is in the historical record, but there are two other snippets from history, seemingly peripheral, which might have contributed to the story. One of the best-known women during the late eighteenth century was Moll Dimond Pitcher, a fortune-teller in Lynn, Massachusetts. Sailors and shipowners would come from afar to consult Moll Pitcher before casting off to sea. John Greenleaf Whittier published a poem about her in 1832, and a popular melodrama entitled *Moll Pitcher, or the Fortune Teller of Lynn* played on stages in Boston, New York, and Philadelphia from 1839 until after the Civil War.[19] Clearly, this Moll Pitcher had nothing to do with Mary Hays, Margaret Corbin, or the Battle of Monmouth—but her name was out there, a household word. Perhaps the renown of this prophetess, a legend in her own right, played some role in the evolution of Revolutionary folklore. Throughout the late nineteenth century, the heroine at Monmouth was often called "Moll Pitcher."[20]

We might also conjecture a link between the Molly Pitcher story and a similar tale from the Napoleonic Wars. In 1808–1809, when a French army was laying siege to the Spanish town of Saragossa, a young woman named Augustina Domonech carried drinks to thirsty soldiers, then took the place of a dead artilleryman. Later, when her husband or lover was shot, she took his rifle and resumed his position in battle. Afterward, the "Maid of Saragossa" became something of a sensation; unlike Mary Hays, she did not have to wait until after her death to receive her accolades. The similarity between the Maid of Saragossa and the final evolution of the Molly Pitcher tale might not be coincidental—as Molly's fame grew through the nineteenth century, she was often compared to her European counterpart.[21]

We do not know, nor can we ever know, how these shreds of "evidence" became blended in folkloric reminiscences to produce "Molly Pitcher," but we can trace the evolution of the legend in written accounts.

The storyline gelled before the name. Curiously, "Molly Pitcher" started her legend-life as "Captain Molly." Half a century after the

Battle of Monmouth, George Washington Parke Custis, Martha Washington's grandson through her first marriage, set to print the broad outlines of the story:

[W]hile Captain Molly was serving some water for the refreshment of the men, her husband received a shot in the head, and fell lifeless under the wheels of the piece. The heroine threw down the pail of water, and crying to her dead consort, "lie there my darling while I revenge ye," grasped the ramrod the lifeless hand of the poor fellow had just relinquished, sent home the charge, and called to the mattresses to prime and fire. It was done. Then entering the sponge into the smoking muzzle of the cannon, the heroine performed to admiration the duties of the most expert artilleryman, while loud shots from the soldiers ran along the line, . . . and the fire of the battery became more vivid than ever. . . .

[T]he next morning . . . Washington received her graciously, gave her a piece of gold and assured her that her services should not be forgotten. This remarkable and intrepid woman survived the Revolution, never for an instant laying aside the appellation she has so nobly won . . . the famed Captain Molly at the Battle of Monmouth.[22]

This rough draft of historical storytelling deviates from the final version in two ways. First, and most noticeably, is Molly's appellation. Second, Custis has Molly carrying a pail. During a battle, of course, water was transported in a pail or bucket, not in a dainty vessel used at the dinner table—but years later, when Molly acquired the surname of Pitcher, the pail would have to go.

In 1850 Benson Lossing visited Custis at his home, seeking out lore and artifacts to display in his forthcoming *Pictorial Field-Book of the Revolution*. Lossing discovered there a painting entitled *The Field of*

Monmouth, featuring George Washington riding a horse and Captain Molly ramming shot into a cannon. Custis, clearly enamored of the story, had created this canvas himself. When Lossing published his book two years later, he included an engraving of Custis's painting, accompanied by a recitation of the Captain Molly story.[23]

Elsewhere on his journey, while traveling to the Hudson Highlands near West Point, Lossing talked to three informants who claimed to have known or seen a woman named Captain Molly.[24] Here, the legend touches base with reality, for there was in fact a woman known as "Captain Molly" residing in the Hudson Highlands shortly after the Revolutionary War. According to official army records, between 1785 and 1789 the government provided "Captain Molly" with such items as a "bed-sack" and an "old common tent." She was unable to care for herself, and money for her support was paid directly to her caregiver.[25]

Who was this "Captain Molly"? She certainly wasn't Mary Hays McCauly, who resided hundreds of miles distant in Carlisle, Pennsylvania. But she could have been, and probably was, Margaret Corbin, the heroine of Fort Washington. Corbin had been granted a military pension, and she had also been the only woman in the Invalid Regiment at West Point, which disbanded in 1783. We pick up "Captain Molly" two years later, in the military records, only three miles from where Corbin had been living.

Margaret Corbin, however, was not present at Monmouth; indeed, she was already an invalid by the time of that battle. Yet stories proved more mobile than the particular women involved. The legendary Captain Molly moved freely from battlefield to battlefield, propelled by the frailties of memory or the whimsies of imagination. We know for sure that Margaret Corbin took the place of her fallen husband at Fort Washington. With time, this incontrovertible act of heroism, attributed to Captain Molly of the Hudson Highlands, was transposed to Monmouth and attached to one of the women who hauled buckets of water in the heat. The story also paid a visit to other battlefields.

After the war, a letter from the Commissary Department placed Corbin's exploits at Brandywine.[26] One of Lossing's informants placed the "Captain Molly" he knew from the Hudson Highlands not only at Monmouth but also at Fort Clinton, where she supposedly fired the last cannon before the American retreat.[27]

Perhaps, more than one woman took the place of her husband or lover during battle. Very likely, several women participated in the crews that fired cannons.[28] Certainly, many women hauled water and everything else needed in the logistics of warfare. In the mid-nineteenth century, all these exploits were attributed to one woman, Captain Molly.

The "real" Captain Molly, however, was not a likely heroine. According to one of Lossing's informants, she was also known as "Dirty Kate" (see note 24, page 287), and she "died a horrible death from the effects of syphilitic disease."[29] In 1850, when Elizabeth Ellet cast about for women to include in the saga of the Revolutionary War, she failed to include Captain Molly, a poor invalid. Her stories filled three volumes—but the tale that would soon dwarf them all was notably absent.[30] Even George Bancroft, in his multivolume magnum opus on the history of the Revolution, said nothing about Captain Molly, the heroine of Fort Washington and alleged heroine of Monmouth, Fort Clinton, and Brandywine. Although touted in folklore, Captain Molly needed to acquire a more appealing persona before she could be enshrined as the Revolutionary War's premier woman warrior.

THE STORY REFINED

Molly's new image came in the form of a name. The earliest recorded references to "Molly Pitcher" are attributed to artists, not writers. Nathaniel Currier, if not the first to use the name, was certainly among the vanguard. In 1848, seventy years after the battle, Currier entitled a canvas "Molly Pitcher, the Heroine of Monmouth." In the

1850s Dennis Malone Carter followed suit with two paintings, one of Molly by a cannon, the other of Molly being presented to Washington. By 1860 reproductions of engravings were beginning to bear the caption "Molly Pitcher" instead of "Captain Molly."[31]

In the 1860s several written accounts of the Revolutionary War included accounts of Molly Pitcher's heroics at Monmouth, using Custis's basic storyline but changing the name of the protagonist. The revised 1862 edition of Dr. James Thacher's *Military Journal of the American Revolution,* originally published decades earlier, contained some brand new material—an account of Molly Pitcher—even though Thacher himself had died in 1844.

The name change worked wonders. Molly was no longer a poor, vulgar camp follower, but a respectable woman in service of men. She had traded in her heavy pail for a more delicate container, in keeping with her recently acquired surname. Defined by both a cannon and a pitcher of water, Molly now embraced a perfect blend of masculine and feminine attributes. That such a creature could be found in the middle of a Revolutionary battlefield was cause for wonder and celebration.

The legend was almost perfect, save for one element: an actual heroine, a person who had once lived and breathed. As Molly Pitcher came to life in the minds of her many fans, she demanded to be reified. People began to wonder: Who *was* Molly Pitcher, anyway?

Immediately before the centennial celebration of 1876, in the town of Carlisle, an old-time resident named Wesley Miles volunteered an answer. Forty-four years earlier, he recalled, he had been present at the funeral of a local woman whom he claimed had been buried with military honors. He wrote to the local paper: "Reader, the subject of this reminiscence is a prototype of the 'Maid of Saragossa.' The heroine of Monmouth, Molly Pitcher."[32]

That's all it took. Town promoters immediately claimed the legendary figure as their own. After Miles had identified the unmarked grave site, residents of Carlisle raised $100 to place a new headstone by the bones of their forgotten heroine:

MOLLY MCCAULEY
RENOWNED IN HISTORY AS
"MOLLY PITCHER,"
THE HEROINE OF MONMOUTH.
DIED JANUARY 22, 1833
AGED SEVENTY-NINE YEARS [33]

Years later, somebody pointed out that the date of death on the tombstone was a year off. What if the site of the grave, as indicated by Wesley Miles, was off as well? In 1892, just to be sure, concerned citizens of Carlisle dug up the grave and discovered the skeleton of an adult female; they carefully placed it back, certain that those bones had once worked a cannon at Monmouth. [34]

Once Carlisle had discovered and declared the true identity of Molly Pitcher, elderly residents began to come forth with tales they had never told. One former neighbor, a young girl when Mary Hays McCauly was an old woman, recalled her saying, "You girls should have been with me at the Battle of Monmouth and learned how to fire a cannon." Another suddenly remembered that she had met Mary in 1826, when "she was known as 'Molly Pitcher.' " [35] (That was actually during the reign of "Captain Molly," two decades before the first recorded use of "Molly Pitcher.") In a book published for the Patriotic Sons of America in 1905, local historian John B. Landis used these recovered memories to confirm Carlisle's claim to the "real" Molly Pitcher. "No imaginary heroine was Molly Pitcher," Landis wrote, "but a real buxom lass, a strong, sturdy, courageous woman." [36] Today, if people suddenly came forth with recovered memories about the exploits of soldiers during the Spanish-American War in 1898, the veracity of their stories might be questioned—but few people at the time seemed to care that more than a century had elapsed between deed and memory. In 1911, when the prestigious *Journal of American History* published Landis's findings, the McCauly / Molly Pitcher connection was anointed with a quasiofficial stamp of approval. [37]

With her identity revealed and confirmed, Molly Pitcher began to accumulate physical artifacts. In 1903 a great-great-granddaughter of Mary Hays McCauly made a generous gift to the local historical society: "Molly Pitcher's pitcher," an ornate piece featuring oriental pagodas, some sort of fortifications, and figures floating in thin air.[38] In 1905 the Patriotic Sons of America placed a flagstaff and a cannon by Molly's tombstone; the cannon, acquired from an arsenal in Watertown, Massachusetts, had supposedly been used at Monmouth.[39] Meanwhile, at Monmouth, history enthusiasts constructed two signposts declaring "Mollie Pitcher's Well" on either side of the water source she supposedly used to fill her pitcher. (Years later, Monmouth's most prominent historian, William Stryker, revealed that the marked well had been dug fifty years after the battle.)[40]

Amid all the fanfare, one man wasn't buying it. Jeremiah Zeamer, himself a resident of Carlisle, did not think it appropriate to honor a woman who had been described as vulgar and profane, while many "Revolutionary heroes who lived useful and respected lives" remained obscure. "Molly McCauley is neither the historical nor moral character to hold up to young Americans for emulation," he argued. Using careful genealogical research, he went on to shoot holes in the Molly Pitcher = Mary Hays McCauly equation.[41]

But the public showed no concern for Jeremiah Zeamer's quibbles. Rather than scrap the legend, those who believed in their local heroine chose to change her image. Just as the vulgar Captain Molly had been transformed into a more genteel Molly Pitcher, so did Mary Hays McCauly take on a more gracious persona. The new monument placed by her grave in 1916 referred to her as an "army nurse" who became known for "her many acts of kindness." Years later, a newspaper article described "Pennsylvania's Number One Revolutionary Heroine" as a "cheerful" person.[42] No longer a hard-drinking, cursing old woman with bristles in her nose, Mary was now fit to become a respectable heroine, an appropriate model for impressionable young girls.

Spurred by the dramatic rise to fame of her compatriot in Carlisle, Margaret Corbin—the "real" Captain Molly—staged something of a renaissance. On March 16, 1926, at the urging of the Daughters of the American Revolution, her bones once again saw the light of day. ("A few decayed fibers of wood and several rusty hand-forged nails were the only traces of a coffin," wrote a witness at the disinterment. "The bones of the skeleton were complete except the small bones of the feet and the bones of the right hand which had disintegrated.") Twenty minutes later, the remains of Margaret Corbin were placed back underground in the cemetery of the United States Military Academy at West Point, only a few miles from her original grave site. A tablet identified her definitively as "Captain Molly." [43]

And so it was. By 1926 both Captain Molly and Molly Pitcher had been identified, properly reburied, and honored with the appropriate monuments. Their legends were literally sealed in stone. One tale, however, had subsumed the other. Although the "real" Captain Molly stood in for her husband at Fort Washington, this heroic deed was not quite enough. It took the cannon and pitcher together to warrant the title of "Number One Revolutionary Heroine."

Ever since John Landis and the town of Carlisle made Molly Pitcher their own, her story has been firmly attached to a real, dead woman. [44] The 1948 *Dictionary of American Biography* (*DAB*) included an entry for Mary Ludwig Hays McCauley, "better known as Molly Pitcher." [45] The recently updated *American National Biography,* superceding the old *DAB,* has taken the process of reification one step further by including an entry for "PITCHER, Molly (13 Oct. 1754?– 22 Jan. 1832)." John K. Alexander, the author, treats "Molly Pitcher" as an actual resident of Carlisle, Pennsylvania, with dates of birth and death. The details of her life, he admits, remain uncertain—"only her actual first name, Mary, is accepted as definite"—but like the other entries that fill this twenty-four-volume authoritative reference shelved in most respectable libraries, "PITCHER, Molly" is assumed to have been a real person. [46]

Today, Molly Pitcher is as celebrated as she was in the late nineteenth century. As of this writing, a Google search on the Internet reveals 16,300 sites—and this number is increasing rapidly. Students hoping to write reports on Revolutionary heroines can find a wealth of information on the Net, including digitalized reproductions of Molly Pitcher paintings and the poem engraved on her tombstone in Carlisle:

> O'er Monmouth's field of carnage drear,
> With cooling drink and words of cheer
> A woman passed who knew no fear,
> The wife of Hays, the gunner. . . . [47]

Many of these enterprising young scholars, following a folkloric tradition appropriate for our times, post their own minibiographies of Molly Pitcher on the Web. Also in keeping with current mores, Molly now lends her name to those who hope to keep our economy alive: mollypitcher.com promises to connect consumers with everything they might need in the way of home mortgages, gambling, job searches, cruises, life insurance, golf, skin care, cell phones, pets, dating, or divorce.

THE RETURN
OF CAPTAIN MOLLY

Even if the legend is flawed, Molly Pitcher does introduce women "camp followers" into the core narrative of the Revolutionary War. But these women—there were thousands of them—enter the story under false pretexts. In truth, they were more like the historic Captain Molly from the Hudson Highlands than the fanciful Molly Pitcher. They were poor and "vulgar," in the parlance of the times. Like Mary Hays, Margaret Corbin, and the soldiers themselves, many drank and swore. They were part of camp life, not above it. As noted earlier, they hauled water not in delicate pitchers but in heavy wooden buckets—and they hauled everything else as well. They tended to the logistics of war in every respect, both on and off the battlefield. They cooked and cleaned, but they also loaded and fired cannons, whether or not their husbands had fallen. Just ask Joseph Plumb Martin, who showed no surprise at a woman tending the artillery.

Unlike the fabled Molly Pitcher, these women were never honored by Washington for their deeds. Quite the reverse. Starting on July 4, 1777—on the first anniversary of the Declaration of Independence—Washington issued orders for the women who accompanied the Continental Army not to ride on the wagons. Again and again he repeated these orders: women should walk, not ride, and they should stay in the rear with the baggage. For a general trying to put together a respectable army, camp followers were to be tolerated at best—and the fewer the better, as far as the commander-in-chief was concerned. "The multitude of women," he wrote in 1777, "are a clog on every movement. . . . Officers commanding brigades and corps [should] use every reasonable method in their power to get rid of all such as are not absolutely necessary." [48]

Common soldiers, on the other hand, appreciated the women among them. Contrary to general orders, they let women ride in the wagons clear to the end of the war. The only "reward" bestowed on female camp followers was the respect of their male peers. After the war, these men kept the memory of "Captain Molly" alive. When telling old stories, they recalled their own "Captain Mollies," those courageous camp followers who braved the heat of the action at Fort Washington, Fort Clinton, Brandywine, Monmouth, and other historic battlefields. Decades later, when these stories congealed into one and were set in print, veterans who were still alive came forth proudly: "Yes, that must have been her. I saw that woman. I knew the heroine myself." [49]

While Captain Molly has a legitimate place in the story of our nation's birth, Molly Pitcher does not. This conjured heroine is no more than a male fantasy: a woman who serves men but can also fight tough. She does not adequately represent the female presence in the Revolutionary War. The problem is, nobody can. Women's contributions, however real and important, cannot readily be revealed through heroic, martial stories, for they were marked by drudgery, not high drama.

We prefer to imagine otherwise. Today, some Americans would like to show that women can be warriors, just like men. Others prefer to emphasize a more traditional image of female service. Molly Pitcher pleases both camps, so we continue to tell her story, even though she didn't exist, and even though her conjured tale masks the hard work of hundreds of thousands of *real* women who labored for eight years as our nation struggled for independence.

3

THE MAN WHO MADE
A REVOLUTION: SAM ADAMS

In A. J. Langguth's popular book *Patriots: The Men Who Started the American Revolution,* one patriot stands out from the rest. Samuel Adams is the instigator of every revolutionary event in Boston, while all the other patriots are merely his "recruits," his "legions," his "roster," his "band." [1] In *Liberty!*—the companion volume to the 1997 PBS series on the American Revolution—Thomas Fleming proudly proclaims, "Without Boston's Sam Adams, there might never have been an American Revolution." [2] Children's book author Dennis Fradin makes this point even more emphatically: "During the decade before the war began, Samuel Adams was basically a one-man revolution." [3]

Samuel Adams was not always the hero we make him out to be today. "If the American Revolution was a blessing, and not a curse," wrote John Adams, Samuel's cousin, in 1819, "the name and character of Samuel Adams ought to be preserved. A systematic course has been pursued for thirty years to run him down." [4] From Revolutionary times to the middle of the nineteenth century, Boston's most celebrated idol was not Samuel Adams but his close friend and colleague, Dr. Joseph Warren, the nation's first martyr. John Trumbull's 1786 painting, currently known as *The Battle of Bunker Hill,* was in fact ti-

"Without Boston's Sam Adams,
there might never have been an American Revolution."

Samuel Adams. Engraving based on
John Singleton Copley's portrait, 1772.

tled *The Death of General Warren at the Battle of Bunker's Hill*. These days the eminent Doctor Warren is rarely celebrated, while we take considerable pride in our most famous mischief-maker, the troublesome Mr. Adams. One modern biography is affectionately titled, *Samuel Adams's Revolution, 1765–1776: With the Assistance of George Washington, Thomas Jefferson, Benjamin Franklin, John Adams, George III, and the People of Boston.*

Why the shift? In the aftermath of the War for Independence, Americans were embarrassed by any radical taint, so they did not talk kindly about notorious political activists. But with the passage of time, radicals, like gangsters, can turn into heroes. Contemporary Americans, settled and secure, need not feel threatened by stories of illegal, outlandish activities such as the destruction of shiploads of tea. Indeed, we are titillated by tales of our nation's errant youth. The Boston Tea Party elicits knowing smiles, and Sam Adams, our Revolutionary bad boy and favorite rabble-rouser, brings forth fond feelings.

Ironically, this troublemaker imbues the American Revolution with design and purpose. There are two key components to his mythic story: he advocated independence many years before anybody else dared entertain the notion, and he worked the people of Boston into a frenzy to achieve his goal. These are not incidental to our telling of the American Revolution; our view of the nation's conception leans heavily upon them. Because Adams supposedly had the foresight to envision independence, we are able to perceive the tumultuous crowd actions in pre-Revolutionary Boston as connected, coherent events pointing toward an ultimate break from England. Without this element of personal intent, the rebellion would be a mindless muddle, purely reactive, with no sense of mission. Without an author, the script becomes unwieldy; without a director, the crowd becomes unruly—but Sam Adams, mastermind of independence, keeps the Revolution on cue. He wrote the script, directed the cast, and staged a masterful performance.

The beauty of the story is that Adams was not some autocrat, remote and aloof from the people he directed. He was one of the crowd—one of *us*. Perhaps that is why we like to call Samuel "Sam," although none of his contemporaries did. (In this book, "Sam" denotes the legend, "Samuel" the historical person.) Unlike many a Revolutionary patriarch, he was supposedly at home on the streets, mixing with the people, raising toasts in the taverns. How fitting that his face now adorns no coins or bills—only a bottle of beer.

Sam Adams, who both represents and controls the crowd, allows us to celebrate "the people." Or so it would seem. In fact, while the Sam Adams story appears to celebrate the people, it does not take them seriously. That's why the story was first invented by Adams's Tory adversaries, who wrote "the people" out of the script by placing Adams—a single, diabolical villain—in charge of all popular unrest. To understand the damaging implications of the Sam Adams story, and to see how it distorts what really happened in Revolutionary Boston, we have to examine its genesis.

THE TORIES' TALE

Not wanting to grant legitimacy to any form of protest, conservatives in the 1760s and 1770s maintained that all the troubles in Boston were the machinations of a single individual. In the words of Peter Oliver, the Crown-appointed chief justice who was later exiled, the people themselves "were like the Mobility of all Countries, perfect Machines, wound up by any Hand who might first take the Winch." Mindless and incapable of acting on their own, they needed a director who could "fabricate the Structure of Rebellion from a single straw." [5]

According to this mechanistic view, one man led and everyone else followed. At the outset, that master of manipulation was not Samuel Adams but James Otis Jr. According to Oliver, the mentally deranged Otis had vowed in 1761 "that if his Father was not appointed a Justice of the superior Court, he would set the Province in a Flame." This he proceeded to do, using the unruly yet pliable Boston rabble to fight his battle. [6] Thomas Hutchinson, the man who was chosen over

James Otis Sr., told a similar tale, although less bombastically than Oliver.[7]

When Otis's insanity rendered him ineffectual, the role of puppeteer was supposedly assumed by Samuel Adams, who was also motivated by family loyalty: his father had been defeated in the progressive Land Bank scheme many years before, and Samuel vowed to seek justice by deposing the regime that terminated his father's dreams. Early on, according to Oliver and Hutchinson, Adams decided to foster a revolution that would lead to independence. The Stamp Act riots in 1765, the *Liberty* riot in 1768, the resistance to occupying soldiers, the Boston Massacre in 1770, the Tea Party in 1773, and various lesser-known demonstrations were all orchestrated by Samuel Adams, master Revolutionary strategist.

"His Power over weak Minds was truly surprising," wrote Oliver. Some of the "weak Minds" manipulated by Adams were those of lower-class Bostonians:

[H]e understood human Nature, in low life, so well, that he could turn the Minds of the great Vulgar as well as the small into any Course that he might chuse . . . & he never failed of employing his Abilities to the vilest Purposes.

But the puppets whose strings he pulled also included Boston's most illustrious patriots, people like John Hancock:

Mr. Hancock . . . was as closely attached to the hindermost Part of Mr. Adams as the Rattles are affixed to the Tail of the Rattle Snake. . . . His mind was a meer *Tabula Rasa*, & had he met with a good Artist he would have enstamped upon it such Character as would have made him a most useful Member of Society. But Mr. Adams who was restless in endeavors to disturb ye Peace of Society, & who was ever going about seeking whom he might devour, seized upon him as his Prey, & stamped such Lessons upon his Mind, as have not as yet been erased.[8]

By attributing all rebellious events first to Otis and then Adams, disgruntled Tories like Oliver and Hutchinson exhibited the classic conservative denial of social protest: the people, if left to their own devices, will never rise up on their own. Without ringleaders, organizers, rabble-rousers, troublemakers, or outside agitators, the status quo will not be challenged because nothing is basically wrong. All protests and rebellions can be dismissed; demands and grievances need never be taken seriously.

It's easy to see why his Tory adversaries cast Samuel Adams in the leading role. Adams was a marvelous politician in every respect, equally at home in political chambers and on the Boston waterfront. An accomplished writer, he demonstrated his mastery of the art of political polemic in a steady stream of articles published in the local newspapers. He could also wheel and deal behind the scenes. As an influential member of the Boston caucus, he exerted considerable influence on the selection of local officers and the direction of the town meeting; as clerk of the Massachusetts House of Representatives, he figured prominently in that body's continuing resistance to the dictates of Crown-appointed governors. He was, in sum, an extremely effective partisan of the "popular party," and this caused his opponents in the "court party" great consternation. In the words of a contemporary Bostonian, John Andrews: "The ultimate wish and desire of the high Government party is to get Samuel Adams out of the way when they think they may accomplish every of their plans." [9]

To get Adams "out of the way," his adversaries called him a traitor. On January 25, 1769, a Tory informer named Richard Sylvester swore in an affidavit that seven months prior, the day after a large crowd had protested the seizure of John Hancock's ship *Liberty,* he had overheard Adams say to a group of seven men on the street, "If you are men, behave like men. Let us take up arms immediately and be free and seize all the King's officers." Later, Sylvester claimed, Adams had said during one of his many visits to his home, "We will destroy every soldier that dare put foot on shore. His majesty has no right to send troops here to invade the country. I look upon them as foreign enemies." [10]

Sylvester's trumped-up allegations were sent to London, but the evidence appeared questionable, and the charge of treason was not upheld.[11] Sylvester's testimony was then archived; many years later, in the middle of the nineteenth century, the preeminent historian George Bancroft uncovered the affidavit, accepted it as fact, and repeated it word for word, no questions asked: "[Adams] reasoned that it would be just to destroy every soldier whose foot should touch the shore. 'The king,' he would say, 'has no right to send troops here to invade the country; if they come, they will come as foreign enemies.' "[12] Historians ever since have taken Bancroft at face value, just as Bancroft accepted Sylvester. Today, this discredited accusation continues to provide the basic "documentation" that Adams was a hellfire revolutionary, "Godfather" to the "mob," inciting riots at every available opportunity.

SAM ADAMS'S REVOLUTION

Based on the word of his Tory foes, we have granted Samuel Adams superhuman powers. This one man, we say, set Boston all ablaze—but the historical record tells a different story. Consider the various Sam Adams tales that have emerged over the years.

Stamp Act Riots: "Adams's Waterfront Gang"

In 1765 Boston crowds gathered on two different occasions to protest the new Stamp Tax. On August 14, a crowd of approximately three thousand colonists burned an effigy of the tax collector, Andrew Oliver, and destroyed his office. Twelve nights later, a more violent crowd demolished the home of the wealthy Tory official Thomas Hutchinson. Following the lead of Hutchinson and other contemporary Tories, modern writers attribute these mob actions to "Adams's waterfront gang." According to William Hallahan in *The Day the American Revolution Began*, Sam Adams "had his revenge on Hutchinson for humiliating his father."[13]

In fact, Adams had nothing to do with either event. He approved of the August 14 demonstration after the fact, but he did not organize it—that was the work of the Loyal Nine, a group of Boston activists that did not include Adams. He was appalled by the riot of August 26 because of its "truly *mobbish* Nature," and he acted swiftly "to assist the Majistrate to their utmost in preventing or suppressing any further Disorder." [14]

Boston Massacre: "An Adams-Inspired Mob"

In *Red Dawn at Lexington,* author Louis Birnbaum states that the confrontation that resulted in the Boston Massacre was the work of "an Adams-inspired mob"—but there is nothing in the historical record suggesting that Adams had anything to do with the seamen, laborers, and apprentices who threw snowballs at British soldiers and taunted them to shoot.[15]

Adams did become involved in the aftermath of the massacre. The Boston town meeting demanded that royal officials remove two regiments from the city to an island in Boston Harbor, and it appointed Adams to serve as one of its spokesmen. When the military commander offered to remove one regiment, Adams responded: "If he could remove the 29th regiment, he could remove the 14th also, and it was at his peril to refuse." According to Thomas Hutchinson, acting as governor at the time, Adams said that if the troops were not removed, "the rage of the people would vent itself "—not just against the soldiers, but against Hutchinson "in particular." [16] Later writers and historians have used this incident, as reported by Hutchinson, to prove the immense powers of Samuel Adams, for the troops did leave. In truth, as Adams himself would be the first to observe, Hutchinson relented not because of one man's words, but because he feared "the rage of the people" who awaited his response.

Boston Tea Party: "The Signal"

On December 16, 1773, as three ships sat in the harbor laden with tea, several thousand angry patriots gathered in Boston's Old South Meeting House to figure out what to do. Suddenly, Sam Adams climbed on top of a bench (or so the mythic version goes) and announced to the crowd: "This meeting can do nothing more to save the country." Everybody knew what he meant: that was the signal for the "Tea Party" to begin. "Instant pandemonium broke out amid cheers, yells, and war whoops," one recent narrative declares. "The crowd poured out of the Old South Meeting [House] and headed for Griffin's Wharf." [17]

This story, now included in virtually every narrative of the Boston Tea Party (including my own *People's History of the American Revolution*), was fabricated ninety-two years later to promote the image of an all-powerful Sam Adams, in firm control of the Boston crowd. According to the most complete eyewitness account, Adams did in fact state "that he could think of nothing further to be done," but this was not some "signal," for the timing was way off. Not until ten or fifteen minutes later did Indian yells trigger a mass exodus from the meeting, and at that point Adams and others tried to stem the tide, quiet the crowd, and continue the meeting.[18] George Bancroft, writing in 1854, took this source information and condensed the timeline, thereby suggesting an element of causality; by stating that the "war-whoop" followed immediately, he hinted that Adams had given some sort of signal.[19] In 1865 William V. Wells, Adams's first biographer, took Bancroft's hint and created what would ever after be accepted as dogma: Adams's statement was "the signal for the Boston Tea Party," he pronounced definitively. "Instantly a shout was heard at a door of the church from those who had been intently listening for the voice of Adams. The war whoop resounded. Forty or fifty men disguised as Indians . . ."[20] This is the ultimate Sam Adams story: the people of Boston had been trained to follow a secret, coded message issued by their master.

Lexington: "O! What a Glorious Morning!"

At Lexington on April 19, 1775, while Samuel Adams and John Hancock were escaping the British troops, they heard the first volley of fire. Like a boy hankering for a fight, Sam allegedly turned to John and exclaimed: " 'O! what a glorious morning is this!' in the belief that it would eventually liberate the colony from all subjection to Great Britain."[21] Today, these words are echoed on the official seal of the town of Lexington: "WHAT A GLORIOUS MORNING FOR AMERICA," placed within quotation marks.

This story comes from William Gordon, who in 1788 published a four-volume history of the American Revolution. Because Gordon was a contemporary, historians ever since have assumed him to be a credible source.[22] He was not. How could Gordon be apprised of this private conversation? Indeed, how could anyone know? Hancock wrote nothing of it, nor, of course, did Adams. It did not appear in Paul Revere's firsthand accounts of the Adams-Hancock escape from Lexington.[23] Gordon himself did not include the story in a detailed account of the outbreak of hostilities at Lexington, which he wrote only a month later and which he based on firsthand interviews with informants whose memories were still fresh; instead, he added the incident thirteen years later, well after the fact.[24]

Most likely, Gordon gleaned this Sam Adams tale from local folklore—and the first to dream it up were probably Tories, who had a vested interest in discrediting the man they felt to be their nemesis. Imagine the horror of the moment: guns blasting, men and boys running, eight militiamen shot dead. Imagine then the great sorrow, the mourning, of those in Lexington who witnessed the scene, friends and kin of the deceased. This was the context in which Samuel Adams supposedly rejoiced. At the time, any insinuation that Adams celebrated the massacre of his countrymen could only have been made by his dedicated foes, those who would say anything to bring their nemesis down. The story we now celebrate would have been deemed irreverent, and Adams himself would have been disgraced. Only once the mourning had subsided, after memories had played tricks with events, could such a tale, conjured by his enemies, be given a patriotic spin.[25]

The Architect of Independence

Some say 1765, others 1768, but all popular renditions of the Sam Adams story state categorically that he favored independence several years before it was declared in 1776 and long before any other patriot entertained such a notion.[26] This is what supposedly made him such an effective leader—he had a vision and stuck to it. This is also why we promote him as our hero—he gives force and direction to the saga that terminates with the birth of a new nation.

According to his own writings, however, Samuel Adams did not advocate independence until the winter of 1775–1776, the same time many others started favoring it. Following the lead of historian Pauline Maier, we can trace Adams's record on the issue of independence:[27]

- In 1765 Adams argued that the colonists were and always had been "good Subjects" who had "bought with them all the Rights & Laws of the Mother State"; they had never made any "Claim of Independency," he boasted, despite their geographic isolation.[28] At that time, there was no reason that Adams and his fellow colonists would even consider abandoning the country they deemed to be the freest in the world.

- In 1768, when British troops started occupying Boston, Adams wrote forcefully that colonists should be "restored to the rights, privileges and immunities of *free subjects.*"[29] Boston's problems, he asserted, were caused "by the Vile insinuations of wicked men *in America*"—not by any structural irregularities of the British Constitution.[30]

- In 1771 Adams argued, "By our compact with our King, wherein is contain'd the rule of his government and the measure of our submission, we have all the liberties and immunities of Englishmen. . . . It is our duty therefore to contend for them whenever attempts are made to violate them."[31]

- In 1773 Adams still clung to the notion that problems with the British government stemmed from "a few men born & educated amongst us, & governd by Avarice & a Lust of power." If these men—people like Thomas Hutchinson and Peter Oliver—could be "removed from his Majesty's Service and Confidence here," peace might be restored.[32]

- In 1774, writing from the First Continental Congress, Adams urged Joseph Warren, his associate in Boston, to oppose country radicals who were moving "to set up another form of government." Even at this late date, and while writing to his closest compatriot, he dismissed as "groundless" the charges that Adams, Warren, and other Boston patriots were aiming at "a total independency."[33]

Not until patriots and Redcoats had engaged in pitched battles for the better part of a year did Samuel Adams publicly advocate a total break from Britain.[34] By this time, as Adams himself stated, declaring independence was something of a moot point. We have no way of ascertaining when he privately started wishing for independence. Even if it was sooner than his public pronouncements indicate, his increasing radicalization probably stemmed from his frustration with British obstinacy, not from a grand vision he possessed from the start.

The Man Who Made a Revolution

Sam Adams gives our Revolution some punch. The rest of the famous patriots, Patrick Henry and Tom Paine excepted, come across as cautious, rational men. Most were also very rich. These dignitaries make honorable founders but poor revolutionaries—and so we turn to Sam Adams, a tried-and-true incendiary.

The real Samuel Adams does not live up to the image of a flaming revolutionary. Throughout a political career that spanned four decades, he opposed violent acts that threatened a well-ordered society:

- In 1765 Adams forcefully condemned the riots on the night of August 26, which destroyed private property. At the town meeting that followed, he agreed with the "universal Consternation" and "Detestation" of the event.[35]

- In 1768, in response to crowd action induced by the seizure of John Hancock's vessel, *Liberty*, Adams wrote in the *Boston Gazette*: "I am no friend to '*Riots, Tumults and unlawful Assemblies.*' "[36] Further, he argued that most colonists were "*orderly* and *peaceable* inhabitants" whose only aim was to enjoy the rights of Englishmen.[37]

- In 1772 Adams told a compatriot that he "feard that this unhappy Contest between Britain and America will end in Rivers of Blood," and he pleaded that patriots do everything in their power "to prevent if possible so dreadful a Calamity."[38]

- In 1774 Adams counseled his friend James Warren "to avoid Blood and Tumult" and to oppose "Rash Spirits" who would "by their Impetuosity involve us in unsurmountable Difficulties."[39]

- In 1776 Adams pronounced with great pleasure that independence had been achieved "without great internal Tumults & violent Convulsions."[40]

- In 1780 Adams served on a three-man committee that drafted a constitution for Massachusetts which included steep property requirements for voting. Only men of considerable

means could serve as senators—this was important, Adams
said, for the people themselves were prone to excessive
"passions and whims," which had to be held in check by
propertied interests.[41]

- In 1786 and 1787 Adams advocated the suppression of the
popular uprising known as Shays' Rebellion. As president of
the state senate, he pushed to suspend writs of habeas corpus.
Afterward, when many of his contemporaries advocated
leniency, Adams wanted to hang the rebels. Again in 1794,
Adams endorsed the squashing of the Whiskey Rebellion. In
a republican government, he proclaimed, people should
never break the laws, but work to change them by legal
means.

- In the 1790s Samuel Adams served three terms as governor of
Massachusetts. He made no great waves during his tenure in
office; instead, he continued to proclaim, as he always had,
that piety and virtue were the essential ingredients of public
life. Biographies, textbooks, and popular histories routinely
ignore the later years of Adams's political life, which they
cannot bend to fit the profile of a revolutionary.

Samuel Adams never advocated "revolution" in the modern sense,
a complete overthrow of the government and a radical restructuring
of the social order. He was indeed a "revolutionary" in the parlance of
the times—a firm believer in the values promoted by England's Glorious Revolution of 1688, which rooted sovereignty in the people
rather than in a monarch—but we read history backward when we su-
perimpose later meanings onto earlier times.[42]

The misreading of Adams reached its zenith with John Miller's biography, *Sam Adams: Pioneer in Propaganda,* which continues to influence popular history today. (Miller was the first to change Samuel's
name to "Sam.") Writing in the 1930s, Miller based his portrait on a

conception of "revolution" current at the time. Since Adams was allegedly a revolutionary, he was "by nature . . . passionate, excitable, and violent." This "notorious riot lover . . . continually drenched the country with propaganda." He "summoned" the town meeting "for whatever purpose he chose." Citing Sylvester's charges as fact, Miller wrote that Adams was active in the streets, haranguing listeners "to make a bold attack upon the royal government." His command over the people was absolute: "Boston was controlled by a trained mob and . . . Sam Adams was its keeper." By this reading, one man alone was responsible for all the unrest—everyone else was "brought into the revolutionary movement against their own . . . wishes." [43]

In all the Sam Adams stories, we distort the historical record. Curiously, the revisions bear an uncanny resemblance to those of Adams's political opponents. "Without Boston's Sam Adams, there might never have been an American Revolution," the Tories once said, and today we are saying it again. [44] This is not a good sign. The reason we can pass off Tory tales as truth is that we have unconsciously adopted their way of looking at political processes. The Tory way of thinking, to which we have regressed, sees common people as "perfect Machines" who need someone else to tell them what to do. One man leads, while the rest follow adoringly. [45] Thomas Hutchinson and Peter Oliver certainly subscribed to this hierarchical notion, but why should we?

A COLLECTIVE AFFAIR

Bostonians had all sorts of reasons to oppose British policies, and they did not need Samuel Adams to set them in motion.

Merchant-smugglers like John Rowe, William Molineaux, Solomon Davis, Melatiah Bourn, Edward Payne, and William Cooper had much to gain by opposing British mercantile policies that restricted free trade. These men, articulate and politically effective, were certainly capable of acting on their own behalf—in fact, they had been doing so for several years before Samuel Adams ascended to a position of influence in 1765. Five years earlier, they had organized themselves into the Boston Society for Encouraging Trade and Commerce, which sent numerous petitions to Parliament. During the non-importation movement of 1768, a resurgent group called Merchants and Traders emerged to promote the collective interests of its members. "We feel for the Mother Country as well as our selves," wrote Cooper, "but charity begins at home." [46] In 1770 a third group, the Body of the Trade, reached out to include all those in town with a stake in trade issues—but Samuel Adams played no role in this organization.

During the Stamp Act riots, Boston's lower classes had their own motivations for ransacking the home of Thomas Hutchinson, who justified poverty because it produced "industry and frugality." According to William Gordon, "Gentlemen of the army, who have seen towns sacked by an enemy, declare they never before saw an instance of such fury." [47] This fury was their own, not Adams's.

Starting in 1768, laborers and seamen had personal reasons for resenting the presence of British Regulars in their midst. Troops routinely stopped them in the streets, roughing them up or demanding swigs of rum. Off-duty privates competed with local workers for employment on the docks. Little wonder that these people jeered the Redcoats whenever they could.

Longshoremen and sailors had good reasons for opposing British restrictions of trade. Shipping was the backbone of Boston's economy; if the ships didn't sail, "Jack Tar" would have no work. Little wonder that ordinary men who wanted jobs responded to the confiscation of the *Liberty* or the monopolization of the tea trade by British interests.

These people did not take orders from a single authoritarian leader. Patriots worked with each other in a wide array of activist groups and political organizations, and every one of these groups engaged in collaborative processes. The Boston Caucus had been meeting since the 1720s to promote candidates who were sympathetic with popular issues, such an increased availability of hard currency; by the 1770s scores of citizens were active in three caucuses, one each for North, Middle, and South Boston. In 1765 the Loyal Nine, a group of artisans and shopkeepers who met in Speakman's distillery, expanded into the Sons of Liberty; together with similar groups in other colonies, they formed a fledgling infrastructure for coordinated resistance. Throughout the 1760s and 1770s, the St. Andrews Lodge of Freemasons met in the Green Dragon Tavern to discuss politics and plan political actions. Like the Sons of Liberty, the community of Masons helped give some sense of cohesion and purpose to revolutionary unrest.

Samuel Adams was not a member of the Sons of Liberty or the Masons, but he did belong to the Long Room Club, a group of seventeen patriots, mostly professionals, who met above the printing press of John Gill and Benjamin Edes, publishers of the patriotic *Boston Gazette*. He was also one of the founders of the Boston Committee of Correspondence, which joined with similar groups in other Massachusetts towns and other colonies to carry the torch of resistance in the 1770s. Garry Wills, one of the most respected minds of recent times, calls the committees of correspondence Adams's "own wire service,"[48] but this organization, like all the others, brought together many dedicated and talented patriots in common cause: James Warren, among the first to suggest the idea; Joseph Warren, the doctor from Harvard with great rhetorical flare; Josiah Quincy, the talented young lawyer; Joseph Greenleaf, the printer who had called the presence of British troops in Boston "an open declaration of war" against liberty; and Thomas Young, the flamboyant political activist who urged resistance at every turn.[49]

Many other tradesmen, artisans, and laborers met in the taverns of Boston to engage in collective action. Butchers, bakers, and leather workers sent petitions to the General Court and Boston's selectmen. Daily, during their 11:00 A.M. break, shipyard workers gathered in taverns and in the streets to talk over the state of affairs. These people, working in concert, had become political actors.[50]

All these people, and many more, came together for the Boston town meeting, the local governing organization that invited the participation of "the whole body of the people"; during the height of Revolutionary fervor, this came to include apprentices, women, and others who were not granted the formal right to vote. Each year, the town meeting elected representatives to the Massachusetts House of Representatives, and each year these people were handed specific instructions, approved by the town meeting, as to how they should respond to the key issues of the day.

The entire edifice was heavily weighted at the bottom. This was a politicized population, and that was part of the problem: British officials and local Tories found it difficult to accept, or even comprehend, the degree of popular participation in politics in Revolutionary Boston.

Samuel Adams functioned within this framework. He was one of the leaders of the Boston Caucus, the Long Room Club, and the Committees of Correspondence. He sometimes served as moderator for the town meeting. From his position as clerk of the House of Representatives he wielded considerable power at the provincial level. More a polemicist than a street leader, he drafted many letters and resolutions, giving sentiments that were shared by many a concrete expression. He was intelligent, dedicated, persuasive, and savvy—an effective activist and master politician.[51]

But he did not run the show, because nobody could. Revolutionary Boston simply didn't function that way—and no self-respecting patriot, certainly not Samuel Adams, *wanted* it to function that way. Authoritarian government was seen as the problem, not the solution.

Royal officials and Tories never did grasp the Revolutionaries' distinction between "the body of the people" and a mindless mob. Because they knew no other way, they interpreted Boston's politics as a top-down chain of command. In the process, they transformed Samuel Adams into a detestable demon. Now, we honor the mythological figure his enemies created.

Mercy Otis Warren—sister of James Otis, wife of James Warren, political colleague and personal friend of Samuel Adams—knew very well that Adams owed much of his renown to the fuss made by his enemies. When General Gage singled out Adams and Hancock for proscription, she claimed, he revealed his great ignorance of "the temper of the times, the disposition of the people at large, [and] the character of the individuals":

> His discrimination, rather accidental than judicious, set these two gentlemen in the most conspicuous point of view, and drew the particular attention of the whole continent to their names, distinguished from many of their compeers, more by this single circumstance, than by superior ability or exertion. By this they became at once the favorites of popularity, and the objects of general applause, which at that time would have been the fortune of any one, honored by such a mark of disapprobation of the British commander in chief.[52]

Warren seemed amused that Adams's enemies made him into a hero—but she had no way of foreseeing that people like Gage and Hutchinson would successfully blind later generations of Americans to the importance of democratic political behavior during the Revolutionary era. Passionately committed to the cause of popular government, Mercy Otis Warren, Samuel Adams, and the rest of Boston's patriots would be quite surprised to learn that America's "patriotic" history has been imbued with a Tory perspective.

DAVID AND GOLIATH

"British professionals . . . pump[ed] shot into
the backs of fleeing Minute Men."

The Battle of Lexington. Reduced engraving by Amos Doolittle,
1832, from his original engraving, 1775,
based on a sketch by Ralph Earl.

4

THE SHOT HEARD
'ROUND THE WORLD:
LEXINGTON AND CONCORD

Every year, over one million Americans commemorate "the shot heard 'round the world" with a patriotic pilgrimage to Minuteman National Historical Park on the outskirts of Concord, Massachusetts. On April 19, the anniversary of the famous event, reenactors dress up as colonial Minutemen and march from nearby towns to Lexington and Concord, where they exchange make-believe musket fire with friends and neighbors dressed as British Redcoats. Throughout the state, and in Maine and Wisconsin as well, "Patriots' Day" is celebrated as an official holiday.

The story is classic David and Goliath, starring rustic colonials who faced the world's strongest army. At dawn in Lexington on April 19, 1775, several hundred British Regulars, in full battle formation, opened fire on local militiamen. When the smoke had cleared, eight of the sleepy-eyed farmers who had been rousted in the middle of the night lay dead on the town green.

In the wake of the bloodbath, to mobilize popular support, patriots proclaimed far and wide that the Redcoats had fired first. The Massachusetts Provincial Congress collected depositions from participants and firsthand witnesses, then published those accounts that conformed to the official story under the title *A Narrative of the*

Excursion and Ravages of the King's Troops. British authorities countered with their own official version: the Americans had fired first. Not surprisingly, this story received little circulation in the rebellious colonies.

Because of the biases and agendas of the witnesses, we can never know for sure who fired the first shot at Lexington. But we do know that the patriots won the war of words. "The myth of injured innocence," as David Hackett Fischer calls it, became an instant American classic.[1] We have all learned that the British started the American Revolution when they opened fire on outnumbered and outclassed patriot militiamen on the Lexington Green. But this makes no sense. Revolutions, by nature, are proactive—they must be initiated by the revolutionaries themselves. The American Revolution had begun long before the battle at Lexington.

In 1836 the poet and essayist Ralph Waldo Emerson coined a catchy phrase that has signified the event ever since: "the shot heard 'round the world." Actually, Emerson's poem "Concord Hymn" commemorated the fighting at the North Bridge in nearby Concord, and his celebrated "shot" was fired by Americans:

> By the rude bridge that arched the flood,
> Their flag to April's breeze unfurled,
> Here once the embattled farmers stood,
> And fired the shot heard 'round the world.

Over time, however, Emerson's poem was relocated to Lexington, a site more hospitable to the story we wish to hear. At Lexington the farmers were clearly the victims, while at Concord they were not. The David and Goliath tale, highlighted by the image of bullying British troops mowing down Yankee farmers, has prevailed. Current textbooks routinely refer to "the shot heard 'round the world" at Lexington, not Concord, while popular histories still repeat the story as it was first told by American patriots: "British professionals . . . pump[ed] shot into the backs of fleeing Minute Men."[2]

But what if the roles were reversed? What if American Revolutionaries were actually Goliath, and the British David?

A PEOPLE'S REVOLUTION

In fact, the American Revolution did not begin with "the shot heard 'round the world." It started more than half a year earlier, when tens of thousands of angry patriot militiamen ganged up on a few unarmed officials and overthrew British authority throughout all of Massachusetts outside of Boston. This powerful revolutionary saga, which features Americans as Goliath instead of David, has been bypassed by the standard telling of history. By treating American patriots as innocent victims, we have suppressed their revolutionary might.

To understand why the story of this monumental insurrection is no longer told, we have to go back to the Boston Tea Party. On December 16, 1773, patriots dressed as Indians dumped 342 chests of tea, worth £15,000, into Boston Harbor. Although we take considerable pride in recounting the story today, in the years that followed the event Americans never celebrated it, and they certainly didn't call it a "tea party." [3] While some patriots rejoiced at the boldness of the affair, they could hardly capitalize on this act of vandalism in their propaganda. The East India Company could easily be perceived as the victim, not the antagonist, and even many patriots thought the company should be recompensed for destroyed property.

But when the king and Parliament retaliated for the destruction of the tea with four extreme measures labeled "Coercive Acts," the colonists did indeed become oppressed. Renaming the measures the "Intolerable Acts," radical patriots garnered much support for their cause.

The story of the Coercive Acts and the response they triggered can be told two ways. According to the enshrined version, the first and most important of the measures was the Boston Port Bill, which prohibited all commerce to and from Boston. (The other three measures are sometimes enumerated but rarely discussed.) Parliament intended to isolate Boston and starve its rebellious residents into submission, but this plan backfired when other colonists sprang to the aid of their brothers and sisters. United behind the suffering Bostonians, other colonists heaped aid on their beleaguered friends and braced themselves for a revolution.

Today, this Americanized adaptation of the "Good Samaritan" is repeated in each and every narrative account of the events leading up to the Revolutionary War. But revolutions do not generally stem from acts of charity, and this one was no exception. Our nation came into being because people stood up for themselves and their own best interests.

There is another story, although it has rarely been told in the past hundred and fifty years. According to this version, it was not the Boston Port Bill but one of the "other" coercive measures that turned most Massachusetts citizens into revolutionaries. The Massachusetts Government Act, passed a month after the Port Bill, dictated that people could no longer come together in their town meetings without permission from the Crown-appointed governor, and they could not discuss any items the governor had not approved. The act further stipulated that the people's elected representatives would no longer determine the Council, which comprised the upper house of the legislature, the governor's cabinet, and the administrative arm of provincial government. Also, elected representatives no longer had the power to approve or remove judges, juries, or justices of the peace—the local officials who could put people in jail or take away their property.

After a century and a half of local self-government, citizens of Massachusetts were suddenly deprived of the power of their votes. The Massachusetts Government Act affected not only the 5 percent of the populace who resided in Boston but also the 95 percent who lived in towns and villages clear across the province. Common farmers feared that judges, no longer responsible to the people, might be corrupted and foreclose on land for the slightest debt. The new act eliminated the sovereignty of the people of Massachusetts and threatened their economic solvency.

The people would not allow it. They refused to be disenfranchised.

The Massachusetts Government Act was due to take effect on August 1, 1774. The first court under the new provisions was scheduled to sit in remote Berkshire County, on the western edge of the province, but the court never met. When the Crown-appointed officials showed up for work on August 16, they found themselves shut out of the Great Barrington courthouse by 1,500 committed patriots.[4]

Two weeks later, in Springfield, 3,000–4,000 patriots marched "with staves and musick" and again shut down the court. "Amidst the Crowd in a sandy, sultry place, exposed to the sun," said one observer, the judges were forced to renounce "in the most express terms any commission which should be given out to them under the new arrangement."[5]

In Cambridge, on September 2, 4,000 patriots forced the lieutenant-governor of Massachusetts to resign his seat on the Council. Responding to rumors that the British army had fired at and killed six patriots, an estimated 20,000–60,000 men from throughout the countryside headed toward Boston to confront the Redcoats. In some towns, nearly every male of fighting age participated in the "Powder Alarm," as it was called.[6]

Governor Thomas Gage, who was also commander-in-chief of the British forces in North America, had vowed to make a stand in Worcester, where the court was scheduled to meet the following week. After the Powder Alarm, however, Gage changed his mind and let the judges fend for themselves. On September 6, 4,622 militiamen from 37 surrounding communities gathered in Worcester (a town with fewer than 300 citizens) to depose the Crown-appointed officials. The insurgents lined both sides of Main Street as the officials, in a ritualistic display of humiliation and submission, were forced to walk the gauntlet, hats in hand, reciting their recantations thirty times each so all the people could hear.[7]

As in Great Barrington, Springfield, and Worcester, patriots shut
down the governmental apparatus in Salem, Concord, Barnstable,
Taunton, and Plymouth—in every county seat outside Boston. From
the time the Massachusetts Government Act was supposed to take effect, no county courts, which also functioned as the administrative
arms of the local governments, were allowed to conduct any business
under British authority. According to merchant John Andrews, rebels
in Plymouth were so excited by their victory that they

> attempted to remove a Rock (the one on which their fore-fathers
> first landed, when they came to this country) which lay buried in
> a wharfe five feet deep, up into the center of the town, near the
> court house. The way being up hill, they found it impracticable,
> as after they had dug it up, they found it to weigh ten tons at
> least.[8]

Meanwhile, all the Crown-appointed Councillors were told by
their angry neighbors to resign. The few who refused were driven
from their homes and forced to flee to Boston, where they sought protection from the British army.

In direct violation of the new law, the people continued with their
town meetings. When Governor Gage arrested seven men in the capital of Salem for calling a town meeting, 3,000 farmers immediately
marched on the jail to set the prisoners free. Two companies of British
soldiers retreated—and throughout Massachusetts meetings continued to convene. According to one contemporary account,

> Notwithstanding all the parade the governor made at Salem on
> account of their meeting, they had another one directly under
> his nose at Danvers, and continued it two or three howers longer
> than was necessary, to see if he would interrupt 'em. He was ac-
> quainted with it, but reply'd—"Damn 'em! I won't do any thing
> about it unless his Majesty sends me more troops."[9]

By early October 1774, more than half a year before the "shot heard 'round the world" at Lexington, Massachusetts patriots had seized all political and military authority outside Boston.

Throughout the preceding decade, patriots had written petitions, staged boycotts, and burnt effigies—but this was something new. In the late summer and early fall of 1774, patriots did not simply *protest* government, they *overthrew* it. Then, after dismissing British authority, they assumed political control through their town meetings, county conventions, and a Provincial Congress. One disgruntled Tory from Southampton summed it all up in his diary: "Government has now devolved upon the people, and they seem to be for using it." [10]

When the Boston Port Bill took effect, other colonists passed the hat for relief, held days of prayer and fasting, and called for conferences to talk things over.[11] These were common forms of political action in British North America. When the Massachusetts Government Act took effect, the people of Massachusetts shut down the government and prepared for war. This was the stuff of revolution. The people of Massachusetts forcibly overthrew the old regime and began to replace it with their own.[12]

The traditional telling, which states that the "American Revolution" started at Lexington, conceals this momentous and historic transfer of political power. If the "shot heard 'round the world" was the *beginning* of the American Revolution, we have no way of accounting for the revolution that preceded it.

The traditional story masks the people's vibrant dedication to their own political survival. Many years later, Levi Preston, a veteran of the Battle of Concord, explained why he had become a revolutionary:

"Were you not oppressed by the Stamp Act?"

"I never saw one of those stamps, and always understood that Governor Bernard put them all in Castle William. I am certain I never paid a penny for one of them."

"Well, what then about the tea-tax?"

"Tea-tax! I never drank a drop of the stuff; the boys threw it all overboard."

"Then I suppose you had been reading Harrington or Sidney and Locke about the eternal principles of liberty."

"Never heard of 'em. We read only the Bible, the Catechism, Watts' Psalms and Hymns, and the Almanack."

"Well, then, what was the matter? and what did you mean in going to the fight?"

"Young man, what we meant in going for those Redcoats was this: we always had governed ourselves, and we always meant to. They didn't mean we should." [13]

PREPARING FOR DEFENSE

As they toppled the old order, the people of Massachusetts realized they might have to defend their Revolution against a counterattack by the British army. With limited material means but a great deal of energy and nerve they prepared for war. By subscribing to the "myth of injured innocence"—the image of professional British soldiers mowing down common farmers ill-equipped for battle—we lose sight of the momentous arming and mobilizing that went on throughout the countryside for the better part of a year.

On July 4, 1774, more than nine months before Lexington, the patriotic American Political Society declared "that each, and every, member of our Society, be forth with Provided, with Two Pounds of Gun Powder each 12 Flints and Led Answerable thereunto." [14]

In August, eight months before Lexington, a convention of Committees of Correspondence, meeting in Worcester, resolved that patriots should supply their neighbors with powder, and that the committees should "ascertain what number of guns are deficient to arm the people in case of invasion. [15]

In September, seven months before Lexington, women as well as men personally participated in arming for war: they rolled cartridges of powder and shot for the tens of thousands of militiamen who marched toward Boston to confront the British. Also in September, a convention of Committees of Correspondence took it upon themselves to reorganize the Worcester County militia into seven new regiments, each with newly elected officers. They recommended that each town "provide themselves immediately with one or more field pieces, mounted and fitted for use," and they urged the towns "to enlist one third of the men . . . between sixteen and sixty years of age, to be ready to act at a minute's warning." [16] These were the famous "Minutemen," formed half a year before they would respond to the call at Lexington. Thus the story of the Minutemen does not begin at Lexington, where we normally put it; it is part and parcel of the Revolution of 1774.

In October, five months before Lexington, patriots from throughout Massachusetts formed their own representative body, the Provincial Congress, which assumed the basic functions of government. Foremost among its duties were to collect taxes and prepare for war. On October 26 delegates listed exactly what they would need to defend against a British invasion:

16 field pieces, 3 pounders, with carriages, irons, &c.; wheels for ditto, irons, sponges, ladles, &c., @ £30	£480 0 0
4 ditto, 6 pounders, with ditto, @ £38	£152 0 0
Carriages, irons, &c., for 12 battering cannon, @ £30	£360 0 0
4 mortars, and appurtenances, viz: 2 8-inch and 12 13-inch, @ £20	£80 0 0
20 tons grape and round shot, from 3 to 24 lb., @ £15	£300 0 0
10 tons bomb-shells, @ £20	£200 0 0
5 tons lead balls, @ £33	£165 0 0
1,000 barrels of powder, @ £8	£8,000 0 0
5,000 arms and bayonets, @ £2	£10,000 0 0
And 75,000 flints	£100 0 0
Contingent charges	£ 1,000 0 0
In the whole	£20,837 0 0[17]

All the political and military maneuvers of the next several months would focus on how to procure these armaments and how to keep what the patriots already possessed out of the hands of the British.

In December, four months before Lexington, patriots in nearby New Hampshire made the first offensive move of the war: four hundred local militiamen stormed Fort William and Mary in Portsmouth, took down the king's colors, and carried away approximately one hundred barrels of the king's gunpowder (some of which was later put to use during the Battle of Bunker Hill). The following day, 1,000 patriots marched again on the fort, this time removing all the muskets and sixteen cannon. This armed attack on a British fortress was an act of war, not merely a prelude to war.[18]

Although the offensive against Fort William and Mary was the first frontal military assault, it was not the first time patriots removed British arms and ammunition. Using stealth, cunning, and insider information, patriots had already taken cannon and munitions from British magazines in Boston, Providence, Newport, and New London.[19]

In February 1775, two months before Lexington, British intelligence reported that 15,000 "Minute Men" were "all properly armed." The report noted that the patriots had accumulated thirty-eight field pieces in Worcester and a considerable supply of gunpowder in Concord. If the British tried to seize these, however, they were likely to trigger a massive mobilization of angry patriots.

Although General Gage dared not attack Worcester or Concord, he did try to seize patriot stores he thought were more vulnerable. On Sunday, February 26, he ordered 240 soldiers to find and remove eight field pieces and a supply of powder that patriots were hiding at Salem. Local citizens, gathered in church, learned of the invasion in time to remove the arms and ammunition to a safer location. To stop the British advance, they simply raised a drawbridge that lay on the route of the marching troops. (When the British invaded Lexington seven weeks later, they avoided the mistakes they had made in Salem: they marched by night, not on the Sabbath, and they chose a route that did not have a drawbridge.)

On April 2, seventeen days before Lexington, patriots received word that British reinforcements were on their way to suppress the Massachusetts rebellion. With war imminent, the Provincial Congress voted to establish a regular army. The people of Boston, in anticipation of a military conflict, began to evacuate the city.

By April 19, 1775, the patriots were ready to resist an attack, as ready as they could ever expect to be. They were willing partners in this war-in-the-making. They knew the likely consequences, and they were willing to face those consequences.

The early overthrow of British authority and subsequent preparations for military conflict make the narrative of our nation's founding stronger, not weaker. When local Minutemen showed up on Lexington Green on April 19, and when neighboring Minutemen fought the British at Concord later that day, and when 20,000 others answered the call to arms within a week, they were engaging in conscious, considered political acts. These were not just knee-jerk reactions.

British troops marching toward Lexington and Concord that fateful morning amused themselves by singing *Yankee Doodle,* a pejorative little ditty that depicted their opponents as ignorant, provincial farmers. They failed to grasp that these farmers had turned themselves into soldiers to defend the revolution they had staged many months before. Every time we treat American patriots as no more than unsuspecting victims, we repeat the mistake these British soldiers made.

LOST IN HISTORY

The Massachusetts Revolution of 1774 was the most successful popular uprising in the nation's history, the only one to remove existing political authority. Despite its power—or possibly *because* of its power—this momentous event has been virtually lost to history. It is rarely mentioned even in passing, and it is never included in the core narrative of our nation's birth.

Our most triumphant rebellion did not always suffer such neglect.

The British *Annual Register,* written immediately in the wake of the 1774 revolution, gave considerable attention to the forced resignations, court closures, and preparations for war throughout the countryside of Massachusetts.[20] Early American historians—William Gordon in 1788, David Ramsay in 1789, and Mercy Otis Warren in 1805—covered the response to the Boston Port Act, but they highlighted the Massachusetts Government Act as the major catalyst leading to the American Revolution. According to Ramsay, the Massachusetts Government Act

> excited a greater alarm than the port act. The one effected only the metropolis, the other the whole province. . . . Had the parliament stopped short with the Boston port act, the motives to union and to make a common cause with that metropolis, would have been feeble, perhaps ineffectual to have roused the other provinces; but the arbitrary mutilation of the important privileges . . . by the will of parliament, convinced the most moderate that the cause of Massachusetts was the cause of all the provinces.[21]

Gordon described the popular uprising in considerable and vivid detail. In response to the "obnoxious alteration" dictated by the Massachusetts Government Act, "the people at large" prepared "to defend their rights with the point of a sword," and even the moderates "became resolute and resentful."[22] Warren went even further, calling the 1774 rebellion "one of the most extraordinary eras in the history of man: the exertions of spirit awakened by the severe hand of power had led to that most alarming experiment of leveling of all ranks, and destroying all subordination."[23]

This was too much of a revolution for conservative historians and schoolbook writers of the next generation, who argued that the "American Revolution" was not really revolutionary and that patriots were not to be construed as "rebels." Paul Allen, writing in 1819, devoted seventeen pages to the aid sent to Boston, while he assigned less than a paragraph to the resistance triggered by the Massachusetts Government Act.[24] Salma Hale's 1822 school text emphasized the themes of sympathy and solidarity, with nary a word about the overthrow of British authority.[25] The following year Charles Goodrich, in his popular *History of the United States of America,* wrote about Virginia's "expression of sympathy" with Boston, while ignoring altogether the people's rebellion in Massachusetts.[26]

The Good Samaritan approach certainly played better to children. Stories featuring neighbor-helping-neighbor conformed to educational goals, while those showing bullying crowds did not. Richard Snowden's school history, written in biblical style, made the events of 1774 sound like the story of the three wise men at the nativity: "Now it came to pass, when the people of the provinces had heard that their brethren in town were in a great strait, they sent to speak comfortable words unto them, and gave them worldly gifts." [27]

By midcentury, the patriotic historian George Bancroft was comfortable enough with the idea of a people's revolution to pay some respect to the uprising of 1774. Although Bancroft spoke of "sympathy" for Boston, he also devoted the better part of three chapters to the dramatic resistance to the Massachusetts Government Act. He did not, however, embrace its democratic character: it was under the direction of Boston's Joseph Warren, he claimed, who was told what to do by an absent Samuel Adams.[28] With this imaginary chain of command, Bancroft placed the first overthrow of the British firmly in the hands of America's favorite revolutionary. (See chapter 3.)

In 1865 William Wells followed Bancroft in placing Adams at the forefront of affairs in Boston, even though he was in Philadelphia at the time. But with no credible evidence linking Adams to the revolution in the countryside, Wells simply ignored those events.[29] For Wells and most subsequent writers, Samuel Adams had to be the prime mover of all crowd actions—and if Adams was not present, the tale was not told. Historians for the past century and a half have followed the lead of British officials of the time, who simply could not believe that authority had been overturned by "a tumultuous Rabble, without any Appearance of general Concert, or without any Head to advise, or Leader to Conduct." [30]

One might think that progressive historians of the early twentieth century—people like John Franklin Jameson, Charles Beard, and Carl Becker—would have been attracted to this popular uprising, but since it did not appear at first glance to be a classic "class struggle," it eluded their attention. While radical historians failed to pick up on this all-but-forgotten revolution, moderates saw no need to rock the boat. In their monumental, 1,300-page compilation of primary sources published in 1958, Henry Steele Commager and Richard B. Morris failed to document this vital episode. Instead, they included a complete section titled "All America Rallies to the Aid of Beleaguered Boston," another on the debates within the First Continental Congress, and over thirty pages on Lexington and Concord. [31]

That's how we stand to this day: "helping beleaguered Boston" and "the shot heard 'round the world" remain firmly anchored in our core narrative, while the actual toppling of the British-controlled government in Massachusetts is neglected entirely, or, at best, reduced to a sentence or two about "crowd actions" or "rural unrest." In six current elementary and middle school textbooks, there is not one word about the termination of British rule in 1774. [32] Eight of ten texts at the secondary and college levels ignore the first transfer of political authority to the Americans. [33] Of the remaining two, one states that "in most colonies . . . revolutionary committees, conventions, and congresses, entirely unauthorized by law, were replacing legal governing bodies," but it says nothing about the revolt in Massachusetts that deposed the official bodies. [34] The other does refer to the "full-scale rebellion" in Massachusetts, but instead of featuring the dramatic acts of the people themselves, it highlights only the formation of a Provincial Congress and the election of John Hancock "to lead it." [35]

Popular historians either neglect the Revolution of 1774 or misread its nature. In *Patriots: The Men Who Started the American Revolution*, A. J. Langguth makes no mention of it, while he includes an entire chapter on how other colonists helped the Bostonians. [36] In *Liberty!*

Thomas Fleming places Samuel Adams solidly in control of all crucial events; Adams allegedly "convened" the Provincial Congress, even though he was hundreds of miles away.[37] Benson Bobrick, in *Angel in the Whirlwind*, reduces the 1774 revolution to a single document, the Suffolk Resolves, which he attributes to the leadership of Joseph Warren.[38] No current popularization of the American Revolution treats the overthrow of British authority in rural Massachusetts as the work of an aroused populace, acting in accordance with democratic traditions and principles.[39]

Why has the story of the dramatic revolution in Massachusetts been abandoned? Why do we think that helping Boston was of greater consequence than shutting down a government, and that the revolutionaries were no more than unsuspecting victims? Why, indeed, have we denied our powerful revolutionary heritage?

There are several overlapping reasons, deeply rooted in our national self-image and the nature of storytelling.

The very strengths of the Revolution of 1774 have insured its anonymity. This revolution was democratic by design; the people not only preached popular sovereignty but practiced it. Although the toppling of authority enjoyed unprecedented, widespread support, there were no charismatic, self-promoting leaders to anchor the story and serve as its "heroes." This made for a stronger revolution, but it simultaneously helps explain why we know so little about it.

This revolution involved no bloodshed, for resistance was unthinkable. The *force* of the people was so overwhelming that *violence* became unnecessary. The handful of Crown-appointed officials in Worcester, when confronted by 4,622 angry militiamen, had no choice but to submit. Had opposition been stronger, there might have been violence; that would have made for a bloodier tale but a weaker revolution.

The Massachusetts Revolution of 1774 was ubiquitous, erupting everywhere at once. General Gage had no idea where or when he might oppose it. But a spontaneous uprising is difficult to chronicle; there is no clear storyline leading neatly from A to Z. This revolution occurred throughout the countryside, while the media of the times were confined to Boston. Again, the very nature of this broad-based revolt led to a stronger revolution but a less compelling tale.

Finally, the Massachusetts Revolution of 1774, like all true revolutions, was a bullying affair. Crowds numbering in the thousands forced a few unarmed officials to cower and submit. This made for a powerful revolution but a scary story. Contrast that to "helping beleaguered Boston," a far gentler tale, or to "the shot heard 'round the world," which features the British, not the Americans, as bullies. Particularly now, when the United States possesses unbridled power, we do not wish our stories to depict patriots as intimidators.

Like the conservatives of the early nineteenth century, we remain fearful of our own revolution. All narratives of early United States history include accounts of an uprising labeled Shays' Rebellion, which was modeled after the Revolution of 1774. In 1786, exactly twelve years after Massachusetts farmers had closed the courts and dismantled the established government, many of the very same people tried to repeat their early triumph. In Great Barrington, Springfield, Worcester—all the same places—disgruntled citizens of rural Massachusetts once again gathered in crowds to topple existing authority. There were two important differences between the uprisings of 1774 and 1786: the latter was much smaller, involving crowds that numbered in the hundreds rather than the thousands, and it failed. In our histories, we have chosen to feature the smaller, failed rebellion in preference to the larger, successful one. Although we like to commemorate the break from Britain, we hesitate to celebrate the raw and rampant power of the people who made this happen.

By shying away, we lose sight of our democratic heritage. Students of history are fond of noting that the United States was founded as a republic, not a democracy, and they accurately point to the views of the Founding Fathers, who feared too much power in the hands of the people. But if we shift our gaze from the Founders to the founders, from gentry in dress suits and wigs to farmers in frocks and mud-caked boots, we find that a very different attitude prevailed. There could never be too much democracy, these people believed. All decisions, even during their mass street actions, had to be approved by "the body of the people." The representatives they selected to deal with recalcitrant officials served for one day only—the ultimate in term limits. These rebels ran their revolution like a mobilized town meeting, each participant as important as any other. At no time in history have people been more passionate about adhering to democratic processes.

At least in Massachusetts, the roots of American democracy go deeper than most of us have ever imagined. The United States owes its very existence to the premise that all authority resides with the people, yet our standard telling of history does not reflect this fundamental principle. The story of the revolution before the Revolution can remind us of what we are all about.

"In the midst of frost and snows,
disease and destitution, Liberty erected her altar."

Valley Forge: March, 1777. Drawing by
Felix Octavius Carr Darley, mid-nineteenth century.

5

THE WINTER AT VALLEY FORGE

To understand the staying power of the Valley Forge story, we need to see it through the eyes of a ten-year-old, for that is the age when Americans first learn it in school. Other Revolutionary tales inspire images of toy-like soldiers and men in wigs; they are alternately inspiring or quaint, but always remote. Not so with the suffering soldiers at Valley Forge. This is a story of elemental forces.

Nowhere is the story told better than in F. Van Wyck Mason's *The Winter at Valley Forge*, one of the "Landmark Books" written for a youthful audience in the mid-twentieth century: "What a miracle was wrought at Valley Forge! This winter encampment with its pain and suffering, its heartaches and despair, might well be called the turning point of the Revolution." Mason's classic work, which introduced the story to an entire generation, depicts dedicated soldiers enduring cold and snow for the good of their country. The winter of 1777–1778, Mason writes, was "one of the cruelest winters in our country's history." As "the blizzards howled" and "the ice thickened," the rebels "found new courage, new resolve, new faith in their cause."[1] This basic impression anchors the traditional telling of the American Revolution: suffering soldiers, fueled by faith, withstood not only the wrath of the British Empire but the worst that God Himself could deal out.

There are two important components to the story. First is the notion of "patient suffering." Patriots were willing to endure extreme hardships, we are told, because they believed so strongly in their country. They were humble folk, not rich and arrogant like the British. Again, we like to see ourselves as David, doing battle with Goliath. The rebels, although outsized and outclassed, had *character*. They would do anything for the cause of freedom.

Second is the notion of the cruel hand of nature. Without the blizzards and the bitter cold, there would be little to celebrate in this winter camp of the Continental Army; militarily, the encampment at Valley Forge was merely an interlude, and in terms of battlefield casualties, those were the quietest months during the entire course of the Revolutionary War.[2]

Both subplots are mistaken. Soldiers did not suffer silently. Routinely, they complained and pillaged; sometimes, they deserted or mutinied. And the weather itself was hardly to blame. The winter spent at Valley Forge was milder than normal. By contrast, two years later, Continental soldiers survived the coldest winter in 400 years on the Eastern seaboard of the United States—and yet, strangely, that story is rarely told.

A LITTLE RESPECT

The Valley Forge story, in its traditional form, is disrespectful to the soldiers who endured years of hardships, endangered their lives, and in many cases actually died so that the United States could gain and retain its independence. To give these patriots the respect that is their due, we have to cease creating idealized fantasies about how well they behaved themselves.

At Valley Forge and throughout the Revolutionary War, Continental soldiers demanded the food, clothing, and pay that had been promised them—and for good reason. Had they not tended to their own concerns and needs, they would not have been able to stay in the field and face the enemy. To appreciate this, we have to understand who these men really were and how they came to serve in the Continental Army.

Although we might like to believe otherwise, the United States won its freedom with the help of hired gunmen. At the beginning of the war, in 1775, all sorts of people showed up to fight. Farmers and artisans, rich and poor, young and old—patriots came forth with uncommon zeal. But this could not last. By the close of 1775, farmers had returned to their farms and artisans to their shops. Since most people had businesses of their own to attend to, Congress found it difficult to induce recruits to fight for their country. "The few who act upon Principles of disinterestedness," George Washington told Congress in September 1776, "are, comparatively speaking, no more than a drop in the Ocean." [3]

Reluctantly, the Continental Congress offered bounties to those who agreed to join the army. This helped, but it did not suffice. Starting in 1777, Congress fixed the number of companies that each state had to recruit for the Continental Army. States and towns, hoping to fill their quotas, added bounties of their own, but even that was not enough. Without sufficient volunteers, most communities resorted to a draft. But the draft worked differently in those days: a draftee had only to produce a body, either his own or someone else's. Those with sufficient means, if called, hired those looking for work to fill their place. In this manner, the ranks of the Continental Army became filled with boys eager for adventure and men without property or jobs. These were the folks who hobbled into Valley Forge on December 19, 1777.

Civilians—those who had not joined up—showed no great love for either the Continental Army or the soldiers who comprised it. They feared standing armies in general (indeed, that was one of the major complaints they voiced against Great Britain), while they looked down upon the men who actually served in this one. As historian John Shy has observed, "The men who shouldered the heaviest military burden were something *less* than average colonial Americans. As a group, they were poorer, more marginal, less well anchored in society." [4] The army became representative not of the American population, but only of its lower orders: poor men and boys, laborers and apprentices, even Indians and former slaves.

This was not truly a citizens' army, as originally intended; it was far closer to the European model than Americans (both then and now) have chosen to admit. Many civilians at the time preferred to look the other way, ignoring rather than supporting the men who had become professional soldiers. Quaker farmers residing near Valley Forge had their own reasons to resent the fighting Presbyterians and Congregationalists, lads whose business it was to kill, while soldiers, on their part, grumbled about the "cursed Quakers" who were "no Friends to the Cause we are engaged in." [5] Soldiers grew to resent the lack of support they received not only from the Quakers but from "Ye who Eat Pumpkin Pie and Roast Turkeys." [6] Increasingly, the hired guns of the Continental Army saw themselves as a class apart.

At Valley Forge, it is often said, Baron von Steuben infused military discipline into the ragtag Continental Army. He turned farmers into soldiers. Although there is some truth in this, farmers became soldiers not only by marching to the commands of their officers, but also by developing a unique sense of identity, separate and distinct from all other Americans. They did indeed become a professional army, with all that that entails.

Ill prepared to support a permanent army, Congress allowed the Commissary Department to fall into a shambles. Food and clothing, much needed, never arrived. Congress, not the raw forces of nature, was accountable for the lack of provisions that caused the soldiers much grief.

Forced to fend for themselves, troops ventured forth from Valley Forge to pillage local civilians. John Lesher, who lived twenty-five miles away, complained that he was "no master of any individual thing I possess." American troops, he said, "under the shadows of the Bayonet and the appellation Tory act as they please." [7] Farmers were so discouraged that they threatened not to plant new crops. Years later, Private Joseph Plumb Martin admitted that " 'Rub and Go' was always the Revolutionary soldier's motto." [8]

At other times during the war, George Washington issued prohibitions against pillaging, but at Valley Forge he was forced to sanction the practice. Although he used the polite term "forage" rather than "pillage" or "plunder," the commander-in-chief ordered soldiers to strip the countryside clean.[9] Farmers were stopped on their way to market, households were raided, and magazines depleted of all provisions. Reluctant local inhabitants, accustomed to being paid real money for their produce, grain, milk, and meat, were given only worthless notes. Private Martin recalled that at Valley Forge he received orders direct from the quartermaster-general "to go into the country on a foraging expedition, which was nothing more nor less than to procure provisions from the inhabitants for the men in the army . . . at the point of the bayonet." [10]

Soldiers tended to their needs in other ways as well. Some simply ran away. According to the traditional tale, all men remained true; in fact, eight to ten men deserted every day from Valley Forge.[11] On February 12, 1778, during a period of extreme shortages, Washington wrote: "We find the Continental troops (especially those who are not Natives) are very apt to desert from the piquets." [12]

The standard story also ignores mutinies as well as desertions. On December 23, 1777, Washington reported that "a dangerous mutiny" two nights before had been suppressed "with difficulty." [13] In February, Washington reported that "strong symptoms of discontent" had appeared, and he feared that "a general mutiny and dispersion" might be forthcoming if complaints were not actively addressed.[14] In April, Washington complained that ninety officers from the Virginia line had just resigned, others were following suit, and he feared for "the very existence of the Army." [15] Although Washington might have been exaggerating for effect, it remains clear that suffering soldiers were not simply enduring their lot, silently and heroically—they were standing up for themselves. If the United States wanted an army, it would have to treat the soldiers better. Privates stated this emphatically by threats of mutiny or by simply running away. Officers threatened to resign, and many did. Actions such as these succeeded in arousing the attention first of Washington, and then, through him, of Congress and state officials. Eventually the complaints of soldiers achieved some results, even if minimal. Had soldiers not voiced their discontent and acted accordingly, the army probably *would* have dissipated.

As the war dragged on, mutinies became a real cause of concern. The famous ones—uprisings within the Connecticut, Pennsylvania, and New Jersey lines, the march on Congress on June 21, 1783, the aborted "Newburg Conspiracy" (see following paragraph)—represent only the tip of the iceberg. Firsthand accounts by both privates and officers reveal that resistance was the rule rather than the exception. Soldiers in the Continental Army repeatedly threatened to take matters in their own hands unless their basic needs were met.

The reporting of acts of resistance within the army is anathema to the illusion of patient suffering. Since soldiers in the Continental Army did desert in great numbers, and since mutinies were far more common than in any war this nation has ever fought against a foreign enemy, the traditional telling of the Valley Forge story necessitates either fancy footwork or an ostrich-like refusal to face what really happened. *Liberty!*, the book that accompanies the PBS six-hour documentary on the American Revolution, announces point-blank that "desertions were relatively few" at Valley Forge.[16] Popular authors often dismiss the subject of mutiny by telling a story of George Washington and the "Newburg Conspiracy." On the ides of March 1783, at his headquarters in Newburg, New York, the beloved commander-in-chief allegedly defused a movement among his officers to march against Congress with a simple offhand remark: "Gentlemen," he is supposed to have said, "you will permit me to put on my spectacles, for I have not only grown gray but almost blind in the service of my country." This, allegedly, was all it took to counter all mutinous or treasonous activities: "It moved the officers deeply, and tears welled in their eyes," the story goes. "Again they felt a tremendous surge of affection for the commander who had led them all so far and long." [17] So much for mutinies in the Continental Army.

This glib refusal to take seriously the grievances of the soldiers is insulting and unpatriotic. To romanticize their experiences in an attempt to honor them dishonors them instead. Without these men, the fledgling United States government would have collapsed. The truly patriotic response, far from denying or ignoring mutinies and desertions, is to examine the real lives and deeds of the soldiers in the fullest possible detail.

To this end, we have no better informant than Joseph Plumb Martin. Although Martin reported that he and others had made it through the Valley Forge winter by pillaging, their hardships did not end the following spring. Martin reported that two years later, in May 1780, "the monster Hunger, still attended us; he was not to be shaken off by any efforts we could use, for here was the old story of starving, as rife as ever." Continental soldiers were forced to confront the most profound dilemma any American has ever had to face:

> The men were now exasperated beyond endurance; they could not stand it any longer. They saw no alternative but to starve to death, or break up the army, give all up and go home. This was a hard matter for the soldiers to think upon. They were truly patriotic, they loved their country, and they had already suffered everything short of death in its cause; and now, after such extreme hardships to give up all was too much, but to starve to death was too much also. What was to be done? Here was the army starved and naked, and there their country sitting still and expecting the army to do notable things while fainting from sheer starvation. [18]

This is the real Valley Forge story, and it lasted for eight long years. It features poor men and boys who fought in place of those were better off. When these soldiers failed to receive adequate food, minimal clothing, or the pay they had been promised, they were forced to weigh their options: Should they endure their hardships silently, grumble among themselves, or create a fuss? If all else failed should they mutiny or simply walk away? All alternatives were possible, none favorable. In addition to staving off hunger and fighting the enemy, soldiers had to deal with this unsolvable problem day by day.

In this particular instance, Joseph Martin and his compatriots chose to act forcibly. "We had borne as long as human nature could endure, and to bear longer we considered folly," Martin continued. One day, while on parade, the privates began "growling like soreheaded dogs, . . . snapping at the officers, and acting contrary to their orders." [19] This led to a series of events sometimes labeled the "mutiny in the Connecticut line." Technically, the soldiers' behavior was mutinous, for privates did challenge the authority of officers; at one point, they even held bayonets to the chests of those in command. But the soldiers were not trying to seize power; they only wanted to gain a little respect and a corresponding increase in rations. They did what they had to do, no more—and they achieved results: "Our stir did us some good in the end," Martin reported, "for we had provisions directly after." [20]

A TALE OF TWO WINTERS

The winter of 1777–1778 was not "one of the cruelest winters in our country's history." We have no record of daily temperatures at Valley Forge, but in nearby Philadelphia, only seventeen miles away, temperatures ran slightly above the historic average (see table). On more than half the winter mornings, there was no frost. Soldiers had to endure only one extended, hard freeze—from December 29 to December 31—and the thermometer dropped below double digits, briefly, only twice. Some snow did fall, but there were no memorable blizzards. Snowfall was "moderate, not heavy," according to weather historian David Ludlum. "On the basis of cold statistics," writes Ludlum, "the winter of 1777–1778 was not a severe one." [21]

Days with Low Temperature Below Freezing—Philadelphia[22]

	1777–1778	HISTORIC AVERAGE
December	17	21
January	15	25
February	13	22
March	5	14

Ironically, soldiers in the Continental Army did have to endure a particularly cruel winter—but it wasn't during their camp at Valley Forge. While camped at Morristown, New Jersey, in 1779–1780, they encountered what Ludlum concludes was "the severest season in all American history." [23] In Philadelphia, the *high* temperature for the day rose above freezing only once during the month of January.[24] On January 20 Timothy Matlack wrote to Joseph Reed from Philadelphia: "The ink now freezes in my pen within five feet of the fire in my parlour, at 4 o'clock in the afternoon." [25] In New York, a thermometer at British headquarters dropped to −16 degrees Fahrenheit; the lowest official reading since that time has been −15.[26] In Hartford, a daily thermometer reading revealed that January 1780, was the coldest calendar month in recorded history. On twenty-one days, the temperature dropped below 10 degrees Fahrenheit; between January 19 and January 31, subzero temperatures were recorded on nine different days, bottoming out at −22.[27]

With temperatures this low, and the cold lasting for such an extended period of time, rivers and bays froze hard. In New York, the Hudson and East Rivers turned to ice. So did New York Harbor, much of Long Island Sound, and some of the ocean itself. To the south, the Delaware River froze, as did large portions of the Chesapeake Bay. In Virginia, the York and James Rivers became solid. As far south as North Carolina, Albermarle Sound froze over. According to David Ludlum, nothing like this had ever happened since the arrival of Europeans, and it has yet to happen again:

During one winter only in recorded American meteorological history have *all* the saltwater inlets, harbors, and sounds of the Atlantic coastal plain, from North Carolina northeastward, frozen over and remained closed to navigation for a period of a full month and more. This occurred during what has ever been called "The Hard Winter of 1780," a crucial period during the war when General Washington's poorly housed, ill-clad, and under-nourished American troops at Morristown in the north Jersey hills were keeping a watchful eye on the British army much more comfortably quartered in New York City some 20 miles distant.[28]

For one winter only, frozen bays and rivers became new roadways. Rebel deserters walked across the Hudson, from New Jersey to British-controlled New York. Hessian deserters from the British army crossed Long Island Sound on foot to rebel-controlled Connecticut. The British carried firewood on sleighs across the Hudson River from New Jersey to Manhattan. They also sent sleighs laden with provisions from Manhattan to Staten Island, and they even rolled cannons across the ice; meanwhile, a detachment of British cavalry rode their horses across the New York harbor in the other direction. Sleighs traversed the Chesapeake from Baltimore to Annapolis. Had Washington decided to make his famous crossing of the Delaware during "The Hard Winter" instead of three years earlier, he could have dispensed with his boats—the troops would simply have marched across the frozen waters.[29]

Along with cold and ice came the snow. The first major fall in Morristown arrived on December 18, 1779, and the ground remained covered for three months afterward. In late December and early January, a series of violent storms swept through the entire Northeast. On December 28–29, the wind toppled several houses in New York City. In Morristown, several feet of snow fell during the first week of January. Joseph Plumb Martin recalled the effects of the storm on the soldiers:

The winter of 1779 and '80 was very severe; it has been denominated "the hard winter," and hard it was to the army in particular, in more respects than one. The period of the revolution has repeatedly been styled "the times that tried men's souls." I often found that those times not only tried men's souls, but their bodies too; I know they did mine, and that effectually. . . .

At one time it snowed the greater part of four days successively, and there fell nearly as many feet deep of snow, and here was the keystone of the arch of starvation. We were absolutely, literally starved. I do solemnly declare that I did not put a single morsel of victuals into my mouth for four days and as many nights, except a little black birch bark which I gnawed off a stick of wood, if that can be called victuals. I saw several of the men roast their old shoes and eat them, and I was afterwards informed by one of the officers' waiters, that some of the officers killed and ate a favorite little dog that belonged to one of them.—If this was not "suffering" I request to be informed what can pass under that name; if "suffering" like this did not "try men's souls," I confess that I do not know what could.[30]

As privates struggled to stay alive, officers worried about the impact on their army. On January 5, 1780, General Nathanael Greene wrote from Morristown: "Here we are surrounded with Snow banks, and it is well we are, for if it was good traveling, I believe the Soldiers would take up their packs and march, they having been without provision two or three days."[31] The following day, Greene's worst fears were almost realized: "The Army is upon the eve of disbanding for want of Provisions," he reported. On January 8 Ebenezer Huntington reported, "the Snow is very deep & the Coldest Weather I ever experienced for three weeks altogether. Men almost naked & what is still worst almost Starved."[32] Huntington, at that point, was unaware that the coldest weather was yet to come.

That same day—January 8, 1780—Washington himself offered a

very bleak assessment: "The present situation of the Army with respect to provisions is the most distressing of any we have experienced
since the beginning of the War"—and that included the winter spent
at Valley Forge.[33] Johann de Kalb, who served as an officer under
Washington, stated definitively: "Those who have only been in Valley
Forge and Middlebrook during the last two winters, but have not
tasted the cruelties of this one, know not what it is to suffer." [34] For all
those who experienced both winters, there could be no doubt: Morristown was by far the worst.

Hardships continued. Since the snowpack hindered the shipment of
supplies, soldiers had to face much of the winter cold and hungry.
How long could they endure? On February 10 General Greene once
again reported: "Our Army has been upon the point of disbanding for
want of provisions." [35] Finally, in mid-March, the weather warmed
and the snow melted. Supplies arrived, and the worst was over. On
March 18 Washington summed up the experience in a letter to General
Lafayette: "The oldest people now living in this Country do not remember so hard a Winter as the one we are now emerging from. In a
word, the severity of the frost exceeded anything of the kind that had
ever been experienced in this climate before." [36]

For the soldiers, it had never been worse than at Morristown. Yet
the Continental Army made it through intact. According to those on
the ground at the time, not those who would tell the story generations
later, Morristown was truly the low point of the war—the real-life
"Valley Forge."

Why, then, do we make such a big deal of "The Winter at Valley
Forge," while the "Hard Winter" at Morristown is nearly forgotten?
Revolutionary soldiers, scantily clad and poorly fed, had to brave the
harshest weather in at least 400 years; why is this not a part of our
standard histories?

The answer, in a nutshell, is that Valley Forge better fits the story
we wish to tell, while Morristown is something of an embarrassment.
At Valley Forge, the story goes, soldiers suffered quietly and patiently. They remained true to their leader. At Morristown, on the

other hand, they mutinied—and this is not in line with the "suffering soldiers" motif.

As a story, Morristown doesn't work for several other reasons as well. First of all, soldiers in the Continental Army camped there during four different winters, and this is much too confusing.[37] The "Hard Winter" was the second of these. The following winter, on January 1, 1781, the Pennsylvania line staged the largest and most successful mutiny of the Revolutionary War. Although this did not take place during the winter of 1779–1780, any mention of Morristown would necessitate at least some mention of this mutiny, which many narrative accounts conveniently leave out. The New Jersey Brigade also camped at Morristown during that third winter, and they too had just mutinied; this uprising was unsuccessful, culminating with the execution of several mutineers. To include all this would undermine a central feature of the "suffering soldier" lesson: clearly, these patriots had not endured their plight in silence.

Furthermore, to tell the complete Morristown saga would reveal that the soldiers' hardships continued throughout the war, virtually unabated. Soldiers in the Continental Army never did receive the help they needed or the respect they deserved. To admit this would make the civilian population look bad. Why didn't other patriots come to the aid of those who did the fighting?

The story of Valley Forge, on the other hand, tells us what we want to hear. Supposedly, soldiers learned to behave themselves when Baron von Steuben whipped them into shape. There were no major uprisings. The troops were allegedly obedient and well behaved. They remained faithful to Washington when his command was challenged by intrigue. All this looks good.

Also, Valley Forge and the American victory at Saratoga happened in close succession. From the storytelling point of view, this works well. Valley Forge was the "low point," and Saratoga the "turning point," of the Revolutionary War. (Strangely, the low point occurred shortly *after* the turning point, but this technical glitch is generally overlooked.) After Valley Forge, the darkest hour was supposedly

over. Come spring, once the soldiers had proved their worth, their
troubles subsided. This mythic tale is based on the classic image of
seasonal renewal, not historical documentation. Although hardships
continued and even worsened till the end of the war, and although
mutinies became rampant, the Valley Forge story serves to suppress
these later difficulties. Narratives can refer to "suffering soldiers" at a
precise, well-defined time, without including the more serious uprisings that followed. By telling the story of the soldiers' plight there,
writers do not have to visit it later on, when a spirit of resistance swept
through the Continental Army.

Finally, Valley Forge makes for a powerful story because many soldiers died. In fact, the deaths were primarily due to camp diseases—
cold and hunger took few lives—but that is rarely stated, because
disease evokes little sense of drama or patriotic sentiment. (More soldiers actually lost their lives because of disease than at the hands of
the enemy during the Revolutionary War.)[38] Still, a death toll always
helps a story along. The winter at Valley Forge was so severe, we are
led to believe, that people actually perished because of it—and all
without raising a fuss. Such patriots they must have been!

CONSECRATED GROUND: THE STORY ENSHRINED

Nobody celebrated Valley Forge during the Revolution itself. At the
time, the sorry plight of soldiers at this winter camp was a guarded
military secret—kept from the ears of the British, who might seize the
moment to attack, and downplayed to the French, who might deny aid
if they heard too much about the ragtag Continental Army. Just before Christmas in 1777, after setting up camp in Valley Forge, Washington told Congress, "Upon the ground of safety and policy, I am
obliged to conceal the true State of the Army from Public view." But
the members of Congress, he confided, should be aware that there had
been a "total failure of Supplies." Conditions were so bad, he re-

ported, that "we have . . . no less than 2898 Men now in Camp unfit for duty because they are bare foot and otherwise naked." [39]

Washington's complaints to Congress, contained in his letters of December 22 and 23, 1777, comprise the basic documentation for the Valley Forge story. Undoubtedly, Washington issued his bleak reports for very practical reasons: he wanted to shock congressional delegates into action. The Commissary Department was in a state of collapse, unable to provide many essential items. Without "more Vigorous exertions," he warned, "this Army must dissolve." [40] In later years, writers would quote Washington's solicitations as the definitive source on the suffering soldiers at Valley Forge, although most have chosen to ignore his repeated warnings that malcontents were on the verge of mutiny. Without Washington's pleading words, geared for maximum effect, there would likely be no legend of Valley Forge. At Morristown, two years later, Washington painted an equally bleak picture, also geared for effect—but these words have been conveniently overlooked.

After the war, as during the war, civilians chose not to harp on the sorry state of the Continental Army, whether at Valley Forge or Morristown. The very existence of the army was something of an embarrassment to many Americans, who opposed standing armies on republican principles. The decrepit state of this particular assemblage of lower-class men and boys was particularly shameful. If anybody had spun the Valley Forge tale back then, they would have been deemed unpatriotic.

Postwar historians did not romanticize the winter camp at Valley Forge. David Ramsay (1789) devoted only one and a half sentences to Valley Forge in over 700 pages. Although William Gordon (1788) and John Marshall (1804) described the camp and cited Washington's letters, they did not treat it as a defining moment in the history of the Revolution or claim that soldiers always endured their hardships in silence. In fact, Marshall emphasized that soldiers seized provisions from local farmers, and all the early historians included extensive discussions of the later mutinies, indications of the soldiers' discontent. [41]

In the early 1800s, some Americans began to focus on the notion of "patient suffering" and affixed this notion to a particular time and place: the 1777–1778 camp at Valley Forge. In 1805, more than a quarter of a century after the fact, Mercy Otis Warren described the condition of the troops in vivid detail:

> The resolution and patience of this little army surmounted every difficulty. They waited long, amid penury, hunger, and cold, for the necessary supplies. . . . Unprovided with materials to raise their cold lodgment from the ground, the dampness of the situation, and the wet earth on which they lay, occasioned sickness and mortality to rage among them to an astonishing degree.

Warren was perhaps the first to use this experience as a defining characteristic of the Revolution:

> We have seen through the narrative of events during the war, the armies of the American states suffering hunger and cold, nakedness, fatigue, and danger, with unparalleled patience and valor. A due sense of the importance of the contest in which they were engaged, and the certain ruin and disgrace in which themselves and their children would be involved on the defeat of their object, was a strong stimulus to patient suffering.[42]

Any "murmurs" of discontent, she concluded, were quickly quieted by "an attachment to their commanding officers, a confidence in the faith of congress, and the sober principles of independence, equity and equality."

To the actual troops encamped at Valley Forge, "confidence in the faith of congress" would have appeared as a joke in bad taste. Congress failed to pay them as promised, let alone feed and clothe them, and soldiers resented this bitterly. Yet Warren chose to paint a cozy picture: the bedraggled army and Congress united in common cause.

The "patient suffering" story was beginning to take shape, ironically, to demonstrate unity between soldiers and civilians—although the suffering of the soldiers was directly attributable to the lack of civilian support, and this in reality caused no end of ill feeling.

As the notion of "patient suffering" caught on, it attached to the camp at Valley Forge. When David Ramsay came out with his *Life of George Washington* in 1807, he included a much more extensive treatment of Valley Forge than he had in his earlier history.[43] The following year, in the sixth edition of his immensely popular *Life of Washington*, Mason Weems told a new story: the commander-in-chief, while alone in the woods at Valley Forge, was seen kneeling in prayer.[44] For more than a century, this pious image would be repeated again and again, testimony to the faith of the man, the army, and the nation.

After thirty years, civilians no longer perceived the fighting men of the Continental Army as a threat. Quite to the contrary: in the military mobilization that culminated in the War of 1812, patriotic writers and orators found it convenient to extol the virtues of the men who had prevailed in the Revolutionary War. In his July 4, 1812, oration to Congress, Richard Rush praised the "noble achievements" of Revolutionary soldiers, and he then insisted that Americans not "dishonor" their memory by failing to answer the current call to arms.[45]

Veterans who were once scorned suddenly found they were being celebrated. The sites of their brave deeds were consecrated, and this brought Valley Forge into play. The May 1812 issue of Virginia's *Monthly Magazine and Literary Journal* suggested that Valley Forge be sanctified as "classic ground to posterity" because of the "toil" and "sufferings" which the soldiers had experienced there.[46] Morristown, its legacy clouded by mutinies, was not similarly consecrated— "patient suffering" couldn't be attached to such a place.

Revolutionary War veterans naturally welcomed the change of attitude and gave it a practical turn. Yes, they had suffered patiently— so now, at last, they should be recompensed. Calling forth memories of mutinies, at this juncture, would have been counterproductive.

Vets pushed hard to receive pensions, and in 1818, forty years after the camp at Valley Forge, Congress finally allocated money to Revolutionary soldiers who could show proof of both service and need.

From that point on, the patient suffering of the soldiers at Valley Forge became a common refrain in most American histories. Salma Hale, in his 1822 history written for schoolchildren as well as adults, romanticized the experience of the soldiers at Valley Forge: "They passed the winter in huts, suffered extreme distress from want of clothing and of food, but endured their privations without a murmur. How strong must have been their love of liberty?" [47] Charles Goodrich, writing in 1823, contrasted the Continental Army at Valley Forge with the British army in Philadelphia: "While the defenders of the country were thus suffering and perishing, the royal army was enjoying all the conveniences which an opulent city afforded." [48] This disparity between dedicated Americans and decadent Englishmen played well to a patriotic audience.

By the middle of the nineteenth century, scarcely a person was left alive who could accurately remember the severities of "The Hard Winter of 1780." In Revolutionary mythologies, the blizzards and biting cold of that winter were conveniently pushed back two years, to coincide with the camp at Valley Forge—the "severe winter of 1777 and '8," it was called. A newspaper in 1848 reported with an air of authority that this had been "one of the most rigorous winters ever experienced in this country. . . . So intently cold was the weather and so exhausted the soldiers when they commenced their march toward Valley Forge, that some were seen to drop dead under the benumbing influence of the frost." [49]

In 1851, Benjamin Lossing's travelogue of Revolutionary historic sites gave Valley Forge top billing:

Valley Forge! How dear to the true worshiper at the shrine of Freedom is the name of Valley Forge! There, in the midst of frost and snows, disease and destitution, Liberty erected her altar; and in all the world's history we have no record of purer devotion, holier sincerity, or more pious self-sacrifice, than was there exhibited in the camp of Washington. The courage that nerves the arm on the battle-field, and dazzles by its brilliant but evanescent flashes, pales before the steadier and more intense flame of patient endurance, the sum of the sublime heroism displayed at Valley Forge. And if there is a spot on the face of our broad land whereon Patriotism should delight to pile its highest and most venerated monument, it should be in the bosom of that little valley on the bank of the Schuylkill.[50]

Here was the Valley Forge story full blown, much as we know it today.

By the centennial celebrations in 1876, Valley Forge had become ingrained in the national consciousness. In step with the times, the local community prepared to commemorate the one hundredth anniversary of the Continental Army's winter camp of 1777–1778. But what kind of celebration would be appropriate to honor the miserable time at Valley Forge, allegedly the lowest point in the history of the Revolutionary War?

A summer solstice party, of course. On June 19, 1878, thousands of locals joined with national celebrities to revel on the anniversary of "evacuation day," the breaking of camp. Capitalizing on the momentum, the Centennial and Memorial Association of Valley Forge gathered funds to purchase Washington's headquarters, a fixed point where tourists could pay their respects. In the years to follow, additional sites were preserved or restored, and in 1893 Valley Forge became a state park. On "evacuation day" of 1917, the federal government added its stamp of approval with the dedication of the National Memorial Arch, and on July 4, 1976, the day of the nation's bicentennial celebration, the state park was transformed into the Valley Forge National Historical Park, a shrine that remains to this day the destination point for over one million patriotic pilgrims every year.[51]

Over the past century and a half, little has changed in the Valley Forge story. Although Mason Weems's tale about Washington praying in the woods is no longer repeated as fact, and although blacks and Indians are now included among the barefoot soldiers, the broad strokes remain the same. When told to children, the story features the cruel hand of Nature; when told to adults, it sometimes lays the blame on Congress as well as Nature—but in either case, the soldiers proved their patriotism through patient suffering, and the values celebrated are passive obedience and blind devotion. These were deemed prime virtues in the early stages of American nationalism, and they are still seen as virtues in some modern states—but why us, and why now? In a modern democracy, such passivity seems oddly out of sync.

From the beginning, Revolutionary soldiers exhibited the freedom they were fighting for. Understandably, this caused their officers some concern. The rebel soldiers "carry the spirit of freedom into the field, and think for themselves," complained General Richard Montgomery, one of the leaders of the Quebec expedition. Montgomery could not understand why troops called "a sort of town meeting" every time a maneuver was planned. "The privates are all generals," he reported.[52] From a military point of view, this excessive spirit had to be reigned in, at least to some extent. But it never disappeared, nor should it have. Americans cherish initiative and independence. The traditional Valley Forge story belittles these values; the true story of soldiers in the Continental Army embraces them. Throughout the Revolutionary War, American soldiers considered their circumstances, weighed the available options, made decisions, and took actions they deemed appropriate. They made their needs known and stood up for their rights. They behaved like good, patriotic Americans. They did not suffer in silence—instead, they devised means to make things better. They did whatever they needed to do to keep themselves alive, fed, and able to carry on. There is no shame in this, although we have acted as if there is.

WISE MEN

"Jefferson's Declaration of Independence
was great from the moment he wrote it."

Thomas Jefferson Writing the Declaration of Independence.
Painting by Howard Pyle, 1898.

6

JEFFERSON'S DECLARATION
OF INDEPENDENCE

Since the Declaration of Independence was undeniably a great document, we naturally assume that only a great mind could have created it. That mind supposedly belonged to Thomas Jefferson, the genius of the Revolution. Jefferson's image has suffered of late because he fathered children with his slave, Sally Hemings—but few question the quality or cogency of his thinking, or the belief that only a man of Jefferson's intellectual caliber could have drafted the momentous document that set us apart as an independent nation.

In *Liberty!* Thomas Fleming notes that Jefferson did not boast about his authorship of the Declaration of Independence. The document contained no "new principles or new arguments," Jefferson admitted. Instead, it was "intended to be an expression of the American mind."

Too much "modesty," Fleming complains. There was no "American mind" at the time. The Declaration, despite Jefferson's disclaimers, was all his own doing: "Jefferson poured into it his experience as an opponent of aristocratic privilege in Virginia," Fleming argues. Only Jefferson could have said the things he did. The visuals accompanying Fleming's text underline his thesis: we see a portrait of Jefferson brooding over a candlelit draft, followed by a facsimile of the draft itself, with many of Jefferson's deletions and additions.[1]

Joseph Ellis presents a more sophisticated version of the same argument. In *American Sphinx,* winner of the National Book Award for nonfiction in 1997, Ellis notes that Jefferson was in a position to draw on the works of many others, including George Mason, who had just drafted a very similar document, the Virginia Declaration of Rights. Ellis then lists other possible influences on Jefferson: the social contract theory of John Locke, the moral philosophy of the Scottish Enlightenment, and contemporary books on rhetoric and the art of the spoken word.[2]

At this juncture, Ellis offers a startling and apt observation:

> The central problem with all these explanations, however, is that they make Jefferson's thinking an exclusive function of books. . . . There is a long-standing scholarly tradition—one might call it the scholarly version of poetic license—that depends on the unspoken assumption that what one thinks is largely or entirely a product of what one reads.[3]

This point is well taken. Certainly we are more than the sum of what we read. But if not from books, where did Jefferson's ideas come from? "From deep inside himself," Ellis posits. The Declaration of Independence represented "the vision of a young man projecting his personal cravings" for a better world.[4]

Ellis's view of the creative process sets individual imagination above all else. The internal vision of the creator—a "wise man"—is not tarnished by external influences. This romantic notion ignores the political setting in which Jefferson lived. There was a revolution going on, and it had been brewing for more than a decade. People talked and wrote to each other nonstop. They engaged in hearty and contentious debate. They designed and circulated petitions and declarations. In those critical years patriots throughout the British colonies worked themselves up to the climactic fever pitch that revolution requires. Revolutionary phrases were stated and repeated so often that they entered the very language. They became the common currency of what might very rightly be called "The American mind."

Most plain folk in America had not studied John Locke's *Second Treatise on Government*, but in any country tavern, ordinary farmers could recite the principle of the "social contract": government is rooted in the people and rulers who forget this are ripe for a fall.[5] From firsthand experience and incessant repetition, they knew all they needed to know about popular sovereignty. For the antecedents and precedents that influenced the Declaration of Independence, Jefferson had only to look to the nearest tavern or meetinghouse, wherever patriots gathered. The most significant "source" for his forceful statement of popular sovereignty was, appropriately, the people themselves—the "American mind" that he himself rightfully credited.

THE "OTHER" DECLARATIONS OF INDEPENDENCE

On October 4, 1774—a full twenty-one months before the Continental Congress approved the document prepared by Thomas Jefferson—the people of Worcester, Massachusetts, declared that they were ready for independence. Four weeks earlier, they had toppled British authority (see chapter 4). Now they were ready to replace the old government with a new one. Without any input or approval from Parliament or the king, delegates from throughout Massachusetts were preparing to meet in a Provincial Congress, even though it had been outlawed by the royal governor. The Worcester town meeting decided to draft instructions for its representative, Timothy Bigelow. If, they said, the infractions to their rights were not repealed by the very next day—an obvious impossibility—Bigelow was to take the next step:

> You are to consider the people of this province absolved, on their part, from the obligation therein contained [the 1691 Massachu-

setts charter], and to all intents and purposes reduced to a state of nature; and you are to exert yourself in devising ways and means to raise from the dissolution of the old constitution, as from the ashes of the Phenix, a new form, wherein all officers shall be dependent on the suffrages of the people for their existence as such, whatever unfavorable constructions our enemies may put upon such procedure. The exigency of our public affairs leaves us no other alternative from a state of anarchy or slavery.[6]

Ordinary farmers and artisans from the hinterlands of Massachusetts were making practical use of the social contract theory that Jefferson would later espouse in the Declaration of Independence. Once the existing charter had been violated, these people reasoned, the contract was null and void—and it was time to start over.

Patriots in Worcester had a word for their dramatic move: "independency." For the British and the Tories, any mention of "independency" was considered treasonous—and even patriot leaders shied away. Samuel Adams wrote from the Continental Congress to his comrades back home, cautioning them not to "set up another form of government."[7] John Adams, also a member of Congress, wrote that "Absolute Independency . . . Startle[s] People here." Most congressional delegates, he warned, were horrified by "The Proposal of Setting up a new Form of Government of our own."[8] In this particular instance, the people led—the "leaders" would follow along later.

Massachusetts was certainly in the vanguard, but patriots in other colonies also declared their willingness to break from Britain several months before the Second Continental Congress commissioned Thomas Jefferson to draft a formal declaration. In Jefferson's Virginia, the issue of independence preempted all others during the spring of 1776. Common folk, not just the famous patricians-turned-statesmen, came to embrace independence for political, economic, and ideological reasons.[9] Beyond noble principles, fear of slaves and Indians contributed to the desire for independence (see chapter 8). In the April elections voters turned out in great numbers—and they stunned the more cautious politicians. Representatives who opposed independence or a republican form of government were turned out.[10]

Before sending off their new delegates to the Virginia Convention, constituents of several counties gave them specific, written instructions to vote for a declaration of independence. Charles Lee wrote to Patrick Henry: The "spirit of the people . . . cr[ies] out for this Declaration."[11] Jefferson himself was in Virginia during that time. "I took great pains to enquire into the sentiments of the people," he wrote on May 16, 1776, just a few weeks before he would pen his famous draft. "I think I may safely say nine out of ten are for it [independence]."[12] The people had spoken, the stage was set. On May 15, 1776, the Virginia Convention instructed its own delegates to the Continental Congress to initiate a declaration of independence.

Acting more swiftly than the Continental Congress, Virginia proceeded to declare its own independence. George Mason prepared a draft for Virginia's "Declaration of Rights," which circulated widely in June, 1776. It appeared in the *Pennsylvania Gazette* on June 12, the day after Jefferson was appointed to a five-man committee that would draft a national declaration. In Philadelphia, Jefferson and the other members of the committee no doubt examined these words closely. Two weeks later, Jefferson presented his own refinement of Mason's ideas:[13]

DRAFT OF THE VIRGINIA DECLARATION OF RIGHTS (GEORGE MASON)	DRAFT OF THE DECLARATION OF INDEPENDENCE (THOMAS JEFFERSON)
1. That all men are born equally free and independant, and have certain inherent natural rights, . . . among which are the enjoyment of life and liberty, with the means of acquiring and possessing property, and pursuing and obtaining happiness and safety.	We hold these truths to be self-evident; that all men are created equal; that they are endowed by their Creator with inherent and inalienable Rights; that among these are life, liberty, and the pursuit of happiness.

DRAFT OF THE VIRGINIA DECLARATION OF RIGHTS (GEORGE MASON) (*continued*)	DRAFT OF THE DECLARATION OF INDEPENDENCE (THOMAS JEFFERSON) (*continued*)
2. That all power is vested in, and consequently derived from the people. . . . That government is, or ought to be, instituted for the common benefit, protection, and security of the people, nation, or community.	[T]hat to secure these rights, governments are instituted among men, deriving their just powers from the consent of the governed.
3. Of all the various modes and forms of government, that is best, which is capable of producing the greatest degree of happiness and safety, . . . and that, whenever any government shall be found inadequate or contrary to these purposes, a majority of the community hath an indubitable, unalienable and indefeasible right to reform, alter or abolish it, in such manner as shall be judged most conducive to the public weal.	[T]hat whenever any form of government becomes destructive of these ends, it is the right of the people to alter or abolish it, and to institute new government, laying its foundation on such principles and organizing its powers in such form as to them shall seem most likely to effect their safety and happiness.

Although Jefferson's prose flows more smoothly from point to point than Mason's, he certainly introduced no new concepts. Many key phrases were merely rearranged. Jefferson in no sense "copied" the Virginia Declaration, but he was evidently influenced by it. That should come as no surprise. This was a time of frenzied but collective agitation, and the Revolution's participants continually referred to each other's words and propositions. In all likelihood Mason himself was familiar with Jefferson's *Summary View of the Rights of British*

America, written two years earlier. Undoubtedly, both men had read classic English and Scottish works that asserted revolutionary concepts, and both were privy to expressions that were common parlance among their peers. Mason and Jefferson were tapping into the same rich source.

Virginia's Declaration was only one of many. Historian Pauline Maier has discovered ninety other "declarations" issued by state and local communities in the months immediately preceding the congressional declaration.[14] (She does not include the Worcester instructions, written earlier yet.) Taken together, these reveal a groundswell of political thinking in support of independence. Jefferson and Mason drafted their declarations with full knowledge that others were doing the same, even if they did not consult every state and local document.

Most of these declarations took the form of instructions by towns, counties, or local associations to their representatives in state conventions, telling them to instruct *their* representatives in Congress to vote for independence. The chain of command was clear: representatives at every level were to do the bidding of their constituents. The custom of issuing instructions to representatives did not originate with the American Revolution, but never before had local instructions expressed views of such monumental importance. Now more than ever, patriots insisted that the business of government remain under their immediate control. Witness the "Committee for the Lower District of Frederick County [Maryland]":

> *Resolved, unanimously,* That as a knowledge of the conduct of the Representative is the constituent's only principle and permanent security, we claim the right of being fully informed therein, unless in the secret operations of war; and that we shall ever hold the Representative amenable to that body from whom he derives his authority.[15]

Many of the instructions, while granting new powers to Congress, asserted that the states must retain "the sole and exclusive right" to govern their own internal affairs.[16] People were not about to relinquish any of their political "independence," even to other Americans.

Several of the local declarations offer succinct expressions of the social contract theory. From Frederick County, Maryland:

> *Resolved, unanimously,* That all just and legal Government was instituted for the ease and convenience of the People, and that the People have the indubitable right to reform or abolish a Government which may appear to them insufficient for the exigency of their affairs.[17]

Patriots from Buckingham County, Virginia, issued a similar declaration, then followed with an optimistic vision that would have made the visionary Mr. Jefferson proud: they prayed that "a Government may be established in *America*, the most free, happy, and permanent, that human wisdom can contrive, and the perfection of man maintain."[18]

Like the later Declaration, many of these earlier documents listed specific grievances—often more concisely and pointedly than Jefferson would do.[19] Delegates at more than twenty conventions or town meetings signed off by pledging to support independence with their "lives and fortunes," foretelling the famous conclusion to the congressional declaration: "We mutually pledge our lives, our fortunes, and our sacred honor." Some of these added creative touches to this standard oath: Boston delegates pledged "their lives and the remnants of their fortunes," while patriots from Malden, Massachusetts, concluded: "Your constituents will support and defend the measure to the last drop of their blood, and the last farthing of their treasure."[20]

Thomas Jefferson was one of many scribes, not the sole muse, of the American independence movement. To ignore that, ironically, is to obscure the contributions of "the people" themselves.

A SLOW START

Because the proceedings of the Continental Congress were kept secret, Americans at the time had no way of ascertaining who was on the committee to prepare the Declaration of Independence, who among the committee penned the draft, or who edited the final version. This information, even if available, would have been deemed irrelevant. People didn't care to quibble about authorship or craft. All that really counted was the document's conclusion: the United States was declaring its independence.

During the war, even at Fourth of July celebrations, the Declaration itself was rarely quoted. On the first anniversary of independence in 1777, when William Gordon delivered the oration for the festivities in Boston, he used as his text the Old Testament. When David Ramsay delivered the oration in Charleston on the second anniversary, he used a phrase more common to the times: "life, liberty, and property," not "life, liberty, and the pursuit of happiness," the phrase used in the Declaration of Independence. In 1783, after the war had ended, Ezra Stiles mentioned Jefferson by name—but he did not celebrate the author's unique genius. Stiles said only that Jefferson had "poured the soul of the continent into the monumental act of independence." [21]

In fact, during the Revolutionary Era, George Mason's draft of the Virginia Declaration of Rights was copied or imitated far more often than the Declaration of Independence. None of the seven other states that drafted their own declarations of rights borrowed phrasing from the congressional Declaration, but four of them—Pennsylvania, Massachusetts, New Hampshire, and Vermont—lifted exact portions of Mason's text, including "all men are born equally free and independent." [22]

Surprisingly, the Declaration of Independence was not often cited during the drafting of the U. S. Constitution in 1787 or in the subsequent debates over ratification. Notes from the Constitutional Convention make only two references to the Declaration, while essays in

The Federalist Papers contain but one. When Patrick Henry addressed the Virginia Convention during the ratification debate, he asked rhetorically, "What, sir, is the genius of democracy?" He then proceeded to read from the Virginia Declaration of Rights, not the Declaration of Independence.[23]

Both David Ramsay and William Gordon, in their eighteenth-century histories, focused on the political impact of the Declaration of Independence, not the philosophy contained in its preamble. Ramsay failed to mention Jefferson as the author, while Gordon referred to him only as a member of the five-man committee that prepared the draft.[24]

During the 1790s, partisan politics determined Jefferson's standing. Since Federalists vilified Jefferson, they ignored his authorship and regarded the Declaration itself as suspect. Phrases like "liberty," "equality," and "the rights of man"—all too reminiscent of the French Revolution—did not mesh with either their conservative philosophy or their pro-British foreign policy. Anti-Federalists, meanwhile, celebrated Jefferson's authorship in order to promote the leading figure of their own political party. Not until Anti-Federalists staged separate Fourth of July festivities in the late 1790s was Jefferson's name linked to the Declaration of Independence in public discourse.[25]

Two turn-of-the-century historians replicated these divergent stances. John Marshall, a staunch Federalist, mentioned Jefferson only in a footnote: a committee of five was appointed to prepare the document, he wrote flatly, "and the draft, reported by the committee, has been generally attributed to Mr. Jefferson."[26] Rather than focus on Jefferson, Marshall mentioned several of the other declarations of independence, and he quoted extensively from two of them.[27] Mercy Otis Warren, on the other side of the political spectrum, waxed effusive:

[T]he instrument which announced the final separation of the American Colonies from Great Britain was drawn by the elegant and energetic pen of Jefferson, with that correct judgment, precision, and dignity, which have ever marked his character. The declaration of independence, which has done so much honor to the then existing congress, to the inhabitants of the United States, and to the genius and heart of the gentleman who drew it . . . ought to be frequently read by the rising youth of the American states, as a palladium of which they should never lose sight, so long as they wish to continue a free and independent people.[28]

Warren and other supporters of Jefferson enshrined the Declaration's author in the early nineteenth century, when memories of the Revolution were revived and put in the service of a growing nationalism. The Democrat-Republicans, Jefferson's party, would remain in power for six presidential terms, during which the document and its principal author were increasingly celebrated and indelibly linked.

In 1817 Congress commissioned John Trumbull to paint a large canvas commemorating the approval of the Declaration of Independence on July 4, 1776. Trumbull's masterpiece was displayed to large crowds in Boston, New York, Philadelphia, Baltimore, and Washington.[29] With the mood set, two engraved copies of the Declaration competed for public attention in 1818 and 1819. In 1823 Congress distributed an official facsimile far and wide.[30] Historians quickly moved into this promising territory. During the 1820s John Sanderson published a nine-volume series entitled *Biography of the Signers of the Declaration of Independence*, and in 1827 the popular writer Charles Goodrich came out with a single-volume bestseller, *Lives of the Signers of the Declaration of Independence*. The Declaration by then was firmly entrenched in popular culture.

Jefferson himself fed this frenzy. As far back as 1786, he had talked of an artistic commemoration of the Declaration with John Trumbull and had provided a rough sketch.[31] He approved the distribution of the facsimile edition, hoping it would inspire greater "reverence" for the principles it espoused.[32] He even applauded the gathering of artifacts he had used while drafting the document: "Small things may, perhaps, like the relics of saints, help to nourish our devotion to this holy bond of Union, and keep it longer alive and warm in our affections," he wrote to a promoter—and he then indicated where some these "relics" might be found.[33]

All this rankled John Adams, the only other member of the drafting committee still alive during the Declaration's revival. According to Adams, the hard-earned *achievement* of independence should be the object of celebration, not the simple act of *writing* about it. "The Declaration of Independence I always considered as a theatrical show. Jefferson ran away with all the stage effect of that," he wrote— and, he added grudgingly, "all the glory of it" as well.[34]

Starting in 1811, thirty-five years after the fact, these two elder statesmen quibbled over who should receive accolades. Adams argued that he had successfully pushed the motion for independence through Congress. He also noted that Jefferson's draft was discussed, revised, and approved by a five-member committee, then discussed, revised, and approved by the body of Congress.[35] Jefferson countered: "Mr. Adams' memory has led him to unquestionable error." In particular, Jefferson objected to Adams's claim that the two men had constituted a "sub-committee" charged with writing the document.[36]

Despite a paucity of direct sources and the differences in memory, we do know that a five-member committee was appointed to produce a draft for Congress to consider, and we can safely conjecture that the committee discussed the issues and provided some direction before sending Jefferson on his way with quill and ink. Then, when the draft reached the floor of Congress, others certainly had their say. According to Jeffersonian scholar Julian Boyd, "In all there were eighty-six alterations, made at various stages by Jefferson, by Adams and Franklin, by the Committee of Five, and by Congress.[37]

The major thrust of Adams's argument—that the Declaration of Independence was more than a one-man affair—seems correct. Even so, Jefferson won the debate. The telling of history, if not history itself, was on his side. Before he died, he proposed that "Author of the Declaration of American Independence" be inscribed on his tomb. Although he accepted and even sought credit for penning the words, however, never once did Jefferson seek credit for dreaming up the ideas. That unsolicited honor would be bestowed upon him by others, much later.

THE LINCOLN REVIVAL

During the Abraham Lincoln–Stephen Douglas debates of 1858, both participants based their arguments on the alleged authority of the Declaration of Independence. According to Lincoln, the Declaration had stated in "plain, unmistakable language" that "all men are created equal." Douglas countered that these words were never intended to apply to "the Negro or . . . savage Indians, or the Feejee, or the Malay, or any other inferior or degraded race," and he noted that many of the state and local declarations, which had preceded the congressional Declaration, had insisted that the states retain all authority over their own internal affairs.[38] Although Douglas was probably correct on the first count, and certainly correct on the second, Lincoln rebutted both arguments. The second point was easy: Lincoln noted that his quarrel was only with the *expansion* of slavery, and this involved no violation of states' rights.

But what about those slaveholding founding fathers? How could Lincoln seriously maintain that they had believed in the equality of *all* men, including those they were holding in bondage?

Lincoln argued that Jefferson had included the phrase "all men are created equal" for no immediate and practical purpose, but as a "promise" for the future. The "sentiment embodied in the Declaration of Independence" was to give "hope to all the world . . . that in due time the weights would be lifted from the shoulders of all men, and that all should have an equal chance."[39] Since slavery was too firmly embedded at the time to permit practical opposition, Jefferson could do no more than issue this blanket pronouncement in favor of equality—"the father of all moral principles," Lincoln called it—for the use of future generations.[40]

Lincoln's line of reasoning had, and still has, great appeal. Because of their alleged "promise" to the future, the signers of the Declaration of Independence can be released from any charge of moral culpability or hypocrisy.

Historically, however, this is a difficult argument to sustain. Antislavery elements in the North made no mention of "equality" in instructing their delegates to state or federal conventions in 1776. Only in the South did the term "equality" appear. Surely, if slaveholders themselves used the term, they did not do so with the freedom of slaves in mind.

The two largest slaveholding states were Virginia and South Carolina. In Virginia, principal Revolutionary players—Thomas Jefferson, George Mason, and James Wilson—featured the notion of equality in their writings, even though they each enslaved a multitude of other human beings.[41] It is implausible that such proponents of the institution would issue any "promise" of equality for blacks. Nor would such equality be acceptable in South Carolina. When the grand jury of the Cheraws District declared itself in favor of independence on May 20, 1776, it praised the new Constitution because it was "founded on the strictest principles of justice and humanity, where the rights and happiness of the whole, the poor and the rich, are equally secured."[42] In Revolutionary South Carolina, slaves were not seen as part of that "whole," even though they constituted approximately half the population. The grand jury of Georgetown, South Carolina, also praised the new Constitution as "the most equitable and desirable that human imagination could invent":

> The present Constitution of Government, formed by the late Congress of this Colony, promises to its inhabitants every happy effect which can arise from society. Equal and just in its principles, wise and virtuous in its ends; we now see every hope of future liberty, safety, and happiness confirmed to ourselves and our posterity.[43]

Not even Lincoln would have dared to suggest that back in 1776 the white citizens of Georgetown, South Carolina, intended that "promise" to extend to their slaves.

When Lincoln tried to defend the notion of "equality" as the "sentiment" of the nation's founders, he gave full credit to Thomas Jefferson, the author of the words he cherished:

All honor to Jefferson, to the man who, in the concrete pressure of a struggle for national independence by a single people, had the coolness, forecast, and capacity to introduce into a merely revolutionary document, an abstract truth, and so to embalm it there, that today and in all coming days, it shall be a rebuke and a stumbling block to the very harbingers of reappearing tyranny and oppression.[44]

Lincoln was not the first to remake the master of Monticello—a man who ranted against race-mixing and bred slaves for profit until the day he died—into the architect of racial equality in America.[45] During the Senate debates on the Kansas-Nebraska Act in 1853, Benjamin Wade, a senator from Ohio, invoked the Declaration of Independence in a similar manner, and so did other opponents of slavery.[46] But because of Lincoln's presidential status and his role in ending slavery, his interpretation had an indelible, lasting impact.

In establishing Jefferson as a prophet of egalitarian principles, Lincoln displayed great political savvy. He shrewdly co-opted the founder of the opposing political party, while he recruited one of the largest slaveowners in Revolutionary Virginia to argue the antislavery case. Many would agree that Lincoln played his cards well in a game that really counted. The end in this case might justify the means.

But this interpretation, or misinterpretation, of the historical record comes at a cost. By exalting Jefferson as the creative genius who introduced the notion of equality into our nation's founding document, Lincoln was demoting all the other patriots who ushered in American independence. If Jefferson inserted his own, original meaning into the Declaration of Independence, bypassing and even contradicting the will of the people whom he represented, he undermined popular sovereignty—and that, supposedly, was the very basis for independence. According to Lincoln's reading, the Revolution had not created a nation "of the people, by the people, and for the people"; at best, it was a nation of the people and for the people, created by Thomas Jefferson and approved by the rest of the signers of the Declaration of Independence.

The broad strokes of the Lincoln-Jefferson revival remain with us today. Routinely, current textbooks echo Lincoln's notion of a "promise" made by the founders: "All people were not treated equally in America in 1776," one states, "but the Declaration set high goals for equal treatment in the future." [47] Joy Hakim, in her popular *History of US*, writes that on July 4, 1776, "something happened . . . that changed the whole world." That "something" was not the act of declaring independence: "It was the words they used in that declaration that made all the difference. . . . Jefferson's Declaration of Independence was great from the moment he wrote it, but it has grown even greater with the passing of time." [48] With this clever turn of phrase, Hakim celebrates Jefferson's genius, his prophesy, and his ownership of the Declaration of Independence. Jefferson, like the words he penned, seems to have "grown even greater with the passing of time."

TEAM SPIRIT

Although it has been several years since Pauline Maier retrieved from obscurity the other declarations of independence, those documents receive no mention in current school texts or popular histories. Though such books give some ground—they now routinely mention that Jefferson was a member of a committee, for example—they fail to acknowledge the ubiquitous revolutionary upsurge that resulted in Revolution. If they mention any widespread revolutionary feeling, they credit yet one more autonomous perpetrator—Thomas Paine. Tom Paine (as he is casually called) supposedly swayed the minds of a fickle public who could not have attained true revolutionary status without him. In the reckless rush to commemorate Paine's mastery, several texts have recently listed the contemporary sales of *Common Sense* at an astounding half-million, one for every free household in the thirteen colonies—even those with no literate individuals.[49]

According to classic narrative structure, the wise man persuades the rest. Yet this individualistic/heroic model does not accurately describe how history works. A better model features collaborative effort—like that between Jefferson and Mason, who were participating in an ongoing dialogue as they penned their various declarations. An entire population took part in that robust dialogue, and here, the media is indeed the message. The dialogue itself deserves celebration, not just its practical conclusion. If we disregard it, we disregard one of history's finest lessons in active and popular self-government.

It was the fact of independence that shook the world, not the words, later misconstrued, that one man used to describe it. Listen to what Jefferson had to say on the matter in the year before his death, for no one argues the question more persuasively:

> But with respect to our rights, and the acts of the British government contravening those rights, there was but one opinion on this side of the water. All American whigs thought alike on these subjects. When forced, therefore, to resort to arms for redress, an appeal to the tribunal of the world was deemed proper for our justification. This was the object of the Declaration of Independence. Not to find out new principles, or new arguments, never before thought of, not merely to say things which had never been said before; but to place before mankind the common sense of the subject, in terms so plain and firm as to command their assent, and to justify ourselves in the independent stand we were compelled to take. Neither aiming at originality of principle or sentiment, nor yet copied from any particular and previous writing, it was intended to be an expression of the American mind, and to give to that expression the proper tone and spirit called for by the occasion. All its authority rests on the harmonizing sentiments of the day, whether expressed in conversation, in let-

ters, printed essays, or in the elementary books of public right, as Aristotle, Cicero, Locke, Sidney, &c.[50]

Later that year, while supporting the promotion of relics he had used to draft the Declaration, Jefferson again insisted that his words were to be seen as no more than "the genuine effusion of the soul of our country."[51] Unfortunately, his most ardent admirers, in their headlong quest for a solitary visionary, have failed to take seriously Jefferson's honest and forthright pronouncement: the "authority" of the Declaration of Independence rests exclusively on the "harmonizing sentiments" of the American people.

7

FOUNDING FATHERS: THE GREATEST GENERATION

We all know their names—George Washington, Thomas Jefferson, Benjamin Franklin, Alexander Hamilton, John and
Samuel Adams, Patrick Henry, James Madison. People who learned
the story in grade school and never studied it later—that includes
most Americans, as we shall see later on—would probably delete
Madison, the one who had the most to do with the writing of the Constitution, in favor of John Hancock, whose name has come to represent any sort of a signature, and Paul Revere, the midnight rider of
the Revolution. These were America's wise men, the great figures
who gave our nation its bearings.

Regardless of whom we cast in the roles, the principal figures in the
story of our nation's founding would enjoy an elevated status. They
were our *creators,* so they must have been particularly honorable and
judicious. This is a structural requirement of the narrative, not necessarily a reflection of the individual personalities of real people who
once lived on the eastern seaboard of North America.

FOUNDER CHIC

The choice of leading characters has changed over time. Military officers were the first stars of the show. In the immediate wake of the

"They were America's first and, in many respects, its only natural aristocracy."

The Declaration of Independence, 4 July 1776.
Painting by John Trumbull, 1787–1820.

Revolutionary War, the people who brought home victory were naturally considered its heroes. (Ben Franklin, the folk idol, was a notable exception.) George Washington was foremost, then as now, but his supporting cast included people who are almost forgotten today: Israel Putnam, Horatio Gates, Nathanael Greene, Henry Knox. Statesmen like Thomas Jefferson, Alexander Hamilton, and John Adams, deeply immersed in divisive politics, were too controversial to be considered as icons for a new nation in search of a collective identity.

In the second decade of the nineteenth century, Americans began to celebrate those who had signed the Declaration of Independence. These men, the "Signers," became the subjects of numerous biographies. Painter John Trumbull, working on a commission from Congress, immortalized these people with his historic canvas, which depicted a scene of little visual drama but great national significance.

Today, most of the "Signers," like the military figures of the Revolutionary War, are no longer household names; there were simply too many of them. Stories with fifty-six heroes do not have the immediate, compelling force we expect from a creation myth. We need fewer, no more than a dozen or so, if we expect every person in the nation to learn their stories and recite them by rote.

In the second half of the nineteenth century, Americans settled on the small group we still honor today, our "Founding Fathers." Technically, this term seems to denote the men who drafted the Constitution, but in common parlance it connotes an elite corps of venerable men who conjured up the idea of independence, brought the Revolution to its successful conclusion, and then, like Solon or Moses, gave us our laws.

Adulation for the founders has evolved with the times. Today, it is no longer fashionable to be a statue. Posed, formal portraits are out as well. The informality of the late twentieth century has taken its toll on mounted riders cast in stone and the stiff, distant patricians who line up single file on the walls of echoing galleries.

But informality can be seen as irreverence, and the relaxed attitude has proved unsettling for Americans who yearn for the good old days, when the founders were properly honored. "Not so long ago," writes historian Gordon Wood, "the generation that fought the Revolution and created the Constitution was thought to be the greatest generation in American history. . . . Until recently few Americans could look back at these revolutionaries and constitution-makers without being overawed by the brilliance of their thought, the creativity of their politics, the sheer magnitude of their achievement. They used to seem larger than life, giants in the earth, possessing intellectual and political capacities well beyond our own." Yes, those were the days—"but not anymore," Wood bemoans. "The American revolutionaries and the framers of the Constitution are no longer being celebrated in the way they used to be." [1]

In fact, the Founding Fathers *are* being celebrated, although not "in the way they used to be." Popular historians such as Wood, Joseph Ellis, David McCullough, and John Ferling have managed to resurrect America's most respected statesmen by dressing them in more contemporary attire. Like modern celebrities, the founders have been humanized, personalized, and made accessible to the masses. Now, as millions read about the details of their lives, it has become fashionable once again to honor the likes of John Adams, George Washington, and Benjamin Franklin. They have become Founder Chic—America's "greatest generation" despite their human quirks, or, more precisely, because of them.

The Founding Fathers were "human and imperfect; each had his flaws and failing," David McCullough wrote in his July 4, 2002, op-ed piece for the *New York Times*. In the past, flaws and failings were not to be tolerated in our most venerable public figures, but now these very imperfections work in their favor. Because they "were not gods," McCullough argues, we can admire them all the more. Were they gods, "they would deserve less honor and respect. Gods, after all, can do largely as they please." [2]

Joseph Ellis captured the current mood in the title of his bestselling book, *Founding Brothers*. Brothers, unlike fathers, squabble and misbehave—but "their mutual imperfections and fallibilities, as well as their eccentricities and excesses" somehow manage to cancel each other out. Brothers come together in the end, as our founders did when they created a viable blueprint for the United States.

According to Ellis, the young nation's "eight most prominent political leaders" constituted "America's first and, in many respects, its only natural aristocracy":

> [T]hey comprised, by any informed and fair-minded standard, the greatest generation of political talent in American history. They created the American republic, then held it together throughout the volatile and vulnerable early years by sustaining their presence until national habits and customs took root.[3]

The key words here—"the greatest generation"—have been oft repeated during the recent resurgence of patriotic sentiment. The phrase serves as a rallying cry, beckoning us to aspire to their greatness and admonishing us not to waver from our allegiance to the nation these men created. Yet there is a troubling phrase—"by any informed and fair-minded standard"—embedded within Ellis's forthright assertion. What, exactly, might such a standard be? How can we determine who was "great," let alone who was the "greatest generation," now that these gods have become mere mortals?[4]

The *Random House College Dictionary* lists almost a score of common usages for "great," many with numerous synonyms: noteworthy, remarkable, exceptionally outstanding, important, eminent, prominent, celebrated, illustrious, renowned, main, grand, leading, highly significant or consequential, momentous, vital, critical, distinguished, famous, admirable, having unusual merit, of extraordinary powers, of high rank or standing, of notable or lofty character, elevated, exalted, dignified. Which of these meanings do we intend when we call a particular historical personage, or a particular generation, "great"? Most likely, we wish to imply some sort of ill-defined amalgamation. We do not intend specific meanings; we hope only to instill some sense of admiration for the heroes of our choosing. The term "great" serves as a grandiose but generic stamp of approval. Every time we use it, we make a momentous declaration—but without any standards, we can affix no claim of legitimacy upon our pronouncement, nor can we discuss "greatness" intelligently.

To develop standards, perhaps we should follow the lead of the Catholic Church, which has established very precisely who can be called a "saint." To qualify, a candidate must endure the scrutiny first of a specially convened tribunal; then, in succession, of the Congregation for the Causes of Saints; a committee of nine theologians; a committee of cardinals and bishops; and finally the Pope. If these officials all certify that the candidate possessed both the theological virtues (faith, hope, and charity) and the cardinal virtues (prudence, justice, temperance, and fortitude), he or she can be called a "Servant of God." Certification by these deliberative bodies that the Servant of God performed a miracle earns the title of "Blessed," and finally, certification that the Blessed performed a miracle after she or he had died warrants the title of "Saint." It's all cut and dry.

To be fair and precise, we ought to require candidates for historical greatness to undergo some sort of scrutiny like this. Of course we don't—but in the absence of standards, definitions, and procedures, we are free to apply the term "great" promiscuously to our favorite historical personalities. Anyone can call anyone else "great" and get away with it, unchallenged. Ironically, every time we try to speak intelligently about "greatness," we utter nothing but platitudes.[5]

There is no quicker route to the trivialization of history. A recent book published by American Heritage, *Great Minds of History: Interviews with Roger Mudd*, features "greatness" from three angles: a great newscaster interviews great historians about great personalities. In a chapter titled "Gordon Wood on the Colonial Era and Revolution," Roger Mudd asks Professor Wood various questions of great import about our nation's founding moment:

"Back to Ben Franklin, did he dress and speak like a gentleman?"

"What more can you tell me about Benjamin Franklin?"
"What about Alexander Hamilton?"
"What can you tell us about James Madison?"
"John Adams?"
"And what do you think about Thomas Jefferson?"

Here's how Gordon Wood responds to these questions:

"Adams was the most lovable of the Founding Fathers be-
cause he wore his heart on his sleeve."
Hamilton was ". . . the brilliant genius . . ."
Madison was ". . . the most intellectual . . ."
Jefferson was ". . . the most important . . ." [6]

Perhaps we might continue: Who was the best-dressed of the class of
'76? The most likely to succeed? The problem here lies with the questions, not the summary responses they triggered. The posing of such
questions leads directly to glib assessments that bear only indirectly
upon the major events of the "Colonial Era and Revolution," which
are purportedly under discussion. Real history—in this case, the dy-
namic process that led patriotic colonists toward independence—is
masked by "lifestyles of the rich and famous." Focusing exclusively
on stories of allegedly great men produces a level of historical analysis that is frivolous at best.

Although the term "great" does not say or denote anything in particular, and although it leads us away from discussing serious historical processes, it is not used without purpose. By calling people
"great," Founder Chic authors promote attitudes of deference and
reverence. This provides the rationale for the phrase "the greatest
generation"—Americans are still expected to venerate the founders,
despite their personal idiosyncrasies. Deference and reverence, however, are strangely out of step with the rambunctious and assertive
spirit of independence that drove the American Revolution forward.
They contradict our most basic founding principle, that governmental

leaders should be made subservient to the popular will. How strange that now, in a society that places a premium on the active and democratic participation of its citizenry, such submissive attitudes should be deemed patriotic.

CENTRAL PLAYERS

There is one use of the term "great" that does not imply adulation. If a historic personage was important and powerful enough, he (rarely she) will warrant the appellation irrespective of any moral qualities deserving of respect. Alexander the Great, Napoleon, Hitler—these people were in one sense "great," even though we might not approve of what they did.

Although we would be loath to compare the "greatest generation" of Americans with these great but cruel conquerors, Joseph Ellis argues that we must place our founders at the center of the story by sheer virtue of their power and significance:

> The central events and achievements of the revolutionary era and the early republic were political. These events and achievements are historically significant because they shaped the subsequent history of the United States, including our own time. The central players in the drama were not the marginal or peripheral figures, whose lives are more typical, but rather the political leaders at the center of the national story who wielded power.[7]

The key concept here (repeated three times in as many sentences) is "central"—but that notion is entirely dependent on one's field of vision. Characters who appear at the center of one story will be on the periphery of another. While promoting the importance of his eight protagonists, Ellis demotes the other three million Americans—also members of the Revolutionary generation—to the secondary status of "marginal or peripheral." This is politically suspect and historically incorrect. The *central* theme of the American Revolution was popular sovereignty: all power resides with the people. How, then, can "the people" be reduced to the periphery of the story? In fact, regular Americans were at the very center of the drama:

- Common farmers, without any help at all from Ellis's featured players, were the first to overthrow British political authority. (See chapter 4.)

- Poor men and boys fought the British army. Without them, the founders might all have been hanged. (See chapter 5.)

- If it weren't for a popular clamoring for independence, Congress would not have passed their final declaration. (See chapter 6.)

- If it weren't for the labor of hundreds of thousands of "Founding Sisters," American society could never have survived the war. Whatever the "Founding Brothers" were able to accomplish in political chambers would have proven futile. (See chapter 2.)

- The political history of the American Revolution in the southern half of the fledgling nation cannot possibly be understood without reference to slaves and the fears they inspired among whites. (See chapters 8 and 10.)

- The military history of the war in the West cannot be understood without reference to Indians as "central players." (See chapter 13.)

Without the participation of these people, the American Revolution would have been altogether different—or, more likely, there would have been no Revolution at all. By dismissing so many Americans as "marginal or peripheral," Ellis and other practitioners of

Founder Chic both misread history and set a dangerous precedent: when we marginalize common people in the past, we learn how to marginalize common people in the present.

Ironically, since Ellis's stories do not relate to the actual founding of our nation, they are all "marginal or peripheral" to "the central events and achievements of the revolutionary era." Ellis refers to the two "founding moments" in American history, the Declaration of Independence in 1776 and the adoption of a Constitution in 1787–1788, yet he addresses neither of these, for his book commences in the year 1790. There is nothing wrong in this, save for the false packaging. He titles his book *Founding Brothers: The Revolutionary Generation* to give the stories added weight and significance, even though he addresses neither the "Founding" nor the "Revolution." Like so many others, he rides the coattails of America's most special time: the act of national creation.

Joseph Ellis's approach, a common one, is to place himself within the seats of power and then describe what happens when important insiders come up against each other. He assumes that whatever occurs within this narrow and contained world inhabited by famous people must be "historically significant." Fame and significance, however, are not synonymous. Ellis opens his masterfully written book with an intriguing story of a duel between two fading political figures, Alexander Hamilton and Aaron Burr, in 1804—a tragic personal drama of little historical import.[8] He follows with a tale about a dinner party in which a major deal was supposedly struck; this intimacy in the political arena makes for a good story, but Ellis himself admits that the deal was discussed in other venues as well, and his dinner party scenario "vastly oversimplifies the history that was happening at that propitious moment."[9] Another tale features the "silence" of the first federal Congress over the question of slavery; here indeed was an issue of great national importance, yet Ellis's claim that debates within Congress over the question of slavery were "central," while the experiences of the slaves themselves were not, is disingenuous.[10] The final story eulogizes the friendship between John Adams and

Thomas Jefferson during their later years. This reconciliation between elder statesmen affords a poignant conclusion to the book, but
it was hardly central to the founding of our nation or "the subsequent
history of the United States, including our own time." The story of
the Adams-Jefferson friendship, like that of the Burr-Hamilton duel,
appears significant only because the characters had participated in
other important events at previous times. Ellis includes these episodes
not because they are crucial to the history of the United States, but because they can be turned into interesting stories. The lives of heroes
and giants, from birth to death, will always make for a good read—but
biographical sketches of famous personalities should not be presented
as "significant" history.

This insider's approach generates a skewed view of the past. By
ignoring the various forces acting upon insiders from the outside, it
distorts the very nature of political processes. Throughout the Revolutionary Era, representatives who gathered in deliberative bodies
were expected to abide by specific, written instructions from their
constituents. They also had to respond to military victories and de-
feats, the breakdown of the economy, and other extrinsic factors. Political leaders did not operate in a vacuum, determining the fate of
their nation by simple fiat. Lines of influence went both ways, both toward and away from the seats of power.

THE FEW AND THE MANY

By limiting themselves to an insider's view, Founder Chic authors depict political leaders as causal agents who are personally responsible
for all the major events of the times. This is an occupational hazard of
biographers. Since the importance of their stories is determined in
part by the importance of their protagonists, biographers have a
vested interest in endowing their subjects with as much historical significance as the record will bear—and sometimes more. The very nature of their enterprise entices them to portray their chosen heroes as
prime movers of history.

David McCullough, in his Pulitzer Prize–winning *John Adams*, concludes a lengthy discussion of the Declaration of Independence with his own forthright declaration: "It was John Adams, more than anyone, who made it happen." [11] The last three words convey a clear implication of causality: if Adams "made it happen," without him there might never have been a Declaration of Independence. This seems highly implausible. There were many other political figures within the Continental Congress working toward independence, in addition to all those promoting independence on the state and local levels. Other historians, as we have seen in previous chapters, portray Samuel Adams or Thomas Jefferson, not John Adams, as the architect of American Independence. By debating which one of these individuals, "more than anyone," is most responsible for the nation's independence, we participate in a parlor game, not meaningful historical inquiry.

This game is not harmless, for it ignores the hundreds of thousands of people who actually *did* make it happen. Without John Adams, chances are the Continental Congress would still have broken ties with Britain; without a preponderance of popular support for the cause of independence, chances are Congress would have chosen a different path. When Congress finally agreed on independence, it did so in response to a political movement with a broad base of support. Almost two years before, farmers in Massachusetts led the way by deposing British authority and pushing for a new and independent government. Then came the war, and for better than a year tens of thousands of patriots took up arms. When the British government declared the colonies to be in open rebellion, and when they unleashed the largest army and navy ever assembled in the eighteenth century to suppress it, rebellious colonists began to wonder whether the time had come to make a total, formal break with the mother country. In the early months of 1776, with Tom Paine's *Common Sense* as a catalyst, ordinary citizens gathered in taverns and meeting houses throughout the land to debate the issue of independence. By late spring the results were in: most people were ready. As historian Pauline Maier points out, at least ninety state and local communities issued their own declarations of independence, instructing their representatives in higher deliberative bodies to go the full route. (See chapter 6.) By June the majority of delegates in Congress were under pressure from their constituents to declare independence, and many had specific instructions to do so.

To promote the importance of his protagonist, McCullough has to ignore all of this. There was "no sweeping support for rebellion," he states flatly.[12] The notion of independence, he says, enjoyed still less support. McCullough portrays Adams as a lonely hero, willing to defy public opinion. Although the story plays well, it flies in the face of the historical record.

As John Ferling tells it, "Washington and Adams achieved historical greatness in the American Revolution. In some ways, Adams's achievement was the more impressive. His was the more lonely struggle."[13] Ferling sees Adams as "more impressive" precisely because he bucked the tide. If this is to be our standard for "historical greatness," a person is less likely to become great if he or she chooses to engage in common cause with others. Any form of collective action, by definition, is not worthy of the adulation we bestow on solitary heroes who oppose the will of the people—a strange notion for an avowedly democratic society.

Where, if not from the historical record, do we get the notion that John Adams was operating against the will of the people when he pushed for a Declaration of Independence? McCullough gleans his evidence from Adams himself. On March 19, 1812, Adams wrote to Benjamin Rush: "We were about one third Tories, and [one] third timid, and one third true blue."[14] From this single quotation, which he uses as a chapter invocation, McCullough concludes: "So as yet the voices for independence were decidedly in the minority."[15] That left an uphill battle for John Adams and the radicals in Congress, who had to struggle on behalf of an unpopular cause.

But John Adams never stated that only one-third of the people were for independence in 1776. Here are the exact words he wrote to Rush:

> I lament, my dear Friend, that you were not in Congress in 1774
> and 1776. A thousand Things happened there in those years that
> no Man now living knows but myself. Mr Gerry, Mr Lovel was
> not there. Gerry not till 1776. Lovel not till 1777.
>
> 1774 was the most important and the most difficult year of all.
> We were about one third Tories, one third timid and one third
> true Blue. We had a Code of Fundamintal Laws to prepare for a
> whole Continent of incongruous Colonies. It was done; and the
> Declaration of Independence in 1776 was no more than a repeti-
> tion of the Principles, the Rights and Wrongs asserted and
> adopted in 1774.[16]

Adams never mentions the views of "the people" at all—he is discussing only the attitudes of members of Congress, who were divided
into thirds in 1774, not 1776. The difference in dates is no trivial distinction. The central thrust of the second paragraph is to emphasize
the importance of 1774—and to distinguish it from 1776. A statement
about Congress in 1774 does not demonstrate that only a minority of
the American people favored independence two years later. Indeed,
the notion that there were as many Tories as patriots in 1776 is highly
implausible; had this been so, the Tories, allied with the most powerful
army on earth, would certainly have prevailed. And regardless of the
wording of the letter, the estimate of one elderly man thirty-six years
after the fact, can hardly be accepted as proof of the sentiments of an
entire population.[17]

McCullough's contention that there was "no sweeping support for
rebellion" does not jibe with Adams's own writings at the time. On
July 3, 1776, the day after Congress voted for independence, he wrote
to his wife Abigail:

> Time has been given for the whole people maturely to consider
> the great question of independence, and to ripen their judgment,
> dissipate their fears, and allure their hopes, by discussing it in
> newspapers and pamphlets, by debating it in assemblies, con-

ventions, committees of safety and inspection, in town and county meetings, as well as in private conversations, so that the whole people, in every colony of the thirteen, have now adopted it as their own.[18]

According to Adams, independence resulted not from his own "lonely struggle," but from a months-long national conversation—and the people themselves, in overwhelming numbers, decided to make a clean break from Britain.

Curiously, there was a time when Adams had to buck the tide of public opinion—but it was to oppose independence, not support it. Immediately after the people of Massachusetts had overthrown British rule in 1774 (see chapter 4), many of the insurgents pressed for declaring independence from Britain and setting up their own government. This scared both John and Samuel Adams, who were in Philadelphia at the time for the First Continental Congress. Delegates from other colonies, they feared, would be put off if the people of Massachusetts acted too rashly. "Independency" and "the Proposal of Setting up a new Form of Government of our own," John Adams wrote, were ideas that "Startle People here." [19] Samuel Adams urged his colleagues back in Boston to oppose country radicals who were moving "to set up another form of government." [20] Such hesitancy angered the folks back home. "The people in the country begin to be very anxious for the Congress to rise," Abigail wrote to John. "They have no idea of the weighty business you have to transact, and their blood boils with indignation." [21] Far from carrying the torch of independence on their own, both John and Samuel Adams worked to slow things down—*against* the will of their own constituents.

In his July 4 op-ed for the *New York Times,* McCullough extends his treatment of Adams to include all the founders: "Had they been poll-driven, 'risk-averse' politicians gathered in Philadelphia that fateful summer of 1776, they would have scrapped the whole idea of a 'mighty revolution.' " [22] It was a "miracle," he says, "that so few could, in the end, accomplish so much for all humankind." McCullough's founders were all lonely heroes, fighting against the will of the people, the "polls." The majority of Americans during the Revolution, by this reading, are transformed into antagonists. Instead of being treated as heroes themselves, they become the lethargic masses, too slow to share the founders' forward-looking vision. The American Revolution, fought in the name of popular sovereignty, becomes strangely convoluted in stories that not only neglect but denounce the people themselves.

Practitioners of Founder Chic come to this strange place by taking the reminiscences of a handful of prolific writers at face value. The so-called founders sensed they were participating in events of immense historical consequence, and in a sense they wrote their own stories—tales we continue to tell today. Joseph Ellis says as much, quite eloquently:

> [T]he faces that look down upon us with such classical dignity in those portraits by John Trumbull, Gilbert Stuart, and Charles Willson Peale, the voices that speak to us across the ages in such lyrical cadences seem so mythically heroic, at least in part, because they knew we would be looking and listening. All the vanguard members of the revolutionary generation developed a keen sense of their historical significance even while they were still making the history on which their reputations would rest. They began posing for posterity, writing letters to us as much as to one another, especially toward the end of their respective careers. If they sometimes look like marble statues, that is how they wanted to look. . . . If they sometimes behave like actors in a historical drama, that is often how they regarded themselves.[23]

Ellis concludes from this observation that playing to posterity helped the founders remain in line and on cue: "Knowing we would be watching helped to keep them on their best behavior," he states. I draw a very different conclusion: the founders, in writing their own scripts, naturally cast themselves in leading and flattering roles. Although we continue to perform their plays today, much of history gets lost this way. The dramas that Founder Chic authors choose to reenact take place indoors, and the cast is always small—meanwhile, outside, there was a real revolution going on, a majestic spectacle with a cast of thousands.

"Why is it," Joseph Ellis asks rhetorically, "that there is a core of truth to the distinctive iconography of the American Revolution, which does not depict dramatic scenes of mass slaughter, but, instead, a gallery of well-dressed personalities in classical poses?" [24] Here is the fundamental fallacy of Founder Chic, for there is no "core of truth" to this. The "well-dressed personalities in classical poses" certainly engaged in actions of momentous import, but so did the 25,000 soldiers who perished while fighting for the patriot cause, the 300,000 soldiers who placed their bodies in danger, and the 3,000,000 people— the entire population—whose lives were severely disrupted for eight years as the United States labored in birth. To say that the story of the founders supersedes all the rest, that their deliberations were somehow on a higher order than the Revolution itself, is a grievous error. It takes the American Revolution, and with it the nation it created, out of the hands of the people.

DOING BATTLE

" 'Tis true he could talk—Gods how he *could* talk!"

"Give Me Liberty or Give Me Death!" Engraving, 1876.

8

"GIVE ME LIBERTY
OR GIVE ME DEATH"

The time: March 23, 1775.

The place: Henrico Church in Richmond, Virginia—the largest building in town, but still too small to hold all those who wished to attend the second session of the extralegal Virginia Convention. Patriots were gathering in Richmond rather than Williamsburg, the capital, for fear the royal governor might try to disband them.

The reason: Armed hostilities had not yet commenced, but Britain was beefing up its military presence in America with more troops and ships. While moderate patriots were still trying to avoid an armed confrontation, Patrick Henry introduced a series of resolutions that would raise a militia and place the colony in a state of preparedness. In defense of these resolutions, Patrick Henry delivered the most famous speech of his illustrious oratorical career. He addressed his remarks to the president of the Convention, as was the custom. Here are the final passages of his remarkable call to arms:

> Let us not, I beseech you, sir, deceive ourselves longer. Sir, we have done every thing that could have been done, to avert the storm which is now coming on. We have petitioned—we have remonstrated—we have supplicated—we have prostrated our-

selves before the throne, and have implored its interposition to arrest the tyrannical hands of the ministry and parliament. Our petitions have been slighted; our remonstrances have produced additional violence and insult, our supplications have been disregarded; and we have been spurned, with contempt, from the foot of the throne.

There is no longer any room for hope. If we wish to be free—if we mean to preserve inviolate those inestimable privileges for which we have been so long contending—if we mean not basely to abandon the noble struggle in which we have been so long engaged, and which we have pledged ourselves never to abandon, until the glorious object of our contest shall be obtained—we must fight!—I repeat it sir, we must fight!! An appeal to arms and to the God of Hosts is all that is left us!

They tell us, sir, that we are weak—unable to cope with so formidable an adversary. But when shall we be stronger? Will it be the next week or the next year? Will it be when we are totally disarmed, and when a British guard shall be stationed in every house? Shall we gather strength by irresolution and inaction? Shall we acquire the means of effectual resistance by lying supinely on our backs, and hugging the delusive phantom of hope, until our enemies shall have bound us hand and foot?

Sir, we are not weak, if we make a proper use of those means which the God of nature hath placed in our power. Three millions of people armed in the holy cause of liberty, and in such a country as that which we possess, are invincible by any force which our enemy can send against us.

Besides, sir, we have no election. If we were base enough to desire it, it is now too late to retire from the contest. There is no retreat, but in submission and slavery! Our chains are forged. Their clanking may be heard on the plains of Boston! The war is inevitable—and let it come!! I repeat it, sir, let it come!!!

It is in vain, sir, to extenuate the matter. Gentlemen may cry

peace, peace—but there is no peace. The war is actually begun!
The next gale that sweeps from the north will bring to our ears
the clash of resounding arms! Our brethren are already in the
field! Why stand we here idle? What is it that gentlemen wish?
What would they have? Is life so dear, or peace so sweet, as to be
purchased at the price of chains and slavery? Forbid it,
Almighty God!—I know not what course others may take; but
as for me, give me liberty, or give me death! [1]

These words are stirring indeed, but Patrick Henry never uttered
them. The speech was invented many years later, based on distant recollections of those who were present at the time. Although we know
people were moved by Patrick Henry's oratory on March 23, 1775, we
have no text of what he actually said.

In 1805 an attorney named William Wirt resolved to write about
the life of Patrick Henry. This would not be an easy task. Although
Henry had figured prominently in the events leading up to the Revolution, and although he went on to become governor of the nation's
then-largest state, he left few records for historians or biographers to
ponder. He was a speaker, not a writer, and we have no transcriptions,
recorded at the time, for any of the speeches that led to his renown.

In 1815 Wirt wrote to a friend of the difficulties he was having in
finding reliable material about the subject of his book:

It was all speaking, speaking, speaking. 'Tis true he could talk—
Gods how he *could* talk! but there is no acting the while. . . . And
then, to make the matter worse, from 1763 to 1789 . . . not one of
his speeches lives in print, writing or memory. All that is told me
is, that on such and such an occasion, he made a distinguished
speech. . . . [T]here are some ugly traits in H's character, and
some pretty nearly as ugly blanks. He was a blank military commander, a blank governor, and a blank politician, in all those
useful points which depend on composition and detail. In short,
it is, verily, as hopeless a subject as man could well desire. [2]

Undaunted, Wirt filled in the blanks according to his own discretion. He wanted to write a tale that would inspire American youth, and for that he did not need to stick too closely to the historical record. "The present and future generations of our country can never be better employed than in studying the models set before them by the fathers of the Revolution," he wrote to John Adams.[3]

In 1817, twelve years after he started his project, William Wirt published the first biography of Virginia's Revolutionary folk hero: *Sketches of the Life and Character of Patrick Henry.*[4] He dedicated his book "to the young men of Virginia," whom he hoped would emulate the hero of his tale. No matter that he invoked poetic license, his goals were to stimulate patriotism and sell books, and he was successful on both counts. Wirt's book immediately became a mainstay of popular history. Reprinted twenty-five times in the next half-century, it furnished much material that would be used in promoting a nationalist spirit—including the famous "liberty or death" speech, which finally appeared in print forty-two years after it was delivered, and eighteen years after the great orator's death.[5]

How accurate is Wirt's rendition?

Three decades after Henry delivered his inspirational call to arms, Wirt corresponded with men who had heard the speech firsthand and others who were acquainted with men who were there at the time. All agreed that the speech had produced a profound impact, but it seems that only one of Wirt's correspondents, Judge St. George Tucker, tried to render an actual text. Tucker's letter to Wirt has been lost, but we do have a letter from Wirt to Tucker that states, "I have taken almost entirely Mr. Henry's speech in the Convention of '75 from you, as well as your description of its effect on you verbatim."[6]

Scholars have argued for years whether the speech we know is primarily the work of William Wirt or St. George Tucker.[7] But what about Patrick Henry? How much of the speech is his?

Some of those favoring the Tucker hypothesis suggest that the speech published by Wirt is a fairly accurate rendering, since Tucker himself was there at the time. By his own admission, however,

Tucker's account of the speech was based on "recollections," not recorded notes. "In vain should I attempt to give any idea of his speech," he wrote. Tucker attempted a reconstruction of only two paragraphs (the first two in the selection included here), which constitute less than one-fifth of the speech.[8] Even this much is suspect. It seems improbable that St. George Tucker could commit Henry's words to memory, then reproduce them accurately several decades later. He might have captured the basic gist, but what about the diction and cadence, so crucial to the art of oratory? And what about all the rest of the speech, which amounted to 1,217 words? Where did all those words originate?

Imagine, in our own times, the task of trying to recreate the words of a speech delivered forty-two years ago if we had no written record. It has been precisely that long since John F. Kennedy delivered one of the most striking and fateful addresses in the history of this or any nation. On October 22, 1962, President Kennedy told the American people that Russia was trying to place missiles in Cuba, just ninety miles from the United States shore, and that he had just ordered a "quarantine" of Cuban waters. If Russian ships attempted to make any deliveries, they would have to fight American ships. Kennedy's speech brought the world to the brink of nuclear war.

But who, without prompting from the record, can remember the exact words Kennedy said? They too were stirring—something about the path being full of hazards, but the greatest danger would be to do nothing at all—but was that really the way he said it? And what else did he say? Millions watched and heard the speech, some might have even jotted down some notes, but who could reconstruct the speech now, decades later, if they had not done so at the time?[9]

Those of us old enough to remember the speech will recall the emotions—the fears and apprehensions of the moment—much better than the words. We might also recall Kennedy's demeanor, his looks, his deportment while delivering his lines. Two years earlier Nikita Khrushchev, Kennedy's Soviet adversary, had addressed the United Nations in unforgettable fashion—he took off his shoe and pounded it on the table. That was indeed memorable, but Khrushchev's precise words are forgotten. So it was with Patrick Henry. He had delivered an inspiring and very hawkish speech with great dramatic flare—people could remember that. But to recall the words he used to excite those patriotic feelings is another matter altogether.

FEAR AND LOATHING

Henry's speech, as we know it, owes much to the oratorical genius of William Wirt and St. George Tucker, in some combination, and it reflects the agendas of nineteenth-century nationalists who were fond of romanticizing war. To idealize war, however, much has to be left out. In the "liberty or death" speech which these men supposedly resurrected, key components of Patrick Henry's popular appeal are mysteriously absent. Henry's sentiments, and those of the men he addressed, were not always so noble as Wirt wanted his readers to believe.

In fact, we do have one account of Henry's speech that was recorded at the moment, not years later—and this version is seriously out of sync with Wirt's later rendition. In a letter dated April 6, 1775, James Parker wrote to Charles Stewart,

> You never heard anything more infamously insolent than P. Henry's speech: he called the K——— a Tyrant, a fool, a puppet, and a tool to the ministry. Said there was no Englishmen, no Scots, no Britons, but a set of wretches sunk in Luxury, that they had lost their native courage and (were) unable to look the brave Americans in the face. . . . This Creature is so infatuated, that he goes about I am told, praying and preaching amongst the common people.[10]

Even allowing for the biases of an unsympathetic observer, Parker's account is plausible. As in any era, hawkish and xenophobic political figures during the American Revolution probably questioned the enemy's courage, descended to name-calling, and appealed to wide-spread fear. Demagoguery is the underbelly of oratory.

Less than one month after Henry delivered his "liberty or death" speech, fear of slave uprisings helped trigger the onset of the Revolution in the South. In the spring of 1775, white citizens of Virginia believed that African Americans held in bondage were planning to rise up, rebel, and go on a murderous rampage against them. Fearful whites panicked and prepared for the worst—and Patrick Henry, one of the largest slaveholders of his county, was among them. Before dawn on April 21 the royal governor of Virginia, Lord Dunmore, dispatched a party of marines to seize gunpowder stored in the magazine at Williamsburg. Later that day, infuriated patriots gathered to protest. One newspaper reported their reasoning:

> The monstrous absurdity that the Governor can deprive the people of the necessary means of defense at a time when the colony is actually threatened with an insurrection of their slaves . . . has worked up the passions of the people . . . almost to a frenzy.[11]

Governor Dunmore at first claimed he had seized the powder so the slaves couldn't get to it. Shortly afterward, however, he changed his stance: if the patriots harmed a single British official, he pronounced, he would "declare Freedom to the Slaves, and reduce the City of Williamsburg to Ashes."[12]

This only kindled the flames of rebellion. Within the next few days at least seven counties hastily formed "independent companies," partly because the British had shed blood at Lexington and Concord, but also in response to Dunmore's threat. In Fredericksburg on April 29, more than 600 members of these companies prepared to march against the governor in Williamsburg. Dunmore reiterated his threat to raise the slaves, saying he would do so immediately if the companies proceeded with their plans.

Moderates convinced most of these companies to disband, but two companies persisted: Albemarle and Hanover. The Albemarle volunteers voted to continue to Williamsburg "to demand satisfaction of Dunmore for the powder, and his threatening to fix his standard and call over the negroes." [13] But they too soon turned back, leaving the field to the company from Hanover—under the leadership of Patrick Henry.[14]

The Hanover County committeemen were not of one mind, but Henry, with many friends and relatives on the committee, carried the day. Because of "apprehension for their persons and property," they decided to march on the capital. Since Dunmore had threatened to raise the slaves while simultaneously seizing gunpowder that whites could use to defend themselves, Henry and the majority of the Hanover men felt they were likely to suffer "calamities of the greatest magnitude, and most fatal consequences to this colony" unless they went on the offensive.[15] In the end, the incipient rebellion triggered by Dunmore's actions reached a negotiated (albeit temporary) settlement: the British paid for the powder they had seized, and the Hanover company went home.

Later that year, when Lord Dunmore formally offered to free any slaves who joined the British army, Colonel Patrick Henry of the First Virginia Regiment took it upon himself to publicize Dunmore's action far and wide. (For more on Dunmore's offer of freedom, see chapter 10.) This time Henry's exact words were set in writing, and there can be no doubt he used fear as a rallying cry:

> As the Committee of Safety is not sitting, I take the Liberty to enclose you a Copy of the Proclamation issued by Lord Dunmore; the Design and Tendency of which, you will observe, is fatal to the publick Safety. An early and unremitting Attention to the Government of the SLAVES may, I hope, counteract this dangerous Attempt. Constant, and well directed Patrols, seem indispensably necessary.[16]

Slaves were not the only objects of fear—Indians might cause trouble as well. One of the independent companies that threatened to march on Williamsburg noted that Dunmore had tried "to render (at least as far as in his power so to do) this colony defenceless, and lay it open to the attacks of a savage invasion, or a domestick foe [a common euphemism for slaves]." [17] This theme was repeated often in complaints about British policies issuing from the Southern states: the king, Parliament, and royal governors were inciting Indian attacks as well as slave insurrections. The following summer, Congress formalized these complaints in the Declaration of Independence. The king, it said, "has excited domestic insurrections amongst us and has endeavored to bring on the inhabitants of our frontiers the merciless Indian savages."

Patrick Henry, like many white Virginians, coveted Indian land. In 1766 he purchased tracts of 1,400 and 1,935 acres in southwest Virginia, then on the frontier of white settlement. He purchased six more tracts the following year, and in 1769, as a member of the Ohio Company (along with Thomas Jefferson and other leading figures), he petitioned the Crown for 50,000 acres on the Ohio River. Through the early 1770s he continued to speculate in various tracts of western lands, and in 1774 he joined the Transylvania Company, which "purchased" twenty million acres—nearly all of Kentucky, and much of northern Tennessee—from a group of Cherokees for the bargain price of less than two cents an acre. [18]

It is little wonder that Henry advocated military invasions of Indian country. In 1778, as governor of Virginia, he increased the military support for frontier settlements and sanctioned a company of "Volunteers" who set out to raid Indian lands. [19] The following year he authorized an expedition into distant territory inhabited by the Chickamaugas, militant Cherokees who resisted white domination. [20] Following the Revolutionary War, while arguing for American rights to navigate the Mississippi River, he declared he would sooner part with the union than with the Mississippi. [21] Before, during, and after the Revolution, Henry was an unrepentant expansionist. His own self-interest, as well as the interest of many other Virginians, demanded it.

It seems highly unlikely that in his efforts to arouse public opinion against Britain, which had tried to close the frontier to white settlement, Patrick Henry would not make use of the prevailing anti-Indian sentiments. Since western lands would be easier to acquire with Britain out of the way, playing on these sentiments aided the Revolutionary struggle against the Crown and Parliament. (See chapter 13.) It is even more implausible that Henry never played the "slave card"—his ace in the hole—in his politicking. Yet nowhere in any of his speeches, as rendered by later writers, do we see even a hint of pandering to instincts less noble than the love of liberty. His speeches, quite literally, have been whitewashed.

"Liberty or death" was not the only speech to receive a touch-up. Ten years earlier, in his first year as a representative to Virginia's House of Burgesses, Henry had stepped forth to offer a dramatic denunciation of the Stamp Act. According to William Wirt:

> It was in the midst of this magnificent debate, while he was descanting on the tyranny of the obnoxious act, that he exclaimed, in a voice of thunder, and with the look of a god, "Caesar had his Brutus—Charles the first, his Cromwell—and George the third—('Treason,' cried the speaker—'treason, treason,' echoed from every part of the house.—It was one of those trying moments which is decisive of character.—Henry faltered not for an instant; but rising to a loftier attitude, and fixing on the speaker an eye of the most determined fire, he finished his sentence with the firmest emphasis)—*may profit by their example*. If *this* be treason, make the most of it." [22]

In this version of the story, reconstructed a half-century after the fact, Patrick Henry dramatically defied his detractors. At the time, however, a French traveler who observed the event firsthand noted that Henry responded to the charge of "treason" quite differently:

> Shortly after I Came in one of the members stood up and said he had read that in former times tarquin and Julius had their Brutus,

Charles had his Cromwell, and he Did not Doubt but some good American would stand up, in favour of his Country, but (says he) in a more moderate manner, and was going to Continue, when the speaker of the house rose and Said, he, the last that stood up had spoke treason, and was sorey to see that not one of the members of the house was loyal Enough to stop him, before he had gone so far.

[U]pon which the Same member stood up again (his name is henery) and said that if he had affronted the speaker, or the house, he was ready to ask pardon, and he would shew his loyalty to his majesty King G. the third, at the Expence of the last Drop of his blood, but what he had said must be attributed to the Interest of his Country's Dying liberty which he had at heart, and the heat of passion might have lead him to have said something more than he intended, but, again, if he said anything wrong, he begged the speaker and the houses pardon. Some other Members stood up and backed him, on which that afaire was droped.[23]

The discrepancies between these two accounts are striking. While nineteenth-century Romantics depicted Henry as defiant in the face of numerous critics, the firsthand witness stated clearly and emphatically that Henry apologized for his excess not once but twice, and that the charge of "treason" came only from the Speaker of the House, not from a chorus of members. Henry was not a solitary hero standing tall in the face of numerous adversaries; instead, he tried to cover his bases when it appeared he had overreached his bounds. By backpeddling, Henry acted wisely and astutely—but not heroically.

The romantic versions of both these speeches—"liberty or death" and "Caesar had his Brutus"—glorify bold defiance. They also glorify oratory itself. At a time when many Americans did not have the ability to read learned dissertations on politics, everybody could hear and respond to a speech. Oratory was crucial to the creation of American nationalism. It is no surprise that William Wirt was something of an orator himself: he served as the keynote speaker to commemorate the fiftieth anniversary of the Declaration of Independence in Washington, D. C., on July 4, 1826.

Oratory has it uses, but it can also drown out compromise, reasoned consideration, and dissent. Hawkish oratory, taken at face value, is little more than military recruitment. Noble sentiments lead impressionable boys and young men to offer up their lives in service to their nation or cause. This danger intensifies when one orator pumps up the words of another, as with Wirt and Henry. Patriots of the early republic sanctified their nationalism and expansionism by appealing to the hallowed tradition of the Revolution. Even if the words came from Wirt, the "liberty or death" speech played better when attributed to the "Son of Thunder," the legendary orator from a generation past.

In the nineteenth century, countless schoolchildren practiced memorization and recitation by delivering and dramatizing the "liberty or death" speech. Little did they know that the words they spoke did not come from Patrick Henry, or that the noble sentiments they expressed concealed baser motives. Today, we do know these things, yet Henry's call to arms is still featured in roughly half our current texts. Students no longer recite the speech, but they do learn that it is considered very admirable to march off to war. In her *History of US,* Joy Hakim provides a complete stage set for the speech, which she repeats verbatim with no credit to Wirt: "Henry stepped into the aisle, bowed his head, and held out his arms. He pretended his arms were chained." After quoting several sentences, she concludes, "Then Patrick Henry threw off the imaginary chains, stood up straight, and cried out, 'Forbid it, Almighty God! I know not what course others may take, but as for me, give me liberty or give me death!' " [24]

This story works because the words have been teased and the context whitewashed. A speech that called the king a "fool" and Englishmen, Scots, and Britons "wretches" would not still be celebrated today, and a man who played upon fears of slaves and Indians would not be honored. Only by ignoring what actually happened can we tell the story we want to hear.

9

"DO NOT FIRE TILL YOU SEE
THE WHITES OF THEIR EYES"

During the Battle of Bunker Hill, the story goes, Israel Putnam (some say William Prescott) issued a command: "Do not fire till you see the whites of their eyes!" Displaying great courage in the face of the charging Redcoats, the untested patriots obeyed their officers, stood their ground, and withheld their fire until they could gaze into the eyes of the enemy.

According to depositions of those who participated in the battle, American officers issued many commands: "Fire low." "Aim at their waistbands." "Pick off the commanders." "Aim at the handsome coats." "Powder must not be wasted." "Wait until you see the white of their eyes." [1] What is so special about the last one? Why has this particular idiom, which now dominates the story of Bunker Hill, been included among the classic tales of the American Revolution?

Soldiers who see the whites of the eyes of their adversaries must be fighting a very personalized, intimate sort of war. In Revolutionary times, we prefer to believe, the glory of war was not diminished by impersonal slaughter. Man-to-man and honorably, a soldier could prove his valor by facing off against his adversary. Since then, with warfare increasingly industrialized, Americans have yearned nostalgically for more innocent times. The birth of our nation must have

" 'Don't throw away a single shot,
my brave fellows,' said old Putnam,
'till you can see the white of their eyes.' "

The Battle of Bunker Hill. Engraving, 1850s,
based on painting by Alonzo Chappel.

been a cozier affair. This is what "the whites of their eyes" story gives us. It sets the Revolutionary War in a class by itself. Those were the days, we imagine, when a man could look another man directly in eyes before shooting him down.

AN EXPERIMENT

The "whites of their eyes" command was not new to the American Revolution. Prince Charles of Prussia supposedly issued it in 1745, as did Frederick the Great in 1757. They were probably not the only ones. During the Revolution itself, other officers at other battles were said to have spoken these words.[2] "Do not fire until you see the whites of their eyes" was a figure of speech, a common idiom used by eighteenth-century officers to gain control over their soldiers' fire.

The command was never meant to be taken literally. The whites of a person's eyes, under the best of conditions, cannot be deciphered at more than ten yards. On moving targets in the dust and smoke of a battlefield, a person's eyes would scarcely be visible at five yards. To wait that long before firing would be suicidal—after a single volley, those who had waited to gaze into the eyes of an advancing enemy would be overrun before they had a chance to reload. When officers issued this order, as many did, they were telling their soldiers to focus hard on the enemy and hold their fire until further command. They were not telling them to fire only when the enemy had advanced to within five or ten yards.

Once, an American officer did insist that soldiers hold their fire till the enemy was only ten yards away. On May 29, 1780, at Waxhaws, South Carolina, Colonel Abraham Buford ordered his troops not to shoot until the British legion was almost upon them. The single volley proved insufficient to stop the charge, and the patriots were immediately overrun. Banastre Tarleton, the British commander, allegedly ordered the shooting of soldiers who were trying to surrender. One hundred thirteen patriots were killed immediately. Another 203 were captured, most of whom had been wounded. British losses, by contrast, were only five killed and twelve wounded. The experiment at close firing had failed.

Later, patriots would point to the "massacre" at Waxhaws as an example of British cruelty. (See chapter 11.) Perhaps so, but what happened at Waxhaws revealed another face of close combat. When soldiers fought each other with swords, musket butts, and bayonets, battles were likely to turn into slaughters. If "the whites of their eyes" were actually sighted, things could turn nasty indeed.

"CANNONS ROARING MUSKETS CRACKING DRUMS BEATING BUMBS FLYING ALL ROUND"

Sometimes, a Revolutionary soldier could see into the whites of the eyes of the enemy; far more often, he could not. Most men who died never even saw their slayers. In fact, the majority of soldiers who perished died from diseases or while languishing in prisons. With soldiers coming together in crowded and often unsanitary conditions, typhoid fever, typhus, dysentery, and smallpox ran rampant. Close contact with one's fellow soldiers took more lives than close contact with the enemy. According to military historian Howard Peckham, approximately 10,000 patriots died in camp. Another 7,000 died as prisoners of war, primarily by catching diseases from each other. By contrast, Peckham recorded 6,824 deaths from battle casualties.[3]

Those who succumbed in battle were often mowed down by cannons or muskets fired in their general direction by men from afar. The war that brought our nation into existence did not feature direct man-to-man combat nearly so often as we would like to believe; conversely, it did feature distant killing much more often than we prefer to imagine. While soldiers in the infantry were making or resisting a charge, their counterparts in the artillery, working in teams of three to fifteen, were loading cannons, mortars, and howitzers and letting them loose on an anonymous enemy. These weapons featured not only solid shot but also grapeshot, canister shot, and bombs that exploded—antipersonnel ammunition designed to maim or take human life.

The point of soldiering, then as now, was not only to display individual valor but to kill strangers from as safe a distance as possible—the farther away the better. Consider these firsthand accounts by participants in the Revolutionary War:

> Cannons Roaring muskets Cracking Drums Beating Bumbs Flying all Round. Men a dying woundeds Horred Grones which would Greave the Heardist of Hearts to See Such a Dollful Sight as this to See our Fellow Creators Slain in Such a manner.
> —Private Elisha Stevens, the Battle of Brandywine.[4]

> At length we fired the first gun, and immediately a tremendous cannonade—about one hundred and eighty, or two hundred pieces of heavy cannon were discharged at the same moment. The mortars from both sides threw out an enormous number of shells. It was a glorious sight to see them, like meteors, crossing each other, and bursting in the sky. It appeared as if the stars were tumbling down. The fire was incessant almost the whole night, cannonballs whizzing, and shells hissing, continually among us, ammunition chests and temporary magazines blowing up, great guns bursting, and wounded men groaning along the lines. It was a dreadful night! It was our last great effort, but it availed us nothing. After it, our military ardor was much abated.
> —William Moultrie, the first Battle of Charleston[5]

> During the whole night, at intervals of a quarter or half an hour, the enemy would let off all their pieces. . . . I was in this place a fortnight and can say in sincerity that I never lay down to sleep a minute in all that time. . . .
> The cannonade was severe, as well it might be, six sixty-four-gun ships, a thirty-six-gun frigate, a twenty-four-gun ship, a

galley and a sloop of six guns, together with six batteries of six guns each and a bomb battery of three mortars, all playing at once upon our poor little fort, if fort it might be called. Some of our officers endeavored to ascertain how many guns were fired in a minute by the enemy, but it was impossible, the fire was incessant. . . .

The enemy's shot cut us up. I saw five artillerists belonging to one gun cut down by a single shot, and I saw men who were stooping to be protected by the works, but not stooping low enough, split like fish to be broiled. . . .

When the firing had in some measure subsided and I could look about me, I found the fort exhibited a picture of desolation. The whole area of the fort was as completely ploughed as a field. The buildings of every kind hanging in broken fragments, and the guns all dismounted, and how many of the garrison sent to the world of spirits, I knew not. If ever destruction was complete, it was here.

— Private Joseph Plumb Martin, the siege of Fort Mifflin [6]

Even at Bunker Hill, patriots had to brave bombardment from across the river in Boston, as well as from men-of-war and gun batteries anchored offshore. All the firsthand accounts by patriots feature the terror caused by the enemy's distant fire. The cannon shot "buzzed around us like hail" and "were incessantly whistling by us," wrote John Chester.[7] "From Boston and from the ships," wrote Peter Brown, the British were "firing and throwing bombs, keeping us down till they got almost around us." The "brisk" fire from distant weapons "caused some of our young country people to desert."[8] William Prescott complained about the "very heavy cannonading and bombardment" and the "very warm fire from the enemy's artillery," which the patriots had to endure while working on their fortifications.[9] "Our men were not used to cannon-balls," William Tudor confessed to John Adams, "and they came so thick from the ships, floating batteries, &c., that they were discouraged from advancing." [10]

One of the most vivid accounts of the Battle of Bunker Hill comes from Issachar Bates, who had just enlisted in the army at the age of seventeen:

> We had to take our full share of their hot metal—of Cannon Balls—Grape and Cannister shot— . . . I could see them great nasty porridge pots flying thro' the air & cramed as full of Devils as they could hold, come whispering along with its blue tail in the day time, and its firey tail by night and if it burst in the air it would thro its hellish stuff all about ones ears, and if it fell to the ground it would hop about just as if the verry Devil was in it, until it bursted and then look out for shins and all above and at the same times cannon balls flying about once a minuit.[11]

Deeply affected by "these wicked inventions of men to shed blood and bring destruction upon their fellow creatures," Bates became a pacifist and later joined the Shaker sect. (Many others of the Revolutionary generation, like Bates, detested the brutalities of war. Approximately 80,000 people, one in every thirty free Americans, were members of pacifistic religious sects that opposed the taking of human life.)[12]

All this killing-from-afar is left out of the traditional telling, with its emphasis on a more proximate style of warfare. Listening to accounts of those who were there places the Battle of Bunker Hill in a different perspective. There is only one recorded statement mentioning "the whites of their eyes" command (see page 157), but nearly all firsthand descriptions feature the heavy bombardment by British artillery. American soldiers did hold their fire until an appropriate time, and, in the end, a few who had not managed to escape did face hand-to-hand combat. But the notion that the patriots did not engage in battle until they could look the enemy in the eyes is not a fair or adequate characterization of the fighting, either at Bunker Hill in particular or in the American Revolution in general.

Here's what really happened at Bunker Hill, the first pitched battle of the Revolutionary War. After their march against Lexington and

Concord, the British army had retreated to Boston, which it used as a garrison. Approximately 17,000 patriots gathered into an army of their own on the outskirts of town, holding siege. After two months, the patriots received intelligence that the British were preparing to take command of a promontory across the Charles River. American officers issued orders to construct fortifications on Bunker Hill, but the officers charged with executing these orders decided that Breed's Hill would be easier to defend. This is why the Battle of Breed's Hill became known as the Battle of Bunker Hill.

Throughout the night of June 16, 1775, farmers-turned-soldiers worked the soil for military purposes; by dawn on June 17, they had constructed a redoubt "eight rods square." All morning they continued to labor on a series of breastworks that would shield them during an attack, but once the British had spotted their fortifications, patriots had to brave an incessant cannonade while they worked. Approximately 1,500 patriots prepared to defend the position on Breed's Hill against an attack of almost 3,000 British Regulars.

British ships fired not only on the patriots' redoubts, but also on the nearby town of Charlestown, which they committed to flames. Issachar Bates described the conflagration: "And Oh! What a horrible sight, to stand and behold their hot balls, carcases and stink-pots flaming thro' the air for the distance of more than a mile, and in less than an hour that beautiful town was all in flames!" [13]

In the early afternoon, as patriot soldiers braced for the British advance, their officers fired commands like grapeshot. "Do not fire till you see the whites of their eyes," or some variation thereof, was among these last-minute directives hurled at the inexperienced soldiers during this crash course on military discipline.

At around 3:00 in the afternoon on June 17, a vanguard of British soldiers advanced up the hill. Most of the patriots held their fire as commanded; a few did not. (Later, one American officer stated that he had purposely shot early, hoping to induce premature and ineffectual fire from the enemy.) [14] When the British were close enough that musket fire might be reasonably effective—approximately sixty yards, according to contemporary reports—the patriots commenced their first volley. The deadly fire continued unabated, causing the Redcoats to retreat.

The British regrouped and charged the hill once again. This time the patriots held their fire until the enemy was only thirty yards away, still not close enough to gaze into the eyes of the soldiers who were trying to kill them. Since the second charge was not as concerted as the first, there was not as much danger of being overrun, so patriots could wait longer before discharging their muskets. Again the shots hit their marks, and again the British retreated.

Through heavy cannonading, however, the British were able to force the patriots to abandon their breastworks. When the Redcoats charged the third time, the weary and shell-shocked patriots decided to abandon the redoubt. They had not received the reinforcements they had expected. Most patriots were able to run; a few who could not leave the redoubt quickly enough were forced to deflect bayonets with the butt ends of their muskets. This was the only fighting in close quarters during the battle.

The retreat was itself fraught with hazard. Offshore batteries continued to pound away at the narrow Charlestown Neck, which the Americans were forced to cross. "I was not suffered to be touched," wrote Peter Brown, "although I was in the fort when the enemy came in, and jumped over the walls, and ran a half a mile, where balls flew like hail-stones, and cannon roared like thunder." [15]

Technically, the British won the Battle of Bunker Hill, for they took new ground—but their victory game at a horrific cost: 226 killed and another 828 wounded, some of whom later perished. Most of these young men from poor families on the other side of the Atlantic were hit by bullets fired from muskets at midrange. Patriot losses were also significant: 140 killed and 271 wounded. [16] Today, we celebrate this bloodbath with a quaint little story about "the whites of their eyes," which demonstrates how valorous war can be.

THE "EYES" PREVAIL

How did the crude, impersonal slaughter at the Battle of Bunker Hill
come to satisfy our yearning for a more intimate form of combat?

Contemporary accounts referred to Bunker Hill as a defeat for the
Americans. The patriots, however, placed an interesting spin on this
defeat. Soon after the battle, the Massachusetts Committee of Safety
issued a report that claimed a moral victory: "Though the officers and
soldiers of the ministerial army meanly exult in having gained this
ground," wrote the Committee, "they cannot but attest to the bravery
of our troops." The carnage inflicted upon the British, it claimed, had
"blasted" all previous records. "Such a slaughter was, perhaps, never
before made upon British troops." [17]

Crucial to the positive spin placed on the defeat was the willingness of
the rebels to hold their ground against thousands of disciplined Redcoats. Despite glistening bayonets pointed right at them, the committee
declared, the inexperienced, untrained American troops had not panicked. They had obeyed their officers' commands to withhold fire. With
ammunition scarce, no shots had been wasted. Not until the British
"came within ten or twelve rods," wrote the Committee of Safety, did
the Americans commence their first volley. One rod is 16.5 feet, so "ten
or twelve rods" translates to 55 to 66 yards, or 165 to 198 feet.

That number would figure prominently in the early histories of the
Revolutionary War. William Gordon and David Ramsay repeated the
Committee of Safety's estimate verbatim. John Marshall stated more
conservatively that the British had advanced "within less than one
hundred yards" when the Americans opened fire.[18] Virtually all the
early accounts specified the distance that separated the opposing
forces at the time of the first volley, for this constituted proof that the
patriots had both followed orders and displayed great courage in the
face of the advancing Redcoats—but that distance, although it varied
somewhat from one account to the next, was always several times
greater than ten yards, the point at which the whites of the enemy's
eyes might first become visible.

None of the Revolutionary era historians—William Gordon, David Humphreys, John Marshall, or Mercy Otis Warren—mentioned anything about the "whites of their eyes" command. In 1788 Humphreys published a biography of Israel Putnam, the officer from Connecticut who was later said to have issued the order.[19] Humphreys said nothing about the command at Bunker Hill that would later be tied to Putnam's name, but he did tell another story that would become enshrined in Revolutionary lore: "Putnam, who was ploughing when he heard the news [about Lexington and Concord], left his plough in the middle of the field, unyoked his team, and without waiting to change his clothes, set off for the theatre of action."[20] (In later versions of the tale, still with us today, "Old Put" jumped immediately on his horse without even bothering to unyoke his team.) Here was a tale worth telling—this single incident exemplified the eagerness of New England farmers to answer the call to arms. "The whites of their eyes," by contrast, was hardly a story at all, at least in the minds of contemporaries.

The story first found its way into print in Mason Weems's popular biography of George Washington, a quarter-century afterward:

> *"Don't throw away a single shot, my brave fellows,"* said old Putnam, *"don't throw away a single shot, but take good aim; nor touch a trigger, till you can see the white of their eyes."*
>
> This steady reserve of fire, even after the British had come up within pistol-shot, led them [the British] to hope that the Americans did not *mean to resist!* . . . But soon as the enemy were advanced within the fatal distance marked, all at once a thousand triggers were drawn, and a sheet of fire, wide as the whole front of the breast-work, bursted upon them with most ruinous effect.[21]

Few writers over the next half-century echoed Weems's tale. Although most mentioned that the patriots had held their fire, they gave specified distances: Paul Allen in 1819 followed Marshall's estimate of

100 yards; Charles Goodrich in 1823 wrote "within twelve rods"; Salma Hale in 1822 shortened it to "within ten rods"; Noah Webster in 1833 used the official Committee of Safety numbers, ten to twelve rods.[22] Richard Hildreth, a conscientious scholar writing in 1849, set the distance at "within a hundred yards."[23] Even George Bancroft, a popular historian fond of direct quotations and folksy dialogue, said nothing about "the whites of their eyes." Instead, he offered two contemporary estimates: "within eight rods, as [William] Prescott afterwards thought," and "within ten or twelve rods as the committee of safety of Massachusetts wrote."[24] Setting a proscribed distance was deemed critical to the moral of the story, but the precise words of the commanding officer were of little account.

Richard Frothingham, in an exhaustive study of Bunker Hill written in 1849, presented a thesis that would set Weems's story back even farther: Israel Putnam was not even in charge at the time. That honor, he wrote, went to William Prescott, a colonel from Massachusetts.[25] In the middle of the nineteenth century, a furious debate raged through academic circles: who *was* the commander at the Battle of Bunker Hill? Both Putnam and Prescott had their defenders.

One would think that uncertainty over the identity of the commander would have interfered with any story about what this mystery-man actually said. Not so. Following the Civil War, the "whites of their eyes" stories picked up steam—and it has never lost its momentum. In the twentieth century, specific distances began to disappear from school texts; instead, students were told that "untrained militia . . . coolly stood their ground until they saw the whites of the enemy's eyes."[26] A figure of speech had been taken literally and enshrined in the official lexicon of the Revolutionary War. Students had little trouble drawing the obvious conclusion: American patriots, like knights of the Middle Ages, fought their foes eye-to-eye and hand-to-hand.

The "whites of their eyes" tale has shown remarkable endurance. Despite contemporary accounts, all of which state that the patriots fired long before they could have looked into the eyes of their adversaries, the story not only survives but thrives. Even the problem of the commander's identity has proven no obstacle. For those favoring Putnam, he must have said it; for those in Prescott's camp, he was the one. Whoever said it, and however they worded it, the story must still be told.

Louis Birnbaum, in *Red Dawn at Lexington,* goes with Prescott: "Men, you are all marksmen; do not any of you fire until you can see the whites of their eyes." [27] Robert Lieke, in *George Washington's War,* writes with equal certainty: "Burly Israel Putnam rode up and down the lines roaring the immortal words, 'Don't fire until you see the white of their eyes! Then, fire low.' " [28] A. J. Langguth in *Patriots* and Thomas Fleming in *Liberty!* also weigh in with Putnam.[29] Benson Bobrick, in *Angel in the Whirlwind,* hedges. By using the generic term "officers" and writing in the passive voice, he manages to tell the story without favoritism: "Those on the front line were now exhorted by their officers "to be cool" and to reserve their fire until the enemy "were near enough for us to see the white of their eyes." (Contrary to appearances, this is not a direct quotation from a participant, but only a literary device.) Even so, since Bobrick wants to place Putnam at the heart of the action, he has him uttering further commands: "Fire low—take aim at the waistbands—pick off the commanders—aim at the handsome coats." [30]

Those not wishing to show a preference as to the identity of the commander freely attribute these words to both the leading candidates. In his 1858 biography of Israel Putnam, George Canning Hill wrote: "Putnam told the men, as he passed hastily along the lines, dusty and perspiring, not to waste their fire, for powder was very scarce. 'Wait,' said he, 'till you see the whites of their eyes.' " Not wishing to offend the Prescott fans, he then added: "Prescott gave the same orders to those within the redoubt." [31]

Today, little has changed. In the recently published *American National Biography,* a twenty-four-volume compilation that represents state-of-the-art history, Bruce Daniels states definitively: "As field commander of the troops at Bunker Hill, Putnam gave one of the most famous orders in American military history: 'Men, you are marksmen—don't one of you fire until you see the white[s] of their eyes.' " But what does the *American National Biography* say about William Prescott? William Fowler writes: "Tradition has him calling, 'Don't fire until you see the whites of their eyes.' " Although this statement is guarded in tone and not incorrect ("tradition" does say this), the story is passed on nonetheless. Putnam said it, Prescott said it, they both said it—one way or the other, or both ways at once, the legend continues.[32]

Significantly, virtually all modern versions of the story leave out the actual distance between the armies at the time the Americans opened fire. Daniels says nothing about it, while Fowler states only that the British were "within close range." In the absence of concrete numbers, which the early accounts had scrupulously included, we are left only with the evidence of our senses to interpret the now-famous command. The British must have been at a very close range, we assume, if the patriots could see into their eyes.[33] Since the distances mentioned in contemporary accounts would contradict this assumption, they are conveniently omitted.

When the story is repeated in school texts, it is often accompanied by reproductions of Romantic paintings, such as John Trumbull's famous *The Death of General Warren at the Battle of Bunker's Hill*, which show British and American forces within arm's length of each other. We would like to believe that our nation was born in this manner, with no man firing his Brown Bess musket before establishing a kind of personal (if adversarial) relationship with the enemy. Soldiers were brave and fighting was intimate. That's the way they did it in the old days. That's how wars are supposed to be.

The promotional copy for Roger Ford's recent book, *The Whites of their Eyes: Close-Quarter Combat*, plays up this valorous aspect of warfare:

> Here is an anecdotal history of close-quarter combat that brings
> the fear, intensity, and raw courage of close-quarter combat to

real life. Read firsthand accounts of warfare among the ruins of Stalingrad, fighting in tunnels during the Vietnam War, springing an ambush, and even fighting with axes on the Eastern Front in World War II.[34]

That would be ideal, if warfare were somehow reduced to a matter of "raw courage." That's why we cling to traditional images of the Revolutionary War—then, soldiers knew how to fight a good fight, man to man. By including the "whites of their eyes" tale within the core narrative of our nation's founding, we manage to justify and even celebrate the purposive killing inherent in war.

GOOD VS. EVIL

"The relations between master and slave in Virginia were so pleasant that the offer of freedom fell upon dull, uninterested ears."

Life of George Washington the Farmer. Lithograph by Claude Regnier, 1853, based on painting by Junius Brutus Stearns, *Washington as a Farmer at Mount Vernon,* 1851.

10

PATRIOTIC SLAVES

In the popular movie *The Patriot*, a British officer rides up to Benjamin Martin's South Carolina plantation and offers freedom to any slaves who fight in His Majesty's army. This is rooted in historical fact. Early in the war Lord Dunmore, the royal governor of Virginia, pronounced: "I do hereby declare all indented Servants, Negroes, or others, (appertaining to Rebels) free, that are able and willing to bear Arms, they joining His Majesty's Troops as soon as may be."[1] Later on, British general Henry Clinton made a similar offer: "Every Negro who shall desert the Rebel Standard" would enjoy the "full security to follow within these Lines, any Occupation which he shall think proper."[2]

In fact, several thousand bondsmen from South Carolina took these offers seriously and fled to the British in search of their freedom.[3] Not so in *The Patriot*. In the Hollywood version of history, the officer who offered freedom to slaves at Martin's plantation received a most unexpected response from the black field hands he addressed: "Sir, we're not slaves. We work this land as freed men." Here begins a serious stretch of poetic license: we see happy blacks working plantations as freed men in Revolutionary South Carolina, the very heart of the Deep South.

A bit later in the film, a slave named Occam enlists in the militia, serving in place of his master. Although this never happened in South Carolina, Occam proceeds to bear arms on behalf of the patriots in an integrated militia unit. Not until the Korean War, says Dean Devlin, one of the film's producers, would black and white Americans again serve side by side.

Midway through the story, Occam sees a notice posted on a bulletin board in camp. Since Occam, like most slaves, can't read, someone else reads it aloud:

By order of GENERAL GEORGE WASHINGTON and the CONTINENTAL CONGRESS, all bound SLAVES who give minimum ONE YEAR SERVICE in the CONTINENTAL ARMY will be GRANTED FREEDOM and be paid a bounty of FIVE SHILLINGS for each month of service.

Occam then looks wistfully into the air as he whispers to himself: "Only another six months."

The document read to Occam, which is seen onscreen and appears visually authentic, contains more historical errors in a single sentence than at first seems possible. A complete concoction, it seriously misrepresents the participation of African Americans in the Revolutionary War. Neither George Washington nor the Continental Congress issued anything like this emancipation proclamation, which allegedly preceded Lincoln's famous decree by more than fourscore years.

When Washington first assumed command of the Continental forces, he banned the enlistment of all Negroes, both slave and free. Because of serious manpower shortages, however, he soon had to rescind a portion of his order: free blacks who had previously served were permitted to reenlist, but slaves were still banned. Slaves were seen as an embarrassment to a republican army fighting in the name of freedom.[4]

Soldiers were recruited by individual states, not by the Continental Congress, as implied in the notice read to Occam. Later in the war some states permitted blacks to serve as substitutes for whites who had

been drafted, but in South Carolina, not a single black is known to
have enlisted in the Continental Army during the entire course of the
Revolutionary War. Congress had indeed suggested that the state recruit its slaves, but the notion of arming those held in bondage was
seen as preposterous to most white South Carolinians, who rejected
the proposal out-of-hand. "We are much disgusted here at Congress
recommending us to arm our Slaves," wrote Christopher Gadsden.
"It was received with great resentment, as a very dangerous and im-
politic Step." [5]

Unwilling to militarize the slaves, white Southerners confronted
their manpower shortages by offering special bounties. Slaves did figure in the bounty policy, but not as suggested in Washington's alleged
emancipation proclamation: each white man, upon enlistment, was
promised a slave of his own. Even if Congress had recruited slaves,
which it did not, and even if it had offered bounties *to* slaves, instead of
bounties *of* slaves, the bounty would not have consisted of shillings,
which Congress did not possess, but deflated Continental currency,
which it printed at will.

Had Washington and the Continental Congress truly offered freedom for a single year of service, when the standard term for everyone
else was "three years or the duration of the war," slaves by the tens of
thousands would have rushed to sign up.[6] This would have seriously
disrupted Southern society, already reeling from the mass exodus of
slaves fleeing to the British. George Washington, who lost at least
twenty of his own slaves when they escaped to the British, was not
likely to weaken his command over his remaining 300 bondsmen by
offering freedom to those enlisting in the Continental Army.[7]

Besides, had Washington and the Continental Congress offered to
free the slaves, who would compensate their masters? Already broke,
Congress would not be able to afford the expense—but to free slaves
without compensating their masters would surely have provoked an
outright rebellion among Southern whites. The union would have
collapsed at the very beginning had Washington and the Continental
Congress followed the plotline of *The Patriot*.

Why did the creators of *The Patriot* manufacture this specious document, with all the lies it embodied? "The great and painful irony of the American Revolution is the fact that this was a war fought for freedom," explains the screenwriter, Robert Rodat. White Americans, while pursuing their own freedom, denied freedom to their slaves. The only way to resolve this inherent contradiction is to make the freedom struggle for blacks coincide with that of their white masters—but to achieve such an unlikely wedding of interests required the makers of *The Patriot* to break, not merely bend, historical truths.

The desire to reconcile the inherent contradiction of the Revolution led Rodat to create a highly implausible story. Toward the end of the film, Benjamin Martin's family is sheltered by a black Maroon community, composed of his slaves-who-were-not-really-slaves. These joyous people even host a wedding party, to the beat of African drums, for Martin's son Gabriel. This is how we would like to imagine our Revolutionary past: a happy union between former black field hands and a white plantation family.

The conclusion to Occam's tale is even more incredible. As the soldiers prepare to fight and perhaps die at Cowpens, a fellow who has formerly been a bigot observes that Occam has already served his time. (Even by the film's own terms, this does not hold: the alleged emancipation notice applies only to Continental soldiers, while Occam is a militiaman.) Although Occam, unlike white soldiers, is free to go, he refuses to leave, for he has become a true patriot: "I'm here now on my own accord," he announces. The reformed bigot replies: "I'm honored to have you with us. Honored." Then, in the concluding scene, Occam and his new white friend set out to "build a whole new world," starting with a house for Benjamin Martin.

Although the story is made-up, *The Patriot* purports to historical authenticity. "We felt that while we were telling the fictional story," says producer Mark Gordon, "the backdrop was serious history." That's why Gordon and his team decided to consult the Smithsonian Institution, whom they credit in the closing titles. "When you hear the

words 'Smithsonian Institution,' " Gordon explains, "you think serious, you think important."

The mystique of "history" is marshaled in support of fiction. *The
Patriot* tells a story we wish to believe: the American Revolution was
the first step along the long road to the termination of slavery. The
War for Independence, with its promise of freedom and its suggestion
of equality, supposedly served as a blueprint for black independence
as well as white.

In truth, the contradiction between slavery and the American Revolution was not so easily resolved as it was in *The Patriot*. During the
war, Southern white patriots united in opposition to the diabolical de-
signs of the British, who threatened the very roots of their society by
offering freedom to slaves. After the war, the institution of slavery so-
lidified. The Revolution had seriously threatened the very existence
of slavery—tens of thousands of the slaves had actually escaped from
their masters. In response, white owners clamped down. The rigid
slave codes we associate with the period before the Civil War were a
direct outcome of the Revolutionary War. This is "serious history."
The notion that blacks and whites pulled together in the wake of the
Revolution to "build a whole new world" is no more than a self-
serving fantasy.

HISTORY IN BLACK AND WHITE

The celebration of black patriotism is itself a historical phenomenon.
At the time of the Revolution and for decades after, little was said
about the black presence in the Revolutionary War. Early historians
assigned no special role to black patriots, while they either ignored or
downplayed the mass exodus of slaves to the British. When they did
mention slaves fleeing to the enemy, they emphasized the loss inflicted
on white masters. "It has been estimated that between the years 1775
and 1783 the state of South Carolina was robbed of twenty-five thousand negroes, valued at about twelve million five hundred thousand

dollars," wrote Benson Lossing in his *Pictorial Field-Book of the Revolution,* citing the early historian David Ramsay.[8]

Suddenly, in the middle of the nineteenth century, the notion of "colored" patriotism assumed great political significance. Abolitionists pointed to the participation of blacks in the American Revolution to make a strong argument: if these people helped white Americans win freedom, how could they be denied their own?

In 1855 a black abolitionist from Boston, William Nell, authored a book called *The Colored Patriots of the American Revolution.* Nell's work, according to an introduction written by fellow abolitionist Wendell Phillips, was intended "to stem the tide of prejudice against the colored race" and "to prove colored men patriotic."[9] Harriet Beecher Stowe, in a second introduction, claimed that black patriots should be honored even more than whites: "It was not for their own land they fought, not even for a land which had adopted them, but for a land which had enslaved them, and whose laws, even in freedom, oftener oppressed than protected. Bravery, under such circumstances, has a peculiar beauty and merit."[10]

As his title suggested, Nell focused exclusively on the five thousand blacks who fought on the side of the Americans. He made no mention of the tens of thousands of slaves who fled to the British—this would scarcely have won converts to the abolitionist cause. When discussing South Carolina, since he could not point to any black patriot soldiers, he cited the famous Charles Pinckney: "In the course of the Revolution, the Southern States were continually overrun by the British, and every negro in them had an opportunity of running away, yet few did."[11] Instead of running, Pinckney said, South Carolina's slaves worked side by side with their masters to fortify against British attacks. Ironically, abolitionists at that time were in no position to dispute this idyllic picture of happy slaves during the American Revolution.[12]

Following the Civil War and Reconstruction, during the Jim Crow era, blacks in the Revolution once again took a back seat. In 1891 one of the country's foremost historians, John Fiske, spoke for his age

when he ignored the historical record and stated bluntly that happy
slaves had declined Lord Dunmore's offer of freedom:

> The relations between master and slave in Virginia were so
> pleasant that the offer of freedom fell upon dull, uninterested
> ears. With light work and generous fare, the condition of the
> Virginia negro was a happy one. . . . He was proud of his con-
> nection with his master's estate and family, and had nothing to
> gain by rebellion.[13]

One writer during this time, Edward Eggleston, made an intriguing
use of the "happy slaves" myth in his argument for Negro inferiority.
Negroes were so lacking in mental capacities, he claimed, that they
would die out from natural evolutionary processes; this was the "ultimate solution" to the "Negro problem." As proof of their inability to
fend for themselves, Eggleston offered the example of early emancipation efforts around the time of the Revolution—these resulted from
"the improved moral standards" of whites, not the efforts of a "black
race" too feeble to "assert its rights." By failing to acknowledge the
many and varied efforts that blacks had made to gain their freedom
during the Revolution, Eggleston perpetuated one of the greatest of
all historical lies: "The Negro possessed no ability whatsoever to help
free himself. So long as he had plenty of food, and outlets for his ordinary animal passions, he remained happy and content."[14]

Edward Eggleston also wrote textbooks for children; naturally,
none of his texts made any mention of black participation in the
American Revolution.[15] Neither did any of twenty-two other school
texts, written from the end of Reconstruction to the beginning of the
civil rights movement.[16] From the time of Ulysses S. Grant to Dwight
D. Eisenhower, textbook writers totally excluded one-sixth of Revolutionary era Americans.[17]

So did most professional historians. With only a few exceptions
(most notably Herbert Aptheker, a Communist writing in the 1940s
and 1950s), white authors ignored the black presence in the Revolu-

tion for a full century, from the Civil War to the 1960s. It fell upon black historians to tell the story themselves.

In 1883 George W. Williams included in his comprehensive *History of the Negro Race in America, from 1619 to 1880* an extensive discussion of the Revolutionary era. He started by exposing the hypocrisy of white Revolutionaries:

> The sentiment that adorned the speeches of orators . . . was "the equality of the rights of all men." And yet the slaves who bore their chains under their eyes, who were denied the commonest rights of humanity, who were rated as chattels and real property, were living witnesses to the insincerity and inconsistency of this declaration.[18]

Then, rather than limiting his attention to the contributions of black patriots, Williams undertook a serious investigation of the racial politics involved in military recruitment. He showed step by step how Washington and his War Council came to prohibit the enlistment of blacks during the siege of Boston, and he then explained how Dunmore's proclamation of freedom forced them to reverse themselves. He chronicled the flight of slaves to the British and the feeble attempts to quell this exodus by white patriots who claimed to be "true friends" of the people they held in bondage. Suddenly, however, Williams interjected into his forthright analysis a pat display of traditional patriotism: "The struggle went on between Tory and Whig, between traitor and patriot, between selfishness and the spirit of noble consecration to the righteous cause of the Americans," he wrote.[19] Williams tried to negotiate a difficult course: he wanted to tell the story from the black perspective, but he could not evidence anti-American or pro-British sentiments.

Despite his hesitations, Williams arrived at a truly radical conclusion:

> Enlistment in the army did not work a practical emancipation of the slave, as some have thought. Negroes were rated as chattel

property by both armies and both governments during the entire war. This is the cold fact of history, and it is not pleasing to contemplate. The Negro occupied the anomalous position of an American Slave and an American soldier. He was a soldier in the hour of danger, but a chattel in time of peace.[20]

This sobering assessment would not be echoed by white writers for three-quarters of a century.

Although Williams's work was ignored by white scholars, two black scholars writing in the 1920s, Carter G. Woodson and W. E. B. Du Bois, took up where Williams had left off. Woodson, often labeled "the father of Negro history," organized the *Journal of Negro History* in 1916, and in 1922 he published a comprehensive survey that became the standard text for a quarter of a century, *The Negro in Our History.* Woodson treated the flight of slaves to the British in a straightforward manner, without apologies; he also added that "a corps of fugitive slaves calling themselves the King of England's Soldiers harassed for several years the people living on the Savannah River, and there was much fear that the rebuffed free Negroes of New England would do the same for the colonists in their section."[21] At the close of the war in the South, Woodson concluded, "There followed such a reaction against the elevation of the race to citizenship that much of the work proposed to promote their welfare and to provide for manumission was undone."[22] Gone was the fairy tale with a happy ending. The American Revolution had done as much harm as good.

In 1924 Du Bois, a socialist and founder of the NAACP, followed Woodson's basic line in his informal history, *The Gift of Black Folk: The Negroes in the Making of America.* Du Bois discussed openly the idiosyncratic "patriotism" of black soldiers:

His problem as a soldier was always peculiar: no matter for what her enemies fought and no matter for what America fought, the American Negro always fought for his own freedom and for the self-respect of his race. Whatever the cause of war, therefore, his cause was peculiarly just. He appears . . . always with a double motive,—the desire to oppose the so-called enemy of his country along with his fellow white citizens, and before that, the motive of deserving well of those citizens and securing justice for his folk.[23]

In 1947 John Hope Franklin treated the slaves' flight to the British in his popular college text, *From Slavery to Freedom*—but the story remained ghettoized, told only as "Negro history." Despite the work of Williams, Woodson, Du Bois, and Franklin, blacks were still not included in the standard telling of the American Revolution.[24]

Not until the 1960s were blacks once again counted as "present" at our nation's founding. In 1961 another black scholar, Benjamin Quarles, published an account that was both penetrating and thorough, *The Negro in the American Revolution*.[25] The broad lines of argument had been made before, but Quarles added significant detail, and his timing was perfect. Within the history profession, Quarles's masterpiece was considered "a bombshell of a book." [26] Young white historians, influenced by the civil rights movement, embraced and built on Quarles's work. In the decades that followed, black and white scholars have produced a wealth of monographs and in-depth studies chronicling how African Americans experienced the Revolution and the impact of their actions on the politics of war.

Some but not all of this new information has made its way to popular audiences. Today, as in the 1850s, Northern blacks who found freedom by fighting with the patriots are celebrated, while Southern slaves who fled to the British are not. *Liberty!*, the book and PBS series, features James Lafayette, a slave who earned his freedom by serving as valet and groom to the Marquis de Lafayette, as one of the five key "portraits" of the entire American Revolution.[27] (The others are King George III, George Washington, Benjamin Franklin, and, for obvious reasons, Abigail Adams.) The Black Patriots Foundation is currently spearheading an effort to place a "Black Revolutionary War Patriots Memorial" on the Washington Mall—although nobody seems very interested in erecting a monument to slaves who sought freedom by siding with the enemy.[28]

A TALE OF TWO STORIES

There are two stories we can tell: (1) In Northern states during the American Revolution, slaves earned their freedom by fighting side by side with white patriots, and (2) In Southern states during the American Revolution, slaves escaped from patriotic masters to find freedom with the British. The first has considerable appeal for our times, while the second has none.

If we try to cast the American Revolution as a battle between good and evil, we are faced with the undeniable fact that many of the most prominent patriots owned slaves. Slavery is America's original sin— but when we stick to the story we like the best, we hide this blemish on a perfect America. We preserve the good name of the founders by portraying the Revolution as a progressive force that dealt a serious blow to the institution of slavery.

The first story appears to absolve the Revolutionaries of their sins, while the second holds them fully accountable. But to tell the first story while ignoring the second requires serious manipulations of the historical evidence. This is done consciously, not innocently, for ever since the publication of Quarles's *Negro in the American Revolution* over forty years ago, the story of the black exodus at the moment of our nation's inception has been known and embraced within the scholarly community.

The simplest approach is to stonewall. Of thirteen current textbooks for elementary, middle school, and high school students, only one mentions that more blacks served with the British than served with the patriots.[29] Not one mentions that some who fought for the patriots were sent back into slavery at war's end. Not one mentions that twenty of Washington's slaves and at least twenty-three of Jefferson's slaves are known to have fled to the British.[30] Not one mentions that white patriots used the fear of slave flight and slave uprisings to recruit for their cause. As a partial concession to the facts, some do mention Lord Dunmore's proclamation. None of the texts, however, name any individuals who fought with the British, whereas they all identify and celebrate some of those who fought with the patriots.

Another approach is to twist the significance of events by manipulating numbers. Most of the texts boast that 5,000 blacks became American soldiers, but the numbers they provide for the "other" freedom-seeking slaves are smaller. Some mention 300, the number that joined Dunmore within the first five days; one mentions 500, the number that boarded a single British ship.[31] These figures are not technically inaccurate, but they are seriously misleading—the number of black patriots over the course of the entire war is compared with the number of runaway slaves over the course of a few days. One text points out that Lord Dunmore himself owned fifty-seven slaves, but it fails to note that Washington and Jefferson each claimed ownership of several times that number.[32]

By applying a double standard, these texts are able to tell one story and suppress the other. They pronounce proudly that the Revolution, with its rhetoric of "freedom" and "slavery," cracked the institution that held half a million Americans in bondage. Thousands of slaves, they say, were able to negotiate their freedom by fighting with the patriots. Free blacks also became patriot soldiers and sailors, and both slaves and freemen distinguished themselves in battle. On a broader level, the texts state, Revolutionary ideology helped trigger the demise of slavery in the North. In 1777 Vermont stipulated that all slaves born thereafter would be freed upon reaching their maturity (age twenty-two for males and eighteen for females). In 1780 Pennsylvania followed suit with more conservative age limits (twenty-eight for men, twenty-one for women), and by the early nineteenth century all Northern states had taken steps toward the termination of slavery.[33]

The other story, in which slaves owned by famous patriots like Washington and Jefferson fled to the British to seek their freedom, would not play so well to a modern audience. Imagine an alternate plotline for *The Patriot*: halfway through the movie, Benjamin

Martin's slaves run off to fight under Colonel Tavington, the film's sinister British villain; in the next battle scene Martin, the patriot, kills three of his former bondsmen along with the usual seven Redcoats. This is not what we want to see.

The two stories do not easily coexist. They work at cross purposes, one canceling the other. The object of the first story, in which patriots are able to hold the moral high ground, is nullified when we see slaves escaping from their patriot masters to seek emancipation with the enemy. If we are trying to establish who the "good guys" were in the Revolutionary War, we have to choose between the two conflicting tales.

There is another way of looking at these stories. If we focus on the black experience, rather than how the stories portray whites, the two suddenly blend into one.

African Americans in both the North and South used the Revolution to foster the cause of black freedom. In a war between whites, they sided with whichever side offered the best hope of emancipation. They acted strategically in their own best interests, not from any prior commitment to the Americans or the British. In the North, where the British were weak and where the patriots were looking for soldiers, they cast their lot with the Americans. In the South, where the British offered them freedom and appeared (at least in the later years) to be able to make good on that promise, they flocked to the royal standard. Freedom was the name of the game, and they played it however they could.

That's the simple version—the actual plotline has many twists and turns. In the North, slaves had to negotiate carefully to ensure that their contributions to the patriots' cause would actually result in their freedom; in many cases, whites tried to renege on their promises after the war. In the South, slaves had to weigh their options and consider the consequences before fleeing to the British: What were the dangers? Would the British really grant them freedom? Was it worth leaving homes and families for the mere *chance* of a better life?

As it turned out, the dangers faced by Southern slaves who tried to

escape were considerable. Many were captured by patriot slave patrols. Sometimes, when the British were inundated with runaways,
fugitives were turned away. Thousands succumbed to diseases—primarily smallpox, to which they had no immunity. Those who reached
the British and survived were turned into laborers, servants, or soldiers. They toiled on plantations not unlike the ones they had left;
they served the personal needs of British officers, who became their
new masters; they joined the king's army for indefinite terms of service—some later served in the West Indies and even the Napoleonic
Wars. Many were given as slaves to white loyalists in compensation
for lost property. At Yorktown, blacks who had contracted smallpox
were expelled from the British camp, with nowhere to go but the plains
between the opposing armies. Even had they not been turned out,
they would have been captured after the British surrendered and made
to suffer the consequences for joining the losing side.

Many tasted freedom. At the close of the war, the British transported three thousand former slaves from New York to to Canada. As
free persons, not slaves, they were granted plots of land—the worst
available, of course. Others went to London, where they faced hard
times. Some managed to escape to deep woods and dank swamps,
where they survived for years in their own Maroon communities.
(Despite what we see in *The Patriot*, there are no records of white
gentry putting on elaborate wedding ceremonies in these enclaves of
black refugees.) A few thousand eventually wound up in Sierra
Leone, the African colony established for formerly enslaved blacks.

In sheer numbers, more slaves fled from the South during the
American Revolution than in the years preceding the Civil War, during the height of the Underground Railroad. According to the United
States census, sixteen slaves escaped from South Carolina masters in
1850, the year of the Fugitive Slave Act. Since the total number of
slaves residing in the state was 384,984, this amounted to only 1 in
24,061. In 1860, the year Lincoln was elected president, twenty-three
slaves escaped—1 in 17,501.[34] These figures pale in comparison with
those for the Revolution: during the final three years of the war, sev-

eral thousand slaves in South Carolina fled their masters.[35] The Revolutionary emigration was both larger and more concentrated in time. Unlike the Underground Railroad, it seriously threatened the functioning of the plantation system in the Deep South. In the words of historian Gary Nash, black flight during the American Revolution "represents the largest slave uprising in our history." [36]

In our storybook telling of history, these proportions are reversed: the Underground Railroad is celebrated in every school textbook, while the flight to freedom during the Revolution is ignored or downplayed. Indeed, the most dramatic exodus in the annals of American slavery has yet to be honored with a name or label. This is no accident. We don't like to see our enemies, the British, as liberators; in the story of the Underground Railroad, on the other hand, that role is bestowed on good, white Americans—the Abolitionists. The Underground Railroad features racist Southerners like Simon Legree as antagonists—we have no problem with that. But to tell the full Revolutionary saga, slaveowning patriots like George Washington, Thomas Jefferson, and Patrick Henry would have to fill those roles, and so we shy away. To save face, popular American writers pass up an amazing opportunity to celebrate the tenacious spirit of freedom and extend the story of the Revolution to people who have previously been marginalized.

Consider the story of one runaway slave, Boston King. In 1780, to escape the punishment of his master, King placed himself in the service of the British army in Charleston, South Carolina. He fell ill with smallpox; upon his recovery, he became the personal servant first of a British officer, then a militia captain, and finally his commanding officer, who trusted him with an important message which had to be carried through American-controlled territory. If captured he would have been sent back into slavery—but he managed to accomplish his mission. As his reward, he received "three shillings and many fine promises."

He then joined the crew of a British man-of-war. He disembarked at New York, still under British occupation, and was hired out as a carpenter to one master after the next. He received no pay for months and was forced to sign on with a pilot boat. After his vessel was captured by an American whaleboat, he was sent to New Jersey as a prisoner. Although he received sufficient food and was allowed to study the Bible, he was determined to escape confinement. Narrowly avoiding the watch of the guards, he waded a mile across a river at low tide and eventually made his way back to New York. The war was over by that time, and masters from throughout the South came to New York to search for people they claimed had been their slaves. He avoided the slave catchers long enough to gain a berth on a ship headed for Nova Scotia. There he settled in Birchtown, the largest community of free blacks in the Western Hemisphere, and became a preacher.[37]

Here is a true, heroic tale of the American Revolution, but it is not featured in texts or popular histories. There are other stories like it. David George, who also would become a preacher, escaped first from an exceedingly cruel master, then from Indians who had captured him, and once again from an influential patriot, George Galphin. He ran to the British, who soon threw him in prison because they misconstrued his preaching. After his release he contracted smallpox, and while recovering, he narrowly escaped death from the American bombardment of Savannah. He worked as a butcher in British controlled territory, but British soldiers robbed him of his savings. He too received passage to Nova Scotia.[38]

Thomas Peters, a native of West Africa who was enslaved at the age of twenty-two, escaped from his master in 1776 and fought for the remainder of the war in a unit of the British army called the Black Guides and Pioneers. In 1783, at the close of the war, Peters migrated with his family to Nova Scotia. In 1790 Peters traveled back across the Atlantic to hand-deliver a petition from other black refugees to authorities in London: they wanted to move to a more hospitable home and be treated "as Free Subjects of the British Empire." Two years later Peters and almost 1,200 others, including Boston King and David George, set out for Sierra Leone. This was the fourth transatlantic voyage of Thomas Peters's remarkable career.[39]

While stories such as these feature high drama and adventure, and while they celebrate a passionate craving for freedom at any the cost, we deem them unfit to tell in popular histories and schoolbooks because the protagonists were on "the wrong side." This is too narrow a view of our Revolutionary heritage. Boston King, David George, Thomas Peters and countless other runaway slaves were rebels, as much as anyone else. They exemplify the quest for liberty—even more, perhaps, than most of the heroes we normally celebrate. The story of our nation's birth becomes deeper and broader when we choose not censor these intrepid struggles for freedom that the Revolution made possible.

"British parties, . . . the most brutal of mankind, were . . . robbing, destroying, and taking life at their pleasure."

Drawing by Felix Octavius Carr Darley, mid-nineteenth century.

11

BRUTAL BRITISH

We can all picture the enemy in the Revolutionary War: the Redcoats, in full battle formation. These people were "foreign" in the fullest sense. They were soldiers sent from across the seas, bent on putting Americans down.

The enemy, once identified, is easy to villainize. The handiest way to justify intentional killing is to portray the opposition as brutal. In any war, stories abound of atrocities committed by the other side; violent acts committed by the protagonists are merely retaliations for these foul deeds. This is the basic logic of warfare, and the American Revolution was no exception.

GOOD GUYS AND BAD GUYS

The simple juxtaposition of good versus evil gives the movie *The Patriot* its raw power. At the outset of the film Benjamin Martin, played convincingly by Mel Gibson, does not want to fight against the British. Although he was once a hero in the French and Indian War, now he is trying to raise six children (his wife is deceased) and he wants no part of politics or war. "I am a parent," he says at a meeting of patriots. "I haven't got the luxury of principles."

Martin's political apathy does not last long. After a battle is fought in their front yard, Martin and his children and their slaves-who-are-not-really-slaves tend to the wounded, patriots and British alike. Right at this moment Colonel Tavington gallops onto the scene, leading his fearsome British Dragoons. Grinning insidiously, Tavington orders all wounded patriots to be shot on the spot. He also arrests Benjamin's oldest son, Gabriel, for carrying messages. As Gabriel is being dragged away to be hanged, Benjamin protests that his summary execution would violate "the rules of war." Tavington responds: "Rules of war! Would you like a lesson in the rules of war?"—he then points his pistol at the rest of Martin's children. Martin backs off, but when Gabriel's younger brother Thomas bursts forth with a feeble and ill-advised rescue attempt, Tavington shoots Thomas in the back.

Colonel Tavington, we see, is a very bad man. Benjamin Martin is understandably very angry, and he becomes a patriot after all. The cold-blooded killing of his son Thomas must be avenged.

Shortly afterward, Tavington is called to task for these and other barbarous deeds by his superior, General Cornwallis. But after Martin outwits Cornwallis with a cunning scheme, the general abandons his preference for gentlemanly warfare and gives Tavington permission to pursue "brutal" tactics. Sanctioned brutalities become a cornerstone of official British policy.

Tavington, now operating according to orders, proceeds to commit even greater outrages. He gathers the entire population of a village into a church, seals off the door and shutters, then burns it to the ground. Every man, woman, and child—including Gabriel's new bride—perishes in the flames. (Gabriel had earlier been rescued from the gallows by his dad and his two youngest brothers, ages about eight and ten.) A little later, Tavington uses some cunning of his own to kill Gabriel. By now, the viewer is as outraged as Benjamin Martin, who has lost two sons at the hands of the sinister British officer. Tavington and the British must be stopped! We are rooting furiously as our hero, using an American flagpole for a bayonet, faces off against his nemesis in the concluding Battle of Cowpens.

In *The Patriot*, we learn that the British were the bad guys, and Colonel Banastre Tarleton was evil incarnate. (Tarleton, according to the film's writer, Robert Rodat, served as the model for Tavington.) Patriots, by contrast, were the good guys. Americans did not slaughter their prisoners, and they killed no civilians—certainly not a churchful all at once.

At one point, *The Patriot* does show Benjamin Martin's militiamen on the verge of hacking to death British soldiers who had just surrendered—but these excesses are immediately put to a halt by Commander Martin: "Full quarter will be given to British wounded and any who surrender," he commands. Gabriel delivers the moral of this scene: "We are better men than that." That's the basic message of the film: the Americans were better men than those British bullies, like Tarleton, who didn't think twice about hacking prisoners to death.

One scene does equivocate. Back in the French and Indian War, Benjamin Martin had proved himself a hero at "Fort Wilderness." Throughout the film, men praise him for this—but nobody will say what he did. One night at camp, Gabriel asks his father to tell him what happened at Fort Wilderness. Reticent at first, Benjamin finally responds. The French and Cherokee Indians had killed some settlers, including women and children. To avenge this slaughter, Martin and company tracked down the offenders and butchered them. "We took our time," he says softly but deliberately. "We cut them apart, slowly, piece by piece. I can see their faces. I can still hear their screams." He then proceeds with a graphic description of how they mutilated the bodies. "We were . . . heroes," he concludes sardonically.

"And men bought you drinks," Gabriel adds.

"Not a day goes by that I don't ask God's forgiveness for what I did."

Such an admission, coming from the hero of the story, produces a stunning effect. Everything else that happened or will happen in the film takes on an added dimension, for this man is real. But Martin's atrocities were all committed in the past, out on the frontier. He had been fighting for the British at that point—but during the Revolutionary War, at the birth of our nation, no such shenanigans could be tolerated. American patriots were simply too *good* to engage in barbarous behavior. The British thereby serve as scapegoats for the horrors of war.

A simple but deft twist of costuming confirms this thesis. In fact, the dreaded Green Dragoons—American Tories commanded by Banastre Tarleton—wore green jackets with white pants, shirts, and collars; only their sashes and helmet plumes were red. The "special feature" added to the DVD version of the film shows a brief image of this uniform, but in the film itself, green is traded in for a more familiar red. "There were many different kinds of uniforms in the British army," says costume designer Deborah Scott. "We basically settled for one very strong look." Strong and recognizable: the Redcoats. All the men commanded by Colonel Tavington are clearly and unmistakenly British. All the evil deeds are performed by foreigners, not Americans.

This is the way most Americans today have heard the story of the Revolutionary War: the opposition wore no green, only red. In the telling of the war that has evolved over time, the men who fought on the other side were the Redcoats, British antagonists familiar to us all.

THE FIRST CIVIL WAR

The Patriot draws on the interpretation of the war put forth at the time by American patriots. On May 29, 1780, in the Waxhaws district of North Carolina, soldiers under the command of Banastre Tarleton killed American prisoners rather than granting them quarter. For the remainder of the war, the Waxhaws incident provided a rallying cry for angry patriots as they prepared to terminate the lives of other human beings: "Tarleton's Quarter!" they would yell furiously as they stormed into battle. (Sometimes, the cry was "Remember Buford!"—Abraham Buford was the American commander at the Waxhaws.) For patriots toward the end of the Revolutionary War, as for the fictional Benjamin Martin, the enemy's butchery provided reason enough to fight against the British.

This story, proof positive of the enemy's cruelty, has endured for over two centuries. But there has been one important alteration. At the time, the patriots' greatest fury was directed at their local adversaries, the Tories. Now, the adversaries have exchanged green uniforms for red. They must be seen as foreigners, not "us."

In fact, it was Americans who did the slaughtering at the Waxhaws—maybe not patriots, but our countrymen nonetheless. There, Banastre Tarleton led a force of 40 British Regulars and 230 American Tories, primarily from New York. "The British Legion, Americans all, began butchering their vanquished countrymen," writes military historian John Buchanan.[1] This was no isolated event. British officers, on their part, often tried to restrain their American recruits, sometimes to no avail. "For God's sake no irregularities," pleaded British general Henry Clinton, trying in vain to curtail the excesses of Tories who fought under him.[2]

The Revolution in the South was a bloody civil war—even more internecine than *the* Civil War of the nineteenth century, for no geographic boundaries separated the combatants. (Even when patriots fought the Redcoats, they viewed them as "Regulars," not foreigners, as we do today.) In South Carolina alone, local historian Edward McCrady tabulated 103 different battles in which Americans fought Americans, with nary a Brit in sight.[3] At King's Mountain, one of the great victories for the patriots, over one thousand American Loyalists fought under a single British officer.

The impact of this first civil war was devastating. "The whole Country is in Danger of being laid waste by the Whigs and Tories who pursue each other with as much relentless Fury as Beasts of Prey," wrote the American general Nathanael Greene.[4] In some regions all civil society came to a halt. Whenever a band of partisans raged through, inhabitants had to "lay out" in the woods, abandoning their homes to the ravages of soldiers—whatever side they happened to be on. On July 20, 1781, the American Major William Pierce wrote to St. George Tucker:

> Such scenes of desolation, bloodshed and deliberate murder I never was a witness to before! Wherever you turn the weeping widow and fatherless child pour out their melancholy tales to wound the feeling of humanity. The two opposite principles of whiggism and toryism have set the people of this country to cutting each other's throats, and scarce a day passes but some poor deluded tory is put to death at his door.[5]

Partisans on both sides believed they were fighting for their homeland. Many, like the fictional Benjamin Martin, had lost relatives who were to be avenged. Fighting was localized and personalized—and thereby more impassioned. These were not professional soldiers just doing their jobs, but men with scores to settle.

In tales such as *The Patriot,* the fight is between the British, who are cruel or indifferent, and the Americans, who are forced to respond. History was far more complicated than that. Consider: Who is the hero and who is the villain in each of the following tales?

- After the Tories had beaten his mother, William Gipson of South Carolina admitted that he took "no little satisfaction" in torturing a prisoner who was placed in his charge: "He was placed with one foot upon a sharp pin drove in a block, and was turned round . . . until the pin run through his foot."[6]

- A Tory from Georgia, Thomas Brown, was accosted by a patriot mob. Trying to defend himself, he shot one of the patriots in the foot. The mob subdued him, tarred his legs, branded his feet, and took off part of his scalp. Brown lost two of his toes and could not walk for months. Once he had

recovered, he organized a band of Tories and Indians that
raided patriot plantations for the remainder of the war.[7]

• Moses Hall, a patriot from North Carolina, suffered a
"distressing gloom" when he observed his comrades murder
six defenseless prisoners: "I heard some of our men cry out
'Remember Buford,' and the prisoners were immediately
hewed to pieces with broadswords." Reeling with "horror,"
Hall retreated to his quarters and "contemplated the cruelties
of war"—but not for long. On a subsequent march, he came
upon a sixteen-year-old boy, an innocent observer, who had
been run through with a British bayonet to keep him from
passing information to the patriots. "The sight of this
unoffending boy, butchered, . . . relieved me of my
distressful feeling for the slaughter of the Tories, and I
desired nothing so much as the opportunity of participating
in their destruction." [8]

In cases such as these, how can we portray one side as filled with
virtue, the other with vice? Barbarous acts, and the retribution they
inspired, crossed political boundaries. Real-life patriots participated
in this gruesome game of retribution. Frequently, they too slaughtered men who were trying to surrender or had already been taken
into custody. In the aftermath of the patriot victory at King's Mountain, Colonel William Campbell tried to "restrain the disorderly manner of slaughtering and disturbing the prisoners." [9] His orders were
not heeded; prisoners were prodded and trampled to death when they
couldn't keep up with the march. A late-night mock trial ended in the
summary execution of nine Tories. "It is impossible for those who
have not lived in its midst, to conceive of the exasperation which pre-
vails in a civil war," explained Colonel Isaac Shelby, one of the execu-
tioners, as he justified his actions years later. "The execution . . . was
believed by those who were one the ground, to be both necessary and

proper, for the purpose of putting a stop to the execution of the patriots in the Carolinas by the Tories and the British." [10]

MY COUNTRY, RIGHT OR WRONG

Early American historians, members of the Revolutionary generation, could not ignore the obvious: the War for Independence from Britain was also a civil war among Americans, particularly in the South. Tories who had "embodied" as soldiers, wrote William Gordon in 1788, "marched along the western frontiers of South Carolina. They had such numbers of the most infamous characters among them, that their general complexion was that of a plundering banditti." Some of the patriots, he admitted, were little better: "Many of the professed whigs disgraced themselves, by the burnings, plunderings and cruelties, that they practiced in their turn on the royalists." [11] Gordon cited General Nathanael Greene, who bemoaned the "embarrassments" caused by the patriot militia's "savage disposition" and "mode of conducting war." While Gordon confessed that patriots engaged in wrongdoing, his admission contained a disclaimer: officers like Greene and Francis Marion, the good patriots, tried to put an end to all "burnings, plunderings and cruelties." [12]

David Ramsay, in his 1785 *History of the Revolution in South Carolina*, attributed all sorts of foul deeds to Thomas Brown, the Tory who had been tortured by patriots. Brown had hanged prisoners without trial, Ramsay said, and he had turned some over to Indians to be scalped. When a mother offered a passionate plea to spare the life of her son, Brown had turned a deaf ear. [13] The following year, Brown complained directly to Ramsay, denying the atrocities and explaining the hangings: he was under direct orders to hang prisoners who had violated their parole, and the son of the pleading mother had recently engaged in the systematic torture of Tory prisoners before they were executed. [14] In his 1789 *History of the American Revolution*, Ramsay removed all reference to Thomas Brown's villainy—but the rumors he had helped to spread four years earlier did not disappear. In his magnum opus, Ramsay covered the civil war with a more balanced approach:

> Individuals whose passions were inflamed by injuries, and exasperated with personal animosity, were eager to gratify revenge in violation of the laws of war. Murders had produced murders. Plundering, assassinations, and house burning, had become common. Zeal for the King or the Congress were the ostensible motives of action; but in several of both sides, the love of plunder, private pique, and a savageness of disposition, led to actions which were disgraceful to human nature. Such was the exasperation of whigs against tories, and of tories against whigs; and so much had they suffered from and inflicted on each other, that the laws of war, and the precepts of humanity afforded but a feeble security for the observance of capitulations on either side.[15]

Ramsay went on to philosophize about "the folly and madness of war," and he concluded that "war never fails to injure the morals of the people engaged in it"—the patriots were no exception.[16]

Mercy Otis Warren, writing in 1805, admitted that the Revolution had included a "domestic war" and that patriot soldiers, like their adversaries, had evidenced barbarous behavior, but she added a stronger disclaimer: patriotic Americans were never as bad as the British and Tories. Fortunately, she stated, they had lacked "a fierce spirit of revenge." In her concluding remarks, Warren commended the Revolutionaries for their moderation:

> Great revolutions ever produce excesses and miseries at which humanity revolts. In America . . . the scenes of barbarity were not so universal as have been usual in other countries that have been at once shaken by foreign and domestic war. . . . The United States may congratulate themselves on the success of a revolution which has done honor to the human character by exhibiting a mildness of spirit amid the ferocity of war, that pre-

vented the shocking scenes of cruelty, butchery, and slaughter, which have too often stained the actions of men, when their original intentions were the result of pure motives and justifiable resistance.[17]

Patriotic writers of the following generation did not focus much attention on the barbaric civil war in the South. Charles Goodrich, writing in 1823, said not a word of it; the war was only a struggle for independence from Great Britain, not a true "revolution" featuring domestic upheaval here in America. When writers in the early- and mid-nineteenth century did mention the civil war in the Southern backcountry, they, like Warren, issued an immediate qualification:

> But censure ought not to rest equally upon the two parties. In the commencement of the contest, the British, to terrify the people into submission, set an example which the tories were quick, but the whigs slow, to follow; and in its progress the American generals, and they alone, seized every occasion to discountenance such vindictive and barbarous conduct.[18]

The chain of blame was never more clearly stated: the British were the worst, followed in order by Tories and common patriots. Only patriot leaders were beyond reproof. In 1838 John Frost stated flatly, "the British generally conducted the war with cruelty and rancour."[19]

George Bancroft, in the mid-nineteenth century, wrote that British leaders were "the most brutal of mankind," while Americans were "incapable of imitating precedents of barbarity." He singled out Banastre Tarleton and Thomas Brown for particular blame. "The line of [Tarleton's] march could be traced by groups of houseless women and children," he wrote—although in fact this was true in the wake of any march at the time, no matter what the army. He repeated and embellished the rumor that prisoners taken by Brown had been delivered to the Cherokees, who tomahawked them or threw them into fires. Any questionable behavior on the part of the patriots, meanwhile, was excused as justifiable retaliation. After their victory at King's Mountain, patriots had hanged several of the prisoners they took. When describing these executions, Bancroft wrote:

> Among the captives there were house-burners and assassins. Private soldiers—who had witnessed the sorrows of children and women, robbed and wronged, shelterless, stripped of all clothes but those they wore, nestling about fires kindled on the ground, and mourning for their fathers and husbands—executed nine or ten in retaliation for the frequent and barbarous use of the gallows at Camden, Ninety-Six, and Augusta; but Campbell at once intervened, and in general orders, by threatening the delinquents with certain and effectual punishment, secured protection to the prisoners.[20]

Bancroft wanted to have it both ways: the "house-burners and assassins" deserved the worst, yet benevolent patriot officers still protected them—at least those who had not yet been hanged.

Starting in the mid-nineteenth century, some academic historians challenged the traditional patriotic wisdom by refusing to lay greater blame on the British or Tories. "Whigs and Tories pursued each other with little less than savage fury," Richard Hildreth wrote in 1851. "Small parties, every where under arms, some on one side, some on the other, with very little reference to greater operations, were desperately bent on plunder and blood."[21] Forty years later, John Fiske stated bluntly: "There can be no doubt that Whigs and Tories were alike guilty of cruelty and injustice."[22] By the turn of the century, a few American historians were displaying definite sympathies for the loyalists, who had suffered "lawless persecution" at the hands of "irresponsible mobs" of patriots.[23] All crowd actions, even those of the American Revolution, were to be discredited, for they were disruptive to the social order.

Histories that did not favor patriots over loyalists, however, were not always greeted favorably outside academic circles. During the first half of the twentieth century, the views of Progressive historians were perceived as a threat to traditional American values. Attempts by the Progressive education movement to introduce a spirit of relativism in the schools caused traditionalists to recoil. Patriots and loyalists should never be placed on an equal footing, they claimed. An officer of the Daughters of the Colonial Wars, for instance, complained about books that "give a child an unbiased viewpoint instead of teaching him real Americanism. All the old histories taught my country right or wrong. That's the point of view we want our children to adopt. We can't afford to teach them to be unbiased and let them make up their own minds." [24]

In the 1960s, scholars practicing "the new social history" began looking long and hard at the brutal fighting in the South during the later stages of the Revolutionary War, trying to decipher the peculiar local logic that led to the breakdown of civil society. Why, they asked, did particular individuals or groups become partisans to this side or that? How did the differences among neighbors escalate so quickly to such a fever pitch? Professional historians have found no easy answers—and in the absence of any clear alternatives, the simple morality tale lives on.

Indeed, the tale has been embellished. No nineteenth-century writer depicted the brutal British burning a church, with all the inhabitants of a village inside. But the makers of *The Patriot* did, even though there is nothing in the historical record to suggest such a horrific occurrence during the War for Independence. As historian David Hackett Fischer observes, "Something remarkably like this event actually happened, but not in South Carolina during the American Revolution. It happened in the French village of Oradour-sur-Glane on June 10, 1944, during World War II. . . . There were atrocities enough on both sides in the American Revolution, but the German director has converted an 18th-century British and American loyalist army into the S.S." [25]

Sometimes, as in *The Patriot,* the good-versus-bad theme is deafening; often, it is muted but still audible. Popular writers today, in a tone reminiscent of Mercy Otis Warren, give some notice to the brutal civil war, but they find ways of qualifying any condemnation of the patriots. In *Liberty!* Thomas Fleming refers to "the savage seesaw war," but the only examples of savagery he presents were committed by the other side. Thomas Brown, he reports, hanged thirteen wounded patriots "in the stairwell of his house, where he could watch them die from his bed." [26] The reporting of such callousness is calculated to leave a firmly biased impression on the reader. Fleming fails to note that the hangings did not take place in Brown's *own* house, as implied; that if Brown was in bed, it was because he had just been wounded; that the hangings had been ordered by his superiors; and that the man who originally spread the rumor, David Ramsay, later disavowed it. Instead, he restates without question the conventional story about this Tory villain, treating him as the "devil incarnate," in the words of one nineteenth-century historian. [27]

Robert Leckie, in *George Washington's War*, offers a vivid description of patriots mowing down loyalists who were trying to surrender at King's Mountain:

> The rebel blood was up, their vengeance fed by the memory of the Waxhaws. "Buford! Buford!" they shouted. "Tarleton's Quarter! Tarleton's Quarter!" They pursued their frightened victims as they ran to a hollow place on the hilltop and cowered there in horror. One by one, the frontiersmen cut them down, sometimes singling out neighbors by name before they fired. Many of the Patriots thirsted to revenge themselves on the deaths of relatives and friends who were murdered by the Tories. Their eyes glittered maniacally as they loaded and fired . . . loaded and fired . . . At last Major Evan Shelby called on the Loyalists to throw down their arms. They did, but the rebel rifles still blazed. [Ellipses as in the original.] [28]

But were these *real* patriots, who acted so savagely? Not exactly. They were illiterate "Irish and Scots-Irish" who called their rifles "Sweet

Lips" or "Hot Lead." "None of them could have quoted a line from Tom Paine's *Common Sense*," Leckie writes, "and the phrase *Declaration of Independence* meant about as much to them as it did to their livestock." [29] They were animals, not Americans; their deeds need not reflect poorly on the cause.

Today, more than two centuries after the fact, purveyors of popular culture continue to practice a self-imposed censorship. Undue cruelties attributed to the American side must somehow be deflected, if they cannot be defended. But history that hides atrocities behind a cloak of patriotism is complicit in the travesties of war.

On March 3, 1968, United States soldiers in Charlie Company, Eleventh Brigade, Americal Division, brutally massacred more than 300 inhabitants of My Lai, a Vietnamese village. What was the appropriate response? Certainly not to cover it up. Once the story had been exposed by correspondent Seymour Hersh, the American press reported the event in all its grisly details. The public recoiled in horror, investigations followed, and policies changed. Recently, three United States soldiers received full military honors for placing themselves between the attacking American marauders and fleeing Vietnamese villagers. [30] For two decades, veterans have been traveling to Vietnam to help rebuild the country and express their regrets for any harm they caused. All these responses were appropriate, admirable, and patriotic: they gave testimony to a free society at its best.

So it should be in the telling of the American Revolution. The appropriate way to present the story is to be brutally honest about the brutalities of war. Anything short serves as an invitation to more war, with all its attendant sorrows.

Feel-good morality tales, in which the good guys can do no wrong and the bad guys can do no right, are far from harmless. They feed the notion that one side, inspired by righteousness, possesses the right to kill. They fuel the destructive cycle of revenge, for the villainous acts committed by the bad guys must be avenged. The emotions stirred in stories such as *The Patriot* are elemental but base: we want the enemy to go down. Justice is achieved through killing.

The simple, dualistic thinking that works so well in the telling of tales—good doing battle against evil—is easily manipulated to drum up support for war. People who corral innocent civilians into churches and then set them ablaze must surely be punished. Fighting becomes the only legitimate response. We must fight or run—and since nobody wishes to run, we know what we have to do.

Alternative scenarios are written out of the script. Negotiated settlements, mediation, or other pacifistic responses have no place in stories intended to make "us"—Americans—feel like heroes by defeating "them"—the British, people who do unthinkable things. This narrative is easily translated into contemporary idioms: burning villagers inside a church is the eighteenth-century equivalent of blowing up the World Trade Center. Just as September 11, 2001, triggered an instant outpouring of American patriotism, so do conjured or exaggerated accounts of British brutalities give the Revolutionary War, and thereby our nation, a heightened sense of purpose. They bring us together.

But what if the "enemy" cannot be found, or even defined? Stories like *The Patriot* encourage us to lash out, and so we do. The medium is the message: we must stand tough and fight. Today, this appeal to war for its own sake, in the absence of a clearly defined enemy, makes a mockery of the notion of patriotism. War becomes simply a way of life, and our nation, formed in part to resist the presence of a standing army, becomes a permanently militarized society. Tales of the American Revolution, based on the simple opposition of good and evil, delude us into believing that the cycle of revenge will finally come to a halt—after we have had the last word.

HAPPY ENDINGS

"Everyone realized that this surrender meant the end."

The Surrender of Lord Cornwallis at Yorktown, 19 October 1781.
Lithograph by Nathaniel Currier, 1852,
based on painting by John Trumbull, 1787–circa 1828.

12

THE FINAL BATTLE
AT YORKTOWN

On October 17, 1781, Lord Cornwallis, the British commander, surrendered his entire army—some 7,000 troops—to George Washington at Yorktown, Virginia. When Lord North, the British prime minister, heard the news, he exclaimed, "Oh, God, it is all over!" That was the end of the Revolutionary War.

This story is repeated in virtually every narrative account of the American Revolution. The notion of a decisive final battle constitutes a neat and tidy conclusion to the war, placing America firmly in control of her own destiny. "The great British army was surrendering," writes Joy Hakim. "David had licked Goliath. . . . A superpower had been defeated by an upstart colony." [1]

"CARRYING ON THE WAR"

Not everybody at the time saw it that way. In the wake of Yorktown, George Washington insisted that the war was not yet over, and King George III was not ready to capitulate. In fact, the fighting continued for over a year—but this part of history is rarely told. To stick to the story we like, we declare that people who were killing each other in subsequent battles were somehow mistaken—their fighting was some sort of illusion. "Washington considered the country still at war," writes A. J. Langguth in his bestselling book *Patriots*, "and George III was under that same *misapprehension.*"[2]

When King George III heard of Cornwallis's surrender at Yorktown, he did not respond as fatalistically as Lord North. "I have no doubt when men are a little recovered of the shock felt by the bad news," he said, "they will find the necessity of carrying on the war, though the mode of it may require alterations."[3]

Washington was worried that the British Crown might respond this way—so worried, in fact, that he redoubled his efforts to build up the Continental Army. On October 27, only ten days after the victory at Yorktown, Washington urged Congress to continue its "preparation for military Operations"—a failure to pursue the war, he warned, would "expose us to the most disgracefull Disasters."[4] In the following weeks, Washington repeated this warning more than a dozen times.[5] "Yorktown was an interesting event," he wrote, but it would only "prolong the casualties" if Americans relaxed their "prosecution of the war." Candidly, he confessed:

> My greatest Fear is that Congress, viewing this stroke in too important a point of Light, may think our Work too nearly closed, and will fall into a State of Languor and Relaxation; to prevent this Error, I shall employ every Means in my Power.[6]

Heeding Washington's advice, Congress called on the states to supply the same number of soldiers they had furnished the preceding year. But the states were financially strapped, and their citizens were tiring of war. They failed to meet their quotas, and Washington did not receive enough men to undertake the offensive operations he had contemplated.[7]

Meanwhile, the British and French continued to battle for control of the seas. In the West Indies, six months after Yorktown, British seamen crushed the French fleet that had cut off the lines of supply during the siege of Yorktown. With French ships no longer a factor, the

British would be able to regroup and take the offensive—they could move their vast armies by sea to support any land operation they chose. Washington was not the only American general worried about this. Nathanael Greene, who had hoped to lead an attack on Charleston, suddenly expressed concern that the British might attack him instead.[8] On June 5, 1782, more than seven months after Yorktown, Washington wrote to the Secretary of Foreign Affairs about the need to undertake "vigorous preparations for meeting the enemy." [9]

Finally, on August 4, the commanders of the British army and navy in North America informed Washington that the Crown was prepared to recognize "the independency of the thirteen Provinces," providing only that Loyalists receive full compensation for seized property and that no further property be confiscated. It seemed the war was coming to an end at last—but Washington was not buying it.[10] Not until a peace treaty was signed and British troops had returned home, he insisted, would he relax his guard. In his general orders for August 19, 1782—ten months after Yorktown—he wrote: "The readiest way to procure a lasting and honorable peace is to be fully prepared vigorously to prosecute War." [11]

The British then offered to suspend all hostilities, but Washington still wouldn't bite. Right at this moment, Washington received word that Lord Rockingham, the British prime minister believed to be responsible for the peace overtures, had died. The American commander-in-chief, who placed little stock in the fickle nature of British politics, assumed Rockingham would be replaced by a hard-liner. On September 12 he wrote: "Our prospect of Peace is vanishing. The death of the Marquis of Rockingham has given shock to the New Administration, and disordered its whole System. . . . That the King will push the War as long as the Nation will find Men or Money, admits not of a doubt in my mind." [12] On October 17, precisely one year after Yorktown, Washington warned Nathanael Greene:

> In the present fluctuating state of British Councils and measures, it is extremely difficult to form a decisive opinion of what their

real and ultimate objects are. . . . [N]otwithstanding all the pa-
cific declaration of the British, it has constantly been my prevailing sentiment, the principal Design was, to gain time by lulling
us into security and wasting the Campaign without making any
effort on the land.[13]

A preliminary peace treaty was signed on November 30, 1782—but
even that was not enough to satisfy the ever-suspicious American
commander. On March 19, 1783, one year and five months after Yorktown, Washington was still keeping his guard up: "The Articles of
Treaty between America and Great Britain . . . are so very inconclu-
sive . . . that we should hold ourselves in a hostile position, prepared
for either alternative, War or Peace. . . . I must confess, I have my
fears, that we shall be obliged to worry thro' another Campaign, before we arrive at that happy period, which is to crown all our Toils."[14]

Washington saw what we do not. He knew well that Cornwallis did
not command and surrender the entire British army in North America, as most Americans assume. In fact, Cornwallis served under General Henry Clinton, who commanded four times as many British
soldiers in the former colonies as were lost at Yorktown. Although a
fraction of Clinton's forces had surrendered, the vast majority remained ready for battle. The Americans had recently sustained a com-
parable loss, the surrender of about 5,000 soldiers at Charleston, yet
they had continued to fight. So had the British after a similar number
surrendered at Saratoga. From a military perspective, Cornwallis's
defeat at Yorktown was on par with these earlier battles.

The British still maintained a strong presence in and around the
United States. They controlled the St. Lawrence Valley to the Great
Lakes, East Florida, several islands in the West Indies, and the important ports of Halifax, New York, Charleston, Savannah, and St. Au-
gustine. Almost 17,000 British troops were stationed in New York,
11,000 in South Carolina and Georgia, 9,000 in Canada, and 10,000 in
the West Indies—a total of 47,000 men, four times as many as those
serving in the Continental Army.[15]

After the defeat at Yorktown, General Clinton could have un-leashed these forces at any point. New York's Hudson Valley was par-ticularly vulnerable, since Washington had weakened its defense when he moved his army south. The west was still not secure from In-dians, who were now aided by Spanish as well as British forces. Tory bands ruled much of the Southern backcountry. Most importantly, without the French fleet, the British navy continued to control the coastal waters. "Without a decisive Naval force we can do nothing de-finitive," Washington complained shortly after Yorktown.[16]

Washington understood that the outcome of the Revolutionary War depended on continuing French support. The war was being waged with French money. The siege at Yorktown had been con-ducted with French equipment, and over half the regular forces had been French. The siege had been successful only because French ships were able to keep British ships from resupplying the troops. If French support were suddenly withdrawn for reasons beyond the control of the Americans—say, a separate treaty of peace between France and Britain—the Americans would never be able to dislodge the British from their coastal strongholds. If Britain then decided to unleash its vast army against Washington's struggling Continentals, the fledg-ling United States might well be crushed.

This was not idle speculation. Back in London, upon hearing the news from Yorktown, Secretary of State Lord George Germain ar-gued that the British should at least hold onto their coastal enclaves, which could service the West Indies trade and provide a foothold on the continent. Perhaps, if French-American relations turned sour, and if Americans tired of their wartime governments, the opportunity would present itself to mount another offensive. In December 1781, the British ministry decided to continue to defend the positions it held in what it still considered to be its colonies.[17]

Because of military realities and diplomatic uncertainties, the out-come of the Revolutionary War was still very much in doubt after Yorktown. With resolve, the British certainly possessed the resources to continue the fight. Only by reading history backward can we conclude that total British withdrawal was a foregone conclusion. Under the circumstances, Washington had no choice but to continue the war, pushing the temporary advantage the Americans had gained from Yorktown until Britain actually removed all its troops and ships.

He did just that. Immediately following the victory at Yorktown, Washington dispatched a force southward, hoping to put pressure on the British stationed in Charleston and Savannah. He left the French to control the Chesapeake, while he sent the main contingent of the Continental Army northward to counter any offensive by Clinton and the troops under his command in New York. Meanwhile, in the Southern backcountry, the war between local Loyalists and Patriots continued even without a British presence, with each side seeking vengeance for atrocities committed by the other. Across the Appalachians, frontiersmen continued to battle against Indians, who were still supported by the British.

Warfare continued on all these fronts. According to military historian Howard Peckham, 365 Americans lost their lives in the fighting after Yorktown. (As a percent of the population of the United States, this would amount to 36,500 today.) This is undoubtedly a conservative estimate; because of the decentralized nature of the conflict in the South and West, many encounters were never reported. By contrast, during the Battle of Yorktown, only twenty-four American soldiers had been killed. The post-Yorktown death toll exceeded that of the first twelve months of the Revolutionary War, from April 1775 to April 1776, which included the battles of Lexington, Concord, Bunker Hill, and Quebec.[18] Family and friends of the deceased, were they alive today, would be taken aback to discover that we think the deaths of their loved ones had not occurred during the Revolutionary War. Henry Laurens, longtime president of the Continental Congress and one of the negotiators of the peace treaty, would have been particularly surprised: his son John, an aide-de-camp for Washington, perished in battle against British Regulars on August 27, 1782—more than ten months after the war had supposedly been over.

Just as the story of "the shot heard 'round the world" hides the dramatic revolution that preceded it, so does the story of "the final battle" suppress all that came afterward. Our telling of the American Revolution is astoundingly incomplete, leaving out both its true beginning and its true ending.

There are at least three major reasons for this hushing-up of the historical record. First, we want our stories to have neat beginnings and endings, and we are willing to bend the evidence to make this happen. Second, we prefer to view the war as a bipolar struggle between Americans and their foreign oppressors, without acknowledging that the brutal civil war in the South and the fighting against Indians in the West continued unabated after Yorktown. Third, we remain blind to the global nature of the conflict. With no interest in the broader picture, we fail to comprehend why the war went on, long after we think that it did.

THE AMERICAN REVOLUTION: A GLOBAL WAR

The French navy and army that engineered the victory at Yorktown were no strangers to their British adversaries. The American Revolution marked the fifth time in less than a century that Britain and France had been at war with each other. For thirty-six years (1689–1697, 1701–1713, 1744–1748, 1754–1763, 1778–1781) these two colonial powers had battled for dominance in Europe and around the world. The debt Britain accrued during the previous conflict, known in this country as the French and Indian War, led to increased British taxation of her American colonies—this met great resistance, culminating in the Revolutionary War. American rebels, realizing they could not win the war alone, declared their independence in order to receive aid from France. With French money, French troops, French arms and ammunition, and French ships, Americans were able to counter British attempts to squash their rebellion. The causes, the politics, the fighting, and the outcome of the American Revolution were integrally linked to the ongoing struggle for power between two European nations.

In 1763, British victory in the French and Indian War had caused France to lose her stake on the North American mainland. When British colonists declared independence from their mother country thirteen years later, the French monarchy—no great friend to the cause of "liberty"—saw an opportunity to strike back. Once the rebels had proved their mettle with the victory at Saratoga, France jumped into the fray. She had not been able to beat Britain alone, but with the help of others, she might be able to cripple, or at least maim, her arch rival.

France tried to get Spain to oppose Britain. Initially, Spain declined—governmental leaders did not wish to give credence to the American rebellion, fearing it might inspire Spanish colonies to follow suit. But Spain had many good reasons for joining the fight against the world's dominant naval power. Britain had seized Gibraltar, the Spanish fort that controlled the entrance to the Mediterranean. It had also taken the island of Minorca, off Spain's eastern coast. It held the former Spanish colony of Florida, and by controlling Honduras, Jamaica, and several smaller islands, it vied with Spain for dominance in the West Indies. Following the French defeat in 1763, Spain and Britain were the only colonial powers competing for the mainland of North America. If Britain could be expelled, Spain might gain control of the Mississippi and extend its hegemony throughout most of the continent.

In April 1779, Spain allied with France against Britain. It did not formally ally itself with the United States, but by waging war on Britain, Spain played a major role in the American Revolution. Troops, ships, and money that Britain might have used to quell the rebellion had to be used against Spain instead. In the later years of the war, Spain battled against Britain on the American frontier, dislodging the British from West Florida and challenging their control of the Mississippi.

In the summer of 1779, a combined French-Spanish force of sixty-six boats and 10,000 men prepared to invade southern England. For several weeks the allies cruised the English Channel, sending British communities along the coast into something of a panic. But the allies could not overcome logistical problems caused by poor communications, and they called the invasion off. British generals in America, meanwhile, would have liked more troops to stage their offensive in the South—but with the homeland itself in jeopardy, they had to make do with the soldiers they already had.

In fact, British troops and ships at this time were scattered all over the globe. At Gibraltar, French and Spanish forces began a siege that would last for years. The battle for control of the West Indies was heating up, while local armies in southeast India were trying to expel the British who had colonized the coast. British soldiers and sailors were fighting on all these fronts simultaneously.

For Britain, it would only get worse. In December 1780, Holland allied itself with France and Spain. The Dutch, major commercial rivals of the British, controlled the Cape of Good Hope, a key supply station for ships on their way to India or the East Indies. Now that France and Holland were allies, French ships could make use of this station while British ships could not—this would allow France to compete for hegemony in the Indian Ocean. Early in 1781 Britain tried to take the Cape—but the Dutch, reinforced by French ships on their way to India, prevailed. In August, just before the Continental Army and the French converged on Yorktown, British ships engaged Dutch ships in a fierce sea battle for control of the North Sea and command of the critical Baltic trade, rich with naval stores.

Russia was also beginning to display a preference for the allies. What if Russia joined with Holland, Spain, and France in the alliance against Britain? Europe's greatest Continental powers were finding common ground: British power must be contained.

This was the state of European affairs on October 17, 1781, when Cornwallis surrendered the troops under his command at Yorktown. Had the American rebels been their only opponents, the British might well have regrouped, sent more soldiers and ships, and continued the war. They might have staged more offensives, but even if they did not, they could have decided to hold on to the coastal enclaves they al-

ready controlled to maintain a strong presence on the eastern shore of
North America. They were currently holding Gibraltar, part of the
Spanish mainland; soon, they would maintain a port on the mainland
of China—Hong Kong—that could withstand both the Nationalist
and Communist revolutions. New York and Charleston, like Gibraltar and Hong Kong, might have remained in the British empire for decades or even centuries.

It didn't happen that way because the British were tiring of a global
war. With three European powers lined up against them, as well as
strong anti-imperial movements in the United States and India, their
treasury was running dry and their resolve wearing thin. Throughout
the war, a strong opposition within the British Parliament had been
predicting this outcome—and now their predictions were coming
true. It was time to scale back the British Empire to more manageable
proportions.

The defeat at Yorktown, coupled with military setbacks in other
theaters—the Mediterranean, the Cape of Good Hope, and India—
helped to tip the balance and trigger a change in the British ministry.
The new government, formed under Lord Rockingham, initiated the
peace process. This was not a blind surrender but a strategic retreat.
By signing treaties with each of its opponents separately, Britain
hoped to play them off against each other and obtain the best possible
terms.

Even so, the war continued, in America and around the globe.
Gibraltar remained under siege. In February 1782, British soldiers in
Minorca surrendered to 14,000 besieging troops. As soon as this news
arrived in London, Parliament decided at last not to pursue any more
offensives in America. Also in February, British forces surrendered
St. Kitts, an island in the West Indies. In May, 600 British troops in the
Bahamas surrendered to a Spanish expedition sent out from Havana.

In some instances, Britain prevailed. In April, at the Battle of the
Saints, British ships avenged the loss of Yorktown by defeating and
capturing the French fleet, under Admiral de Grasse, that had beaten

them there. In September, the British garrison of more than five thousand men repulsed a massive French-Spanish assault on Gibraltar.

Despite all these battles, in 1782 the main theater of the global war shifted to the East. On the Southeast coast of India, local resistance forces joined with a French fleet to battle against the British army and navy. Hyder Ali, Sultan of Mysore, commanded a large army against the outnumbered British garrisons, while French ships tried to intercept British ships and prevent them from unloading supplies and reinforcements. This situation was reminiscent of that at Yorktown, but there was one essential difference: from the standpoint of British imperialism, India and the East Indies were even more important than the rebellious American colonies. The East India Company, which had triggered the American Revolution by trying to unload tea on the American market, considered the source of that tea more valuable than one particular market for it.

On June 28, 1783—one year and eight months after the Battle of Yorktown—the British forces in India were in a precarious position. They were in danger of losing India as well as the thirteen colonies in North America, but suddenly, they obtained relief: news arrived that a preliminary peace treaty had been signed. By signing with the allies separately, as planned, British diplomats had been able to secure many of their existing possessions. They had lost the rebellious American colonies, but Gibraltar, their islands in the West Indies, and their holdings in India were secure. (Lord Cornwallis, after his defeat at Yorktown, would go on to become governor-general and commander-in-chief in India.) Best of all, war was over, and the threat of an allied invasion of England had passed. In the peace that was to follow, British ships were free to go wherever they pleased and trade with whomever they liked—including the newly formed United States. The empire, although diminished, had been salvaged.

The full story differs markedly from the one Americans tell themselves. According to our texts and popular histories, America was in command of its own destiny, defeating the mightiest empire on earth.

The patriots, like David, slew the giant. Sometimes, we give a grateful nod to France—but never do we view the American Revolution as part of a global war. When we treat Yorktown as the final battle, we ignore not only the warfare that continued here in the United States, but also the conflict that raged in the West Indies, northern Europe, the Mediterranean, South Africa, India, and the East Indies. Had American patriots been fighting Britain alone, Yorktown would not have had the impact it did. In fact, without the other contestants, there would have been no battle at Yorktown at all. Only by ignoring the international context can we tell the story we like.

THE FULL STORY

Historians of the Revolutionary generation, having grown up as Englishmen, took more of an interest in events overseas. They kept a sharp gaze on British politics, after Yorktown as much as before. Nobody at the time would have thought that events leading to the conclusion of the war were somehow irrelevant to the main story. To understand the actions that resulted in the final settlement, early historians paid considerable attention to the global context, which clearly affected Britain's decision to abandon its claims on the thirteen rebellious colonies in North America. They also recognized that in 1782, the year following Yorktown, the British maintained a formidable military presence along the coast, while the civil war in the southern interior continued unabated.

William Gordon (1788) devoted almost two hundred pages to the post-Yorktown events that led to the final settlement.[19] David Ramsay (1789) covered both "the campaign of 1782" and actions of "the other powers involved in the consequence of the American War."[20] Mercy Otis Warren (1805) discussed the Battle of Yorktown in the opening chapter of her third and final volume; in the subsequent 394 pages, she reported in considerable detail about the continuing fight in America, naval battles in the West Indies, the war in the Mediterranean, British politics, mutinies in the Continental Army, negotiations for peace, and the consequences of American independence.[21] John Marshall (1804–1807) followed Washington word for word: after Yorktown, the war was still on. Once the French fleet had gone, he wrote, Americans had little hope of dislodging the British from their coastal strongholds.[22] Reporting on the final year and a half of the war, for these contemporary observers, was more than a mere afterthought.[23]

Popular writers of the nineteenth century began to play tricks with the historical record. Mason Weems, who in 1806 invented the story of Washington and the cherry tree, wrote that King George III, instead of wishing to continue the war, was "graciously pleased" to change leadership in Parliament and pursue peace.[24] Noah Webster (1833) emphasized the "inexpressible joy" experienced throughout the United States upon hearing the news from Yorktown. The celebration of victory, he wrote, was so pervasive that Washington himself, instead of heightening his resolve to fight, "liberated all persons under arrest, that all might partake in the general joy."[25] With Washington celebrating and the king graciously conceding, Yorktown was presented as a happy ending to the war.

Not all authors simplified the story to this extent. John Frost (1838) quoted the king's speech to Parliament, in which he indicated his resolve to continue the war after Yorktown. Frost also discussed the continuing involvement of France, Spain, and the Netherlands.[26] As late as 1875, in the final volume of his monumental history, George Bancroft engaged in a lengthy discussion of the international context of British politics, crucial to an understanding of the end to the war.[27]

But to extend the story beyond Yorktown, and to include a global sweep, presented several problems. First, a story this broad was not very elegant. The intrigues of international politics were more difficult to follow than a simple battle, winner-take-all. Second, any serious discussion of the Revolution in 1782 would entail an admission that the war in the South was essentially a civil war. (See chapter 11.) If Britain had supposedly capitulated after Yorktown, and yet the fighting had continued, who, exactly, was the "enemy"? This raised more questions than could comfortably be answered in simple narrative form. Third, taking the global context in earnest would require the admission that Americans were not totally in control of their own destinies. The basic premise of the favored story—that patriots were able to overthrow the mightiest empire on earth because their cause was so noble—would be called into question.

For all these reasons, popular historians and textbook writers began to ignore the final year and a half of the American Revolution. Resorting to the simplest of narrative devices, they simply decreed that their histories ended at Yorktown. There, the Americans won and the British lost. The Americans celebrated, while the British, following Lord North, declared, "Oh God! It is all over." End of story.

Virtually all twentieth-century textbooks have followed this line.[28] One popular text in 1913 stated flatly, "The surrender of Cornwallis ended the Revolutionary War."[29] Another in 1935 pronounced authoritatively, "In both England and America everyone realized that this surrender meant the end."[30] No student would ever have suspected that "everyone" did not include either George Washington or King George III, both of whom endeavored to continue the war.

Even the most recent texts have followed suit. Of thirteen textbooks displayed at the 2002 convention of the National Conference for Social Studies, not one states that both Washington and King George III vowed to pursue the war after Yorktown, or that a bloody civil war persisted in the South, or that fighting continued across the globe. Instead, eight of the texts conclude their chapters on the Revolution by highlighting Lord North's statement, "Oh God. It is all over," while eight conclude with another tale indicating a final resolution: the surrendering troops marched to the tune of "The World Turned Upside Down." (Four texts include both stories, while only one has neither.)[31] Typically, the final year and a half of the Revolutionary War is abridged to a single subordinate clause, and reduced even further by qualifying adjectives: "Although some fighting continued, Cornwallis's surrender effectively marked the end of the war."[32] All the texts give the impression that the surrender of Cornwallis involved the whole army, not just a small fraction of the British forces stationed in North America: "On October 19, 1781, Cornwallis surrendered his entire army of 7750 regulars, together with 850 sailors, 244 cannon, and all his military stores." [33] This sounds so final that few students, or even teachers, would even think of asking whether Cornwallis's "entire army" and the British army were one and the same.

These omissions have pernicious consequences. By ignoring the global context, simplified histories contribute to the illusion that American history is somehow removed from world history, and, indirectly, that Americans themselves are over and above everyone else. By neglecting the complexities of alliances and treaty negotiations, they portray the Revolutionary War as a straightforward contest between two parties. The Americans won and the British lost. But war stories with simple, happy endings are suspect, for they fuel the dangerous notion that wars provide simple solutions.

"We said, The whole west, clear to the Mississippi, is ours; we fought for it; we took it; we hoisted our flag over its forts, and *we mean to keep it*. We did keep it."

Daniel Boone Escorting Settlers through the Cumberland Gap.
Detail of painting by George Caleb Bingham, 1851–1852.

13

MARCH OF THE
AMERICAN PEOPLE

One perfect war, we are told, created a perfect nation. That nation, so created, was then free to fulfill its destiny. The American Revolution, with its happy ending, set up the rest: first a Constitution, then expansion across the continent, and finally the ascendancy to international prominence. But the story ended happily only for some. For others, the Revolutionary War signaled a loss, not a gain, of popular sovereignty. When we tell the story of the American Revolution from the standpoint of those who lost their land and their sovereign status, it takes on an entirely different aspect.

In 1958 two of the nation's most prominent historians, Henry Steele Commager and Richard B. Morris, concluded their 1,300-page compilation of primary sources for the American Revolution on a bright, optimistic note:

> The American Revolution . . . did little lasting damage, and left few lasting scars. Population increased throughout the war; the movement in the West was scarcely interrupted; and within a few years of peace, the new nation was bursting with prosperity and buoyant with hope.[1]

This view has prevailed for two centuries. The Revolutionary War, by freeing white Americans from their shackles to the east, allowed them to look—and move—to the west. The rest, as they say, is history: the United States grew and thrived as it stretched across the North American continent.

We like to think of the Revolution as a war for independence. It was that, but it was simultaneously something very different: a war of conquest. Commager and Morris were partially correct—the Revolution did promote westward expansion—but the march of white settlers across the Appalachians did not leave all Americans "buoyant with hope." For many Indians, it signaled the end, not the beginning, of nationhood.

The American Revolution was by far the largest Indian war in our nation's history. Other conflicts between Euro-Americans and Native Americans involved only one or two Indian nations at a time—but all nations east of the Mississippi were directly involved in this war. Most fought actively on one side or the other, and many lost their lands as a direct result of the fighting. More sided with the British, but some, particularly those to the east of the Appalachians, thought there was more to gain by joining the rebels. Before and during the Revolution, Indians played off one set of whites against the other as they sought to maintain their own lands; after, with the power of competing European nations on the wane, they were left mostly on their own to face the advance of white Americans.

DIVIDE AND CONQUER

The Revolutionary War looks very different if we stand on Indian lands and look back east.[2] Narratives told from the standpoint of Iroquois or Delaware, Cherokee or Shawnee, bear little resemblance to those accepted, without question, in the dominant American culture.

Not all Iroquois were of one mind about the Revolutionary War. Both British agents and American patriots courted the Iroquois to join their respective sides, the British using presents, the Americans veiled threats. In the end, four of the six nations (Senecas, Cayugas, Onondagas, and Mohawks) cast their lots with the British—they reasoned that American settlers posed a greater threat to their own interests. The other two nations (Oneidas and Tuscaroras), influenced by a missionary named Samuel Kirkland, joined the conflict on the American side.[3]

In 1777 the grand council fire for the League of Six Nations was extinguished. Instead of coming together, Iroquois fought each other as well as their white foes. On August 6 at Oriskany, New York, several hundred Seneca, Cayuga, and Mohawk warriors joined with British rangers and Loyalist volunteers to ambush patriot militiamen and their Oneida allies. To avenge loses at Oriskany, Senecas attacked an Oneida settlement, and the Oneidas, in turn, plundered the nearby Mohawks. A civil war among whites had become a civil war among Indians.

Pro-British Iroquois were far more numerous than their pro-American brothers, and they figured more prominently in the war. In 1778 they staged numerous raids on frontier settlements, most memorably at Wyoming and Cherry Valley. The following year, Congress responded by authorizing a force of 4,500 soldiers, commanded by General John Sullivan, to conduct a scorched-earth campaign against Indian villages. On July 4, 1779, Sullivan's officers offered a toast: "Civilization or death to all American Savages."[4] Then, for the remainder of the summer, they burned every village, chopped down every fruit tree, and confiscated every domesticated plant they could find. In the name of civilization, they tried to wipe out the developed civil society of people they called savages. At the end of the campaign, Sullivan reported triumphantly to Congress:

The number of towns destroyed by this army amounted to 40 besides scattering houses. The quantity of corn destroyed, at a moderate computation, must have amounted to 160,000 bushels, with a vast quantity of vegetables of every kind. Every creek and river has been traced, and the whole country explored in search of Indians settlements, and I am well persuaded that, except one town situated near the Allegana, about 50 miles from Chinesee there is not a single town left in the country of the Five nations.[5]

The Sullivan campaign, which was followed by the "Hard Winter" of 1779–1780—the coldest on record for the eastern United States—created great hardships among the Iroquois people. (For more on the "Hard Winter," see chapter 5.) It did not, however, terminate Iroquois resistance. The following summer, more than 800 warriors staged raids in the Mohawk Valley, killed or captured 330 white Americans, and destroyed six forts and over 700 houses and farms. The Senecas, Cayugas, Onondagas, and Mohawks also forced the Oneidas and Tuscaroras off their lands, causing them to seek refuge on the fringes of white settlements.

The war continued in 1781, with angry Iroquois warriors continuing their raids on whites who tried to occupy their lands. When Cornwallis surrendered at Yorktown, the Iroquois were still fighting, but they couldn't continue forever without British support. In 1782 that support was withdrawn. When Britain sued for peace, it recognized United States sovereignty over the vast region between the Appalachians and the Mississippi, land which was still owned by the Iroquois and other Indian nations. Indians who had fought by the side of the British felt deceived and forsaken. Meanwhile, white Americans felt entitled to settle land that Indians still regarded as their own.

The fate of other Indian nations paralleled that of the Iroquois: the Revolution caused internal divisions, while the termination of the war triggered an onslaught of white incursions. Initially, chiefs from the Delaware and Shawnee pledged friendship with American patriots, for they hoped to work out some sort of accommodation with whites who bordered on their lands. Patriot officials offered these people assurances of support and protection, and they even suggested they would allow friendly Indians "to form a state whereof the Delaware nation shall be the head, and have a representation in Congress"—one of the most disingenuous promises in the history of white-Indian relations.[6] Patriots never did come through with any significant support, and settlers continued to harass rather than protect any Indians, friendly or otherwise, whom they encountered. After Indian-hating frontiersmen murdered four friendly Shawnee who were being held as hostages, the rest of the Shawnee joined with their militant neighbors—the Mingo, Miami, Wyandot, Chippewa, Ottawa, and Kickapoo—in support of Britain.

American acts of aggression alienated the Delaware as well. When white Americans invaded their land and burned their villages, most of the Delaware joined the resistance. A few Christian converts tried to remain out of the fray, but this proved impossible. On March 8, 1782, volunteers from the Pennsylvania militia massacred ninety-six men, women, and children—none of whom were warriors—at the Gnadenhutten mission. As justification for their deeds, the militiamen alleged that their victims had given aid to the British by harboring enemy warriors. This was the crude underbelly of the American Revolution in Indian country.

To the south, the Cherokees waged their own war for independence during the (white) American War for Independence. When Henry Stuart, a British agent, visited the Cherokees early in 1776, he found them in heated debate over how to deal with the advance of Virginians and Carolinians onto their lands. Young warriors argued for immediate resistance: it was "better to die like men than to dwindle away by inches," they argued. Cherokee elders, on the other hand, favored caution. The young hawks were "idle young fellows" who should not be listened to, they told Stuart. Warriors, on the other hand, told Stuart that their elders were "old men who were too old to hunt."[7] The threat to native lands was producing serious stress within Cherokee society.

The warriors prevailed. In the summer of 1776 angry young Cherokees staged numerous raids on frontier white settlements, but their timing could not have been worse. Patriots had just repelled a British attack on Charleston, and since there was no other threat in the region, rebels from the four southernmost states were free to vent their rage on the Cherokee. Six thousand armed men, having trained and mobilized for war against the British, marched against Indians instead. David Ramsay, a South Carolina patriot, explained how the campaign against the Cherokee was used as a training ground for the Revolutionary War:

> The expedition into the Cherokee settlements diffused military ideas, and a spirit of enterprise among the inhabitants. It taught them the necessary arts of providing for an army, and gave them experience in the business of war. . . . [T]he peacable inhabitants of a whole state transformed from planters, merchants, and mechanics, into an active, disciplined military body.[8]

This war had a particularly Southern bent. As in the Sullivan campaign against the Iroquois, the object was to starve the Indians into submission—but once they did submit, some of these Indians were taken as slaves. William H. Drayton, South Carolina's leading patriot, instructed members of the expedition against the Cherokees: *"And now a word to the wise. It is expected you make smooth work as you go*—that is, you cut up every Indian corn-field, and burn every Indian town—and that every Indian taken shall be the slave and property of the taker."[9] Enslavement of captured Indians, however, proved controversial; since this might result in Indians enslaving their white prisoners, the practice was eventually banned. Although whites were forced to turn over Indians they hoped to keep as slaves, the scorched-earth campaign still accomplished its desired result: a total disruption of Cherokee society. Colonel Andrew Williamson, commander of the South Carolina forces, reported back to Drayton on the success of the mission: "I have now burnt every town, and destroyed all the corn, from the Cherokee line to the middle settlements."[10]

The impact on the Cherokee was profound. Elders signed two treaties in which they relinquished over five million acres of land (an area the size of New Jersey) and agreed to end their hostilities—but the young warriors, the ones who initiated the conflict, refused to give in. Instead, many moved to the south and west, and they vowed to continue fighting. These people, called the Chickamaugas after their new home, refused to abide by the treaties negotiated by Cherokee elders. The Cherokee, like the Iroquois, became divided by differing responses to the American Revolution.

For these and all Indian nations in the vast stretch of land between the Appalachian Mountains and the Mississippi River, the War for Independence—*their* independence—continued long after the British conceded defeat. They fought longer because more was at stake. Before the war, Britain had restrained white Americans from settling in the West. After the war, unrestrained, settlers streamed over the mountains at a breakneck pace and claimed Indian land. It had taken Euro-Americans more than a century and a half to settle the thin strip of land between the Appalachians and the Atlantic, but it took them scarcely a decade to extend their reach across a broader area to the west of the mountains. The Revolutionary War had made that possible.

Indian resistance did not fall away, even in the face of this onslaught. In the South, factions within the Creek, Choctaw, and Cherokee nations, including the breakaway Chickamaugas, formed a pan-Indian confederacy dedicated to fighting white encroachments on all of their lands. By procuring arms from Spain, which controlled the mouth of the Mississippi and lands to the south and west, they made a show of force that slowed, but did not stop, white advances. White Americans assumed they now owned the western lands—but many Indians thought otherwise. Alexander McGillivray, a half-Creek, delivered the message of the pan-Indian Confederacy to the United States Congress:

We Chiefs and Warriors of the Creek Chickesaw and Cherokee Nations, do hereby in the most solemn manner protest against any title claim or demand the American Congress may set up for or against our lands, Settlements, and hunting Grounds in Consequence of the Said treaty of peace between the King of Great Britain and the states of America declaring that as we were not partys, so we are determined to pay no attention to the Manner in which the British Negotiators has drawn out the Lines of the Lands in question Ceded to the States of America—it being a Notorious fact known to the Americans, known to every person who is in any ways conversant in, or acquainted with American affairs, that his Brittannick Majesty was never possessed either by session purchase or by right of Conquest of our Territorys and which the Said treaty gives away. . . .

The Americans . . . have divided our territorys into countys and Sate themselves down on our land, as if they were their own. . . . We have repeatedly warned the States of Carolina and Georgia to desist from these Encroachments. . . . To these remonstrances we have received friendly talks and replys it is true but while they are addressing us by the flattering appellations of Friends and Brothers they are Stripping us of our natural rights by depriving us of that inheritance which belonged to our ancestors and hath descended from them to us Since the beginning of time.[11]

To the North, Indian nations from the Great Lakes region—the Mingo, Miami, Wyandot, Chippewa, Ottawa, Kickapoo, Shawnee, and Delaware—continued to fight as well. Officially, the British in Canada could give them no support, but Indians were still able to get unofficial aid in the form of arms and favorable trade. In 1790, Miami Indians defeated an onslaught of soldiers led by Josiah Harmar, first commander-in-chief of the United States Army. In 1791, when white militiamen marched in full force into the Ohio country, warriors from across the North, and even some from the South, stood up to the intruders and killed 630 troops in a single battle along the banks of the Wabash River.

These acts of Indian resistance are rarely noted. White victories, on the other hand, are not only noted but celebrated. Many American history texts do include the story of Fallen Timbers, when Washington sent "Mad Anthony" Wayne and 2,600 soldiers of the United States Army to confront a force of 2,000 Indians—the largest and most diverse force of Native Americans ever assembled against the United States government. This time the Indians lost.

"WHO DEFENDED SETTLERS IN THE WESTERN LANDS?"

Fighting had continued nonstop for two decades in the wars for independence that swept one-third of the way across the North American continent, from the Great Lakes to the Gulf of Mexico. From the perspective of the Indians, the Revolutionary War had been a global war, encompassing all the known people proximate to their world, and it had not ended favorably.

Today's textbooks do not describe the Revolutionary War in these terms. Many now include brief treatments of Joseph Brant, an Iroquois who fought with the British, to fulfill their multicultural requirements, but not one of thirteen elementary, middle school, and secondary texts displayed at the 2002 annual convention of the National Council for Social Studies treats the American Revolution as a war of conquest.[12] This is not the type of history we wish to tell to children.

What kind of history *do* we wish to tell? Consider these two stories about the American Revolution in the West:

(1) In the summer of 1778 and the winter that followed, George Rogers Clark led a band of fewer than 200 frontiersmen down the Ohio River to the Mississippi Valley. This small group of patriots captured three poorly defended British forts along the Mississippi and Wabash Rivers.

(2) In the summer of 1779, the Continental Congress trained and outfitted 4,500 soldiers to take control of the countryside occupied by four Iroquois nations, who had allied

themselves with the British. This expedition, under the command of General John Sullivan, was the only major campaign conducted by the Continental Army in 1779. It destroyed forty Iroquois towns and a major portion of the food supply for the Iroquois people. The following winter (the "Hard Winter" of 1779–1780), as the Continental Army struggled in Morristown, many Iroquois starved and froze to death.

One of these stories has been part of the core narrative of the American Revolution since the nineteenth century; the other has rarely been included in textbooks. One might think that a foray into the wilderness by a small band of frontiersmen would be less note-worthy than a major campaign of the Continental Army, sanctioned by Congress, which included more than twenty times the force—indeed, more than one-quarter of America's professional soldiers at the time. This is not the case. In the traditional telling of the Revolutionary War, George Rogers Clark is treated as a major hero, while Sullivan's campaign is habitually ignored. In twenty-three textbooks published between 1890 and 1955, every single one features Clark, while only three make any mention of Sullivan.[13] "Clark's expedition to the Northwest and capture of Vincennes deserve to be ranked among the world's great military campaigns," boasted *A History of Our Country for Higher Grades,* published in 1923.[14]

From a storytelling point of view, Clark's tale has always been pre-ferred to Sullivan's. Clark can be portrayed as a David, battling against formidable odds. His story appeals precisely because his force was so small. In the traditional telling, Clark and his men braved flooding rivers in the dead of winter to surprise Henry Hamilton, the British commander at Vincennes. The Americans, supposedly out-numbered, yelled and marched back and forth to give the illusion of a much larger army. The ploy worked, and Hamilton surrendered. "Clark belonged to the men of genius who persist in accomplishing tasks which men of judgment pronounce impossible," stated the popular textbook writer David Saville Muzzey in 1934.[15] The authors of a 1942 text pronounced proudly: "The final result of this exploit was to give the Americans the territory that now forms the states of Ohio, Illinois, Indiana, Michigan, and Wisconsin."[16] The story here is that so few—just "a small but effective force of backwoods riflemen"— could accomplish so much. "Clark's victories opened the way for the march of the American people across the continent," wrote William Backus Guitteau back in 1919.[17]

The Sullivan story, by contrast, has little appeal. The Sullivan expedition conducted a terrorist campaign against a civilian population. Even today, textbook writers still promote the romantic image of valiant frontiersmen while suppressing the genocidal policies of the United States government. All six of the elementary and middle school texts displayed at the 2002 National Council for Social Studies convention feature Clark, while not one mentions Sullivan. Five of the seven high school texts include Clark's tale, and, again, none says a word about Sullivan's scorched-earth campaign, sanctioned by the Continental Congress.[18]

Modern texts also suppress the true story of George Rogers Clark, a notorious Indian hater who tortured and scalped his prisoners. When Clark captured Indians outside Vincennes, he and his men tomahawked them and threw them in the river. To avenge the "Widows and Fatherless," he claimed afterward, "Required their Blood from my Hands."[19] Clark, like Sullivan, systematically destroyed Indian food sources, and he allowed his men to plunder Indian graves for burial goods and scalps.[20]

This does not resemble the man described in our texts. Joy Hakim, in her *History of US*, notes that Clark was called the "Washington of the West."[21] The authors of Harcourt's *Horizons* write, "George Rogers Clark helped protect the frontier lands claimed by many American settlers." Then, to insure that students did not miss the message, they ask in their "Review" section: "Who defended settlers in the western lands?" In this one question, a war of conquest is turned on its head.

Not that we don't know any better. Of three current college texts surveyed, all describe the Sullivan campaign in gruesome detail, while only one mentions the frontier heroics of George Rogers Clark.[22] These texts do not sugarcoat the truth. According to *The American Promise* (Bedford/St. Martin's), "Continental army troops under the command of General John Sullivan carried out a planned campaign of terror and destruction. . . . Forty well-established Indian towns met with total destruction; the soldiers looted and torched the dwellings, then burned cornfields and fruit orchards. In a few towns women and children were slaughtered." [23] Such honesty is admirable, but it also gives cause for wonder: If this is what really happened, why do only twenty-year-olds who take history in college learn about it? This constitutes a crucial part of our national heritage. We certainly expect German children to learn about the Holocaust long before they enter the university, so why are American children in such need of protection?

"WE MEAN TO KEEP IT"

Early textbooks did not shy away from treating the Revolution as a war of conquest. George Rogers Clark, they proclaimed proudly, was "the conqueror of the Northwest." [24] Authors assumed that Americans—white Americans, that is—had not only the right but also the moral imperative to take over the continent. In 1899 D. H. Montgomery, one of the most popular writers of his time, wrote in his *Beginner's American History:*

> General George Rogers Clark . . . did more than any one else to get the west for us. . . . By Clark's victory the Americans got possession of the whole western wilderness up to Detroit. When the Revolutionary War came to an end, the British did not want to give us any part of America beyond the thirteen states on the Atlantic coast. But we said, The whole west, clear to the Mississippi, is ours; we fought for it; we took it; we hoisted our

flag over its forts, and *we mean to keep it*. We did keep it. (Italics in the original.)[25]

Today, such outright jingoism would seem too crude—but the jingoism persists, even if it is no longer advertised as such. All current texts follow their chapters on the Revolutionary War with a brief section on "settling the western frontier." Once Britain had ceded the West in the Treaty of Paris, they say, settlers ventured across the mountains to stake their claims. In the Land Ordinance of 1785, Congress ordered that a rectangular grid be superimposed on all newly acquired possessions of the United States to facilitate the private acquisition of land. Two years later, it established a procedure by which settlers in the new territories could form new states. Together, the Ordinances of 1785 and 1787 "opened the way for settlement of the Northwest Territory in a stable and orderly manner."[26] These measures are invariably treated as Congress's crowning achievement during the interval between the Revolution and the drafting of the Constitution. "If you got the impression that the Congress under the Articles of Confederation was a total washout," writes Joy Hakim, "that isn't quite true. That Congress did a few things right, and the Northwest Ordinance was one of them."[27]

This storyline looks quite different from the Indian perspective. Just as the Revolution was the largest conflict between whites and Indians in our nation's history, so was the Ordinance of 1785 the most significant and damaging piece of legislation. It turned opened spaces into lines on a map, harnessing and chaining the earth so land could be bought and sold. In the Treaty of Paris, signed in 1783, the British had ignored Indian rights to the land by stating that the "boundaries" of the United States extended clear to the Mississippi. Then, two years later, Americans effectively ignored Indian tenure by providing that every inch of land be surveyed and labeled, so that it might be distributed to white people. This "happy ending" to the Revolution spelled only doom to native inhabitants.[28]

Right at this crucial juncture, with their fates being sealed by lauded acts of Congress, Indians curiously disappear from the standard narrative. In thirteen current elementary, middle school, and high school texts, not one discusses the pan-Indian resistance to white expansion in the wake of the Revolutionary War.[29] Indians reappear in later chapters, which describe their rearguard, desperate struggles for survival in the nineteenth century—but nary a word at the critical moment, our nation's founding, when Indian claims to their homelands are bypassed and land is passed out to white settlers. Again, this would interfere with the basic storyline: after "we" won the Revolution, we were free to move west and expand.

Current texts fail to see the full impact of the Revolution on Indians because they choose not to treat it as a war of conquest. Unlike our nineteenth-century and early twentieth-century predecessors, Americans today would like to imagine kinder, gentler beginnings for their nation—but in fact, the patriots were neither kind nor gentle to Indians who occupied lands they coveted.

One of the principal objectives of the Revolution was to open the trans-Appalachian West to Euro-American settlement. That's certainly what George Washington, Thomas Jefferson, Patrick Henry, and many other famous patriots had in mind when they challenged British rule. Washington, by trade, was a surveyor, and he knew the value of land. "[T]he greatest Estates we have in this Colony," he wrote in 1767, "were made . . . by taking up & purchasing at very low rates the rich back Lands which were thought nothing of in those days, but are now the most valuable Lands we possess."[30] Washington himself sought to prosper this way. He claimed 35,000 acres as "bounty" for his participation in the French and Indian War, and he purchased rights to an additional 8,000 acres on the cheap from fellow veterans. He also became a partner, along with other Virginia gentry, in the Mississippi Land Company, which sought a 2,500,000 acre grant to the west of the Appalachian Mountains.[31]

The British government, however, had second thoughts about granting western land to rich colonists. If American speculators gained title to land beyond the Appalachians, and American settlers then purchased that land and moved in, Indians were likely to resist, and the British Army would be called out to protect white interests. This would cost money, potentially in large proportions. Also, Americans who moved to the West would be farther removed from British control.

Hence, in 1763, the Crown proclaimed that all lands west of the Appalachian divide would be off-limits for white settlement. Although Washington thought this was only "a temporary expedien[t] to quiet the Minds of the Indians," royal authorities backed up this policy in 1768 with the Treaty of Hard Labor, which guaranteed most of the current state of Kentucky to the Cherokee Indians. The Virginia House of Burgesses unanimously protested, since Virginia speculators held preliminary grants to over six million acres of the ceded land. Assuming their interests would prevail, many speculators—including Washington, Jefferson, and Henry—continued to purchase large tracts of land in the disputed area.[32]

But British policy held firm, and this set the speculators on a collision course with the Crown and Parliament. To acquire western lands, British authority had to be challenged; white settlers, like speculators, eventually came to realize this. In the 1760s, squatters simply ignored the Proclamation Line and moved where they pleased. But the Quebec Act of 1774 placed these lands under new jurisdiction. Henceforth, whites who crossed the divide would be ruled by a government that seemed foreign—and Catholic as well. For many, the Quebec Act was the last straw. American rebels threw off British rule, in large measure, to stake claim to lands that had been placed beyond their reach and control.

Hunger for land set American patriots on a collision course with Indians as well as the British. Whites saw Indians as obstacles to settlement, not rightful proprietors. Whites possessed presumptive rights because they represented a superior civilization. Indians were merely "savages," incapable of putting the land to its highest possible use.

When it suited their needs, as at the Boston Tea Party, patriots usurped the image of the "savage" for their own use. For the most part, however, they utilized the notion of a subhuman race to justify their own wish to subdue the native inhabitants of North America. The Declaration of Independence, which summarized the thinking of the Revolutionary generation, complained that King George III had "endeavored to bring on the Inhabitants of our Frontiers, the merciless Indian Savages, whose known Rule of Warfare, is an undistinguished Destruction, of all Ages, Sexes and Conditions." To mobilize support against Burgoyne's invasion of New York in 1777, patriot officers capitalized on the murder and alleged scalping of a white woman, Jane McCrae. Although McCrae was actually en route to her Loyalist fiancée when she was killed, and although we do not even know for sure who killed her, the image of savages overpowering a white women helped rally patriots to action.

After the Revolution, these attitudes continued. In 1804 John Vanderlyn created a painting, *The Death of Jane McCrae*, that has defined the incident ever since: two muscular, sparsely clad Indians preparing to scalp a voluptuous white woman. Early nineteenth-century schoolbooks instructed students that Indians "listened to the cries of their victims with pleasure" (1804). Their "delight was cruelty" (1831), they exhibited a "diabolical thirst for blood" (1815), and they could not resist the "lust of murderous deeds" (1815).[33] These attitudes prevailed well into the twentieth century. Theodore Roosevelt, in his popular *Winning of the West* (1924), wrote that "the most ultimately righteous of all wars is a war against savages." For Roosevelt, righteousness stemmed from the superiority of the white race: "The conquest and settlement by the whites of the Indian lands was necessary to the greatness of the race and to the well-being of civilized mankind. It was as ultimately beneficial as it was inevitable."[34] In 1927 the most popular textbook writer of his generation, David Saville Muzzey, echoed these themes. Indians exhibited a "stolid stupidity that no white man could match," he pronounced, and "nowhere had they risen above the state of barbarism."[35]

These racist slurs, of course, are no longer in fashion. Most current textbooks, even at lower levels, discuss white-Indian conflicts from a more balanced perspective. They no longer start their narratives with Columbus "discovering" America; instead, they explain how three cultures—American, European, and African—met in the Western Hemisphere in the middle of the last millennium. In later chapters on westward expansion, they do not hide the deceit and cruelty of white conquerors. On the surface, it seems modern texts give fair play to the Native American perspective.

But not in their treatments of the American Revolution. There, the Indian perspective has no place. The War for Independence enjoys a privileged immunity that keeps the full story at bay. Because this was our founding moment, it defines who we are as a nation—and we do not wish to be seen as cruel, uncaring conquerors. To portray Revolutionaries as the oppressors of Native Americans would appear to contradict the basic storyline: (white) patriots were the ones being oppressed, and so they rebelled.

The Revolution, we say, launched this nation on its westward trajectory. After the patriots had gained independence, they provided for the "orderly" expansion into territories they had yet to conquer. This is invariably portrayed as a great advance, followed immediately by the drafting and ratification of a new Constitution. These three achievements of the Revolutionary generation—independence, a blueprint for expansion, and a viable Constitution—set us on our way. Later, some generations would stray from the course: they would treat Indians harshly, fight to maintain slavery, or (temporarily) succumb to governmental corruption. But these are seen as aberrations from the true American way. The path established by the "Founders" is never seriously questioned.

But that path included an acceptance, even an embracing, of the right of conquest. The blueprint for expansion gave license for domination. For almost two centuries following the birth of the nation, most Americans assumed that the superiority of their civilization provided sufficient reason to subjugate other people and take their lands. With a mandate from God, an advanced technology, and a republican form of government, expansionists felt their conquests were both justified and inevitable.

Following the demise of colonialism in the wake of World War II, this sort of blatant chauvinism fell into disrepute. No longer can textbook authors tell students that Americans possessed a mandate to subdue less advanced societies. Even so, the storyline continues to convey the implicit message of "manifest destiny." Once the Revolutionary generation had established the basic track, later Americans had only to stay the course in order to arrive at where we are today. Just as the story of the Revolution had its "happy ending" at Yorktown, so does the megastory—"American History"—end on a positive note. Today, our texts tell us, the United States is the leader of the Free World—the most powerful nation on earth, and also the most devoted to free and democratic government. The story of America has come full circle: from humble beginnings, we have become a great people and a great nation. The final result—the happiest ending of all—is simply *us*, who we are right now. Our very existence as the world's only superpower appears to make all of American history worthwhile.

American Indians told stories that explained how the world came to be as it is: how squirrel got his tail, or how humans acquired fire. We tell these stories too, and we call them history: how America gained its independence, or how slavery was abolished. The stories work because they clarify and vindicate who we are—but they also conceal who we don't wish to be. The "American People," in their march across the continent, strongarmed those who got in the way. This behavior, present from the early seventeenth century to the close of the nineteenth century, did not disappear during the Revolutionary War; indeed, it reached its zenith right at the moment of the nation's inception.

Americans, from the beginning, were both bullies and democrats. Despite the hesitancy of elites, most patriots at the time of our nation's birth believed that ordinary people were entitled to rule themselves and fully capable of doing so. They also believed they had the right, and even the obligation, to impose their will on people whom they deemed inferior. These two core beliefs are key to understanding American history and the American character, and we do an injustice to ourselves and our nation when we pretend otherwise.

"Let the youth, the hope of his country, grow up amidst annual festivities, commemorative of the events of the war."

American Independence, 1859. Anonymous lithograph.

CONCLUSION:
STORYBOOK NATION, OR
WHY WE TELL TALL TALES

The American Revolution, one of the most broadly based political upheavals of all time, spotlighted the notion of popular sovereignty. On the eastern seaboard of the North American continent in the late eighteenth century, political ideas of the European Enlightenment were put into practice on a grand scale. Philosophers for the better part of the century had maintained that all governmental authority resides in the people, but most Old World states, with the notable exception of Switzerland, had yet to follow the logic of this theory and dispense with monarchical or aristocratic power. The United States did.

In time, however, the progressive achievements of the American Revolution would be undermined by narrow, nationalistic interpretations. Nineteenth-century Revolutionary mythologies, which helped define the American experience and the American character, subordinated the notion of popular sovereignty to the celebration of American supremacy. The lesson gleaned from the Revolution would be that one nation was better than the rest, not that all people, of whatever nation, are entitled to rule themselves.

Rather than featuring the collective efforts of hundreds of thousands of Americans, these tales created a tiny pantheon of mythic heroes and highlighted their personal achievements. In the process, they gutted everything revolutionary about the American Revolution. They missed the point of the entire affair.

Why did this happen? How did the national memory of a genuine revolution get reduced to a storybook format?

HARNESSING THE PAST

Our history texts tell us that colonists became "Americans" by sharing the experience of the Revolutionary War, but this is not altogether correct. Soldiers and civilians, Northerners and Southerners, whites and blacks—these people experienced the war in very different ways, and by the end they seemed less enthusiastic about joining together as Americans than they were at the outset.[1] Our magical beginning was already lost in the past—but this past would soon rebound and take on a life of its own. Rediscovered, or rather reconstituted, it would become a vibrant force in the shaping of a nation. It was not the Revolution itself but the use of its image that created a unified, national experience to be shared by all Americans.

To "remember" their Revolution, the people who lived through it first had to learn to forget. "Much about the event called the Revolutionary War had been very painful and was unpleasant to remember," writes historian John Shy. "Only the outcome was unqualifiedly pleasant, so memory, as ever, began to play tricks with the event."[2] This did not come about in a day. The past needed time to *become* a past before it could be selectively recalled in a more positive light and form the basis for national traditions.

Despite the bad memories of war, all patriotic Americans could share one remembrance of unequivocal joy: the declaring of independence. Other war stories would take years of seasoning before assuming their final form, but the recollection of that special moment was put to work from the start. Every year, Americans could revive their commitment to their nation by celebrating the instant of its inception.

John Adams, for one, had a very definite notion of how Americans could commemorate their nation's birth. On July 3, 1776, the day after Congress voted for independence, he wrote to his wife Abigail:

> The second of July 1776, will be the most memorable epocha in the history of America. I am apt to believe it will be celebrated by succeeding generations as the great anniversary festival. It ought to be commemorated as the day of deliverance, by solemn acts of devotion to God Almighty. It ought to be solemnized with pomp and parade, with shows, games, sports, guns, bells, bonfires, and illuminations, from one end of this continent to the other, from this time forward forevermore.[3]

Adams certainly had the spirit right, but he guessed wrong on the date. He had no way of knowing that the official record would soon be altered to change the timeline of history.

Like John Adams, other members of Congress entertained notions of a national celebration, so they conjured an event worth celebrating. The following spring, the committee that printed the official *Congressional Journal* fabricated an entry for July 4 that included a fictive "signing" of the Declaration of Independence, while it omitted the crucial entries for July 19 (the day the New York delegation finally gave its assent) and August 2 (the first day any of the delegates other than President Hancock actually signed the document).[4] According to the official but contrived record, the "Unanimous Declaration of the Thirteen United States" was entered into the books fifteen days *before* it became unanimous, signed even by delegates from New York. This clever invention gave Americans the Fourth of July.[5]

In our nation's first "photo op," an engrossed copy of the Declaration of Independence was presented for signing on August 2. Many members of Congress signed on that day, and over the course of the next several months, others who had been absent or were newly elected affixed their signatures as well.[6] At least fourteen men who were not even present on July 4, 1776, signed their names to the document that appears in the *Congressional Journal* for that date. Eight of these—Matthew Thornton of New Hampshire, William Williams of Connecticut, Charles Carroll of Maryland, and Benjamin Rush, George Ross, James Smith, George Clymer, and George Taylor of Pennsylvania—had not yet become delegates. Oliver Wolcott of Connecticut had taken leave of Congress to assume command of his state's militia, while Lewis Morris and Philip Livingston went home when the British threatened to invade New York. William Hooper of North Carolina, Samuel Chase of Maryland, and George Wythe of Virginia were helping their states constitute new governments. Later, these men would return to sign their names, some not until late that fall. One delegate, Thomas McKean of Delaware, did not sign until after the "official" journal had been doctored the following year.[7]

The signing of the Declaration of Independence was a manufactured event, consciously designed to produce a sort of "overnight antiquity," in the words of historian Garry Wills. A "past" was invented to serve the interests of nation building. "The Fourth includes celebration of some things that happened on different days and of other things that did not happen at all," Wills writes. "The huge glow cast through the years from the Fourth was not visible to the men who worked and argued through the actual July 4 of 1776. It is in every way an *after*glow."[8]

The sleight-of-hand worked. By 1786, the tenth anniversary of independence, Fourth of July rituals in the major cities had assumed an air of tradition. Early in the morning, bells or cannons announced the beginning of commemorative festivities. Militia or volunteer units marched in parade; then, in ritualistic procession, citizens joined the march toward the site of the official oration. There, a prominent citizen preached a secular gospel—often these speeches were placed in print, and some became bestsellers. After the oration, people would join in song, much like parishioners responding with hymns. The Fourth of July was celebrated as a holy day—"the Sabbath of our Freedom," according to one contemporary participant.[9]

Following the formal commemoration, people adjourned to various inns and taverns to break bread and drink. Each group offered thirteen toasts in honor of the body assembled, the state, the nation, and the republican ideal of popular sovereignty. After dinner, with their patriotism revived and their spirits lubricated, Americans caroused in the streets, where they gathered around bonfires and set off fireworks.

Toward the end of the eighteenth century, this "holy day" turned into a "holiday." For the first time, unencumbered by any religious obligations, workers were given a day off. To celebrate the birth of their nation, Americans neither labored nor went to church. The Fourth of July became the liveliest day of the year.

Early Fourth of July rituals helped define the evolving American character. While orators highlighted the "superior advantages" of republican government and "public virtue," the parades and festivities showcased the military aspects of the "American" experience.[10] In 1786 a writer for the *Independent Gazetteer* commented on the proper celebratory mores:

> Let the youth, the hope of his country, grow up amidst annual festivities, commemorative of the events of the war. . . . Let this young hero, at frequent intervals, quit the toils of husbandry, to kindle his public spirit amidst war like exercises; let him learn the use of arms and accustom himself to discipline in the sight of the most respectable citizens. Let him, in their presence, pledge himself to defend his country and its laws.[11]

While the Revolutionary War receded into the past, military men marched in Fourth of July parades, cannons fired, and all paid homage to the Revolutionary dead, creating national martyrs. As Boston poet Barnabas Binney wrote: "With Blood they seal their Cause, / Died to save their Country's Laws."[12]

By paying tribute to the past, Americans affirmed their commitment to the nation that was emerging in the present. The Fourth of July conferred upon the nation a "history," even if it was recent and brief. That was a start. In time, that history would be embellished, set to paper, and codified into a narrative that every American would be expected to learn.

Not coincidentally, two of the orators at early Fourth of July celebrations—William Gordon and David Ramsay—were the first Americans to pen narratives of the Revolution. Gordon led the way with his four-volume tome entitled *The History of the Rise, Progress, and Establishment of the Independence of the United States of America,* published in 1788.[13] The following year, David Ramsay followed with his two-volume *History of the American Revolution.*[14] Both Gordon and Ramsay wrote with political purpose. By chronicling the struggle for independence, Gordon hoped to further his republican ideals. Ramsay, an active Federalist, tried to unify the nation by developing an "American" sense of identity through a shared history. "Joining foot to foot, and hand to hand, . . . with one mind," Ramsay wrote, the American people presented "a solid phalanx opposing their energies and resources to the introduction of arbitrary power."[15]

Other contemporary historians wrote with acknowledged agendas. John Marshall (*The Life of George Washington,* 1804–1807) was a leading political figure in Virginia in the 1790s and chief justice of the United States Supreme Court for more than three decades, starting in 1801.[16] As a staunch Federalist, Marshall wished to minimize regional differences and promote a stronger sense of national pride; to do this, he focused on Washington as a symbol of unity. Mercy Otis Warren (*History of the Rise, Progress, and Termination of the American Revolution,* 1805) was an ardent anti-Federalist, and she too wrote with purpose. Warren's brother, James Otis, and husband, James Warren, had been prominent Massachusetts patriots, and she herself had been an active and communicative Revolutionary. Warren, who still viewed herself as a patriot, tried to revive a sense of public virtue in the post-Revolutionary generation.[17]

The prominent early historians of the Revolution were similar in three respects. First, while professing to seek only the "truth," they consciously promulgated civic values.[18] Although Warren and Gordon focused on public virtue and Ramsay and Marshall on strengthening the nation, their goals certainly intermeshed. All four promoted "America" as the embodiment of republican ideals. Together, they laid the foundations for a coherent narrative of the Revolutionary War, although this rough draft of an American Genesis did not yet include most of the tales featured in these pages. (Gordon's rendition of Samuel Adams, and Warren's celebration of Jefferson's genius and the "patient suffering" at Valley Forge, were notable exceptions.)

Second, they all borrowed liberally from an even earlier work, a narrative set in print years before by an Englishman. Throughout the Revolutionary era an official publication of the British Parliament, the *Annual Register*, chronicled events in the rebellious colonies as part of its annual news-of-the-world report. As luck would have it, during this period the *Register* was under the editorship of Edmund Burke, who wrote many of the entries himself. An outspoken Whig member of Parliament, Burke embraced a perspective that was easy for American patriots to accept: actions adopted by the British government to keep the colonists under tight reins were ill-advised and self-defeating.

Few Americans bothered to read the *Annual Register*, but those who took the trouble perused it carefully—they had to, for they copied it word for word. Sentences, paragraphs, and entire pages reappeared verbatim in the works of Gordon, Ramsay, Marshall, and, to a lesser extent, Warren. In 1789 the *Columbian*, a staunchly patriotic journal, published a "concise history of the late war in America" that lifted large sections from Burke's *Register*, admittedly copied "without change" because of "the superior eloquence of its composition." [19] In 1899 a scholar named Orin Libby exposed this so-called "plagiarism," although during Revolutionary times, intellectual property was not so jealously guarded, and all the alleged culprits had freely acknowledged their sources. [20]

Third, none of the early historians was as successful as he or she had hoped. [21] Only confirmed literati, who already knew the basic story, actually purchased their multivolume tomes—the masses of people whom the authors had wanted to inspire never took much notice. For every person who read their ponderous works, scores of others heard about the glorious deeds of the original patriots only by word of mouth. While Fourth of July rituals celebrated the past in a style accessible to all, written history needed to come down a notch if it was ever to be embraced by common Americans.

ROMANCING THE REVOLUTION

Like his more learned and renowned contemporaries, an itinerant preacher and traveling book salesman named Mason Locke Weems wanted to promote patriotism, but he took the pulse of the American people more accurately. Weems could deliver a sermon, fashion a speech, or play the fiddle—whatever would draw an audience. For thirty years he peddled his "Flying Library" up and down the Eastern seaboard. From New York to Georgia, he worked the crowd at court days and revival meetings. At first he sold books for Matthew Carey, a Philadelphia publisher; later, he pushed his own wares as well—biographies of George Washington, Benjamin Franklin, William Penn, and Francis Marion.[22]

Mason Weems gave the reading public what it wanted: virtuous heroes, lively prose, and cheap books. In 1797 he outlined to Carey the basic strategy that would catapult him to fame:

Experience has taught me that small, i.e. quarter of dollar books, on subjects calculated to *strike* the Popular Curiosity, printed in very large numbers and properly *distributed*, would prove an immense revenue to the prudent and industrious Undertakers. If you could get the life of General Wayne, Putnam, Green &c., Men whose courage and Abilities, whose patriotism and Exploits have won the love and admiration of the American people, printed in small volumes and with very interesting frontispieces, you would, without doubt, sell an immense number of them.[23]

Following his own formula, Weems soon embarked on his personal writing career. In the spring of 1799, as George Washington's health began to fade, Weems propositioned Carey:

> I have nearly ready for press, a piece to be christened "The Beauties of Washington." . . . The whole will make but four sheets and will sell like flax seed at quarter of a dollar. I could make you a world of pence and popularity by it.[24]

Washington died six months later, and Weems wrote immediately to Carey: "Millions are gaping to read something about him. I am nearly primed and cocked for 'em." And so he was: by February 1800 Weems had published his first edition of George Washington's biography, an eighty-page pamphlet which did indeed sell like flax seed at planting time.[25]

Over the next few years Weems peddled his own pamphlet from his "Flying Library." He also took subscriptions for John Marshall's forthcoming *Life of George Washington*. When Marshall's laborious volumes appeared, subscribers complained that there was too much history and too little Washington. Weems listened. He wanted to deliver God and country at an affordable price, but he also knew that his little pamphlet would not serve as a substitute for a full-scale biography, so he started gathering and inventing more material. In 1806, for his fifth edition, he added the fictive "I cannot tell a lie" story about cutting down the cherry tree, and in 1808, the sixth edition, he expanded his product into the full-length book that would introduce the Father of our Country and the Revolutionary War to generations of Americans (*The Life of George Washington; With Curious Anecdotes, Equally Honorable to Himself and Exemplary to His Young Countrymen.*)

To establish his credibility, Mason Weems identified himself on the title page as "Formerly Rector of Mount-Vernon Parish." Although there never was a "Mount-Vernon Parish," the preacher had occasionally delivered sermons at Pohick Church, which Washington might have attended many years before. This supposedly gave the writer an inside connection, and he undoubtedly picked up on some local folklore, but "Parson Weems" (as he was now called) did not hesitate to invent a story from scratch if it could produce the desired result.

Weem's challenge was to present Washington as picturebook-perfect, and to do it in grandiose style. William Gordon had complained that extravagant writing made the reader feel he was "in company with a painted harlot"; if so, Weems was among the most promiscuous of writers.[26] By magically conjuring fantastic and even outrageous images, he entertained as he preached. "He is a most delightful mixture of the Scriptures, Homer, Virgil, and the back woods," wrote Sydney Fisher over a century later. "Everything rages and storms, slashes and tears." [27] For example:

> Then sudden and terrible the charge was made! Like men fighting, life in hand, all at once they rose high on their stirrups! while in streams of lightening their swords came down, and heads and arms, and caps, and carcasses, distained with spouting gore, rolled fearfully all around.[28]

Weems set the standard, and others followed suit. Biography was the name of the game, and the rules were clear: chose a military hero or prominent Revolutionary statesman, build up his virtues while suppressing his vices, and above all, entertain. So it was, in the early 1800s, that fading memories of the Revolution came back to life for the American people. Biographies of Patrick Henry, Thomas Sumter (the Gamecock), and Francis Marion (the Swamp Fox) delighted and inspired. Even David Ramsay jumped onboard, penning a biography of Washington that outsold his original history.[29] During the 1820s John Sanderson came out with a nine-volume series of eulogies entitled *Biography of the Signers of the Declaration of Independence*. All these bestsellers were buttressed by lofty sentiments. Heroic biographies, which provided moral instruction for the young, also promoted a sense of national identity at a time when the United States, still in its adolescence, needed to counter the centrifugal forces of regionalism and rapid westward expansion.

The War of 1812 both reflected and furthered an increased militarism in American culture. Revolutionary War veterans, once scorned, were suddenly celebrated, and the myth of "patient suffering," centering around Valley Forge, was born. In 1817 William Wirt promoted military values with his re-creation of Patrick Henry's speech. Since the United States had been created through acts of war, military virtues became synonymous with patriotism.

The emphasis on military struggles, along with the rage for popular biographies, reduced history to a series of isolated stories with individual protagonists and straightforward plotlines. Battles had definite beginnings and endings, and nobody could mistake a hero for a villain. Events were shaped by personal acts of courage and valor, not by collective action. Separate scenes—"anecdotes," in the parlance of the times—were connected only by the sense of morality they instilled. (One book presumptuously labeled itself "a complete anecdotal history" of the Revolution.)[30] Leading characters assumed godlike proportions in order to serve as appropriate role models for young Americans. The Revolution, in a word, lost all of its dimensions but one.

As those documenting the Revolution searched for heroes with godlike proportions, they eyed the fifty-six delegates to the Continental Congress who had signed the Declaration of Independence. In fact, the Declaration of Independence had been approved by thirteen states, not individual men in dress suits and wigs, and delegates from most states were responding to specific instructions from their constituents. In the popular mind, however, the courageous patriots assembled in Philadelphia had taken the fate of the nation upon themselves. Although countless patriots operating on the state and local levels had also pledged their lives and their sacred honor, these people, along with the collective bodies through which they operated, were eclipsed by "the Signers."

Responding to similar impulses, academic as well as popular writers rendered versions of the past intended to unify the nation. Between 1833 and 1849 Jared Sparks, soon to become president of Harvard, edited a monumental twenty-five-volume series entitled *The Library of American Biography*. He also published a twelve-volume collection of Washington's writings, introduced by a scholarly biography. Here at last were serious works that appealed to the public: altogether, Sparks sold more than half a million volumes. Although Sparks toned down the language and stepped up the documentation, he still dressed up the Revolutionary pantheon for public inspection. Sparks routinely doctored the documents to eliminate offensive material or undignified language. A man of Washington's stature, he reasoned, should not be remembered for such folksy expressions as "not amount to a flea bite." [31]

If the marketplace made its mark on the telling of history, so did the advent of public education. Back in 1790 Noah Webster had argued persuasively that "in our American republics, where government is in the hands of the people, knowledge should be universally diffused by means of public schools." [32] The logic was irrefutable, and by the early decades of the nineteenth century, public education was becoming the norm rather than the exception. Since the need for an informed citizenry necessitated the study of history along with the "three R's," early children's texts included elementary renderings of the American Revolution. One book, *The American Revolution Written in the Style of Ancient History,* imitated biblical language and assigned each of the central characters a biblical name. [33]

In 1820 the American Academy of Language and Belles Lettres offered a prize of $400 plus a medal of solid gold for the best history of the United States designed for schools. [34] Salma Hale, who produced the winning entry, outlined the objectives for his book:

[T]o exhibit in a strong light, the principles of political and religious freedom which our forefathers professed, and for which they fought and conquered; to record the numerous examples of

fortitude, courage, and patriotism, which have rendered them illustrious; and to produce, not so much by moral reflections, as
by the tenor of the narrative, virtuous and patriotic impressions
on the mind of the reader.[35]

Hale's book and many others like it were produced in tiny formats,
four inches by six inches or even less, small enough to fit in a me-
chanic's apron or a frock pocket. Reprinted in mass quantities and sold
for a pittance, they presented a child's version of history to a population that was minimally literate. Addressing two audiences—young
students and adult citizens of a young nation—they performed double duty: character building and nation building.

In their treatments of the American Revolution, books such as
Hale's tread a thin line: they needed to celebrate the break from
Britain, but they could not preach the virtues of rebellion to children
who ought to obey their elders. Coincidentally, this was the same thin
line followed by many Americans of the times. In the decades after the
Revolutionary War, upheavals in France and Haiti, with their infamous massacres, had given revolution a bad name. The earlier meaning of "revolution," prevalent during the War for Independence,
connoted a "revolving turn of events," not an overthrow of the established order; specifically, it referred to the Glorious Revolution of
1688 in England. This is why members of the colonial elite could consider themselves "revolutionaries."[36] In the early nineteenth century,
once the meaning of the word had changed, conservatives faced the
task of derevolutionizing the American Revolution. Paul Allen, writing in 1819, argued that the patriots should not even be called "rebels."
Since they were fighting for no more than "the rights secured by
Magna Charta," they were simply upholding ancient law and tradition.[37] Drawing on folkloric material and the letters of famous leaders
collected by Sparks and others, popular writers presented a sanitized
version of the Revolution, an amalgamation of simple morality tales
depicting courageous displays of valor and great individual achievements. It was at this point that the 1774 revolution in Massachusetts, a

popular uprising that established a dangerous precedent, began to disappear from the saga.

At midcentury, writer-artist Benson Lossing gave this idolatrous, anecdotal history a concrete physical expression. Embarking on an eight thousand mile pilgrimage through the "Old Thirteen States and Canada," Lossing visited "every important place made memorable by the events of the war" in a quest to discover "the history, biography, scenery, relics, and traditions of the War for Independence." His aim was to rescue the "tangible vestiges of the Revolution" from oblivion, before they were swept away by "the invisible fingers of decay, the plow or agriculture, and the behests of Mammon." [38] While researching his historical travelogue, Lossing listened to the tales of countless old-timers, people who had been raised on stories of the Revolution told by firsthand participants. He tapped into an oral tradition strongly linked to a sense of place. Everywhere he went, locals would usher him through battlefields that had turned back to meadows, calling forth the ghosts who still prowled about.

In 1851 and 1852 Lossing published his folkloric compilation, *A Pictorial Field-Book of the Revolution*, accompanied by more than one thousand illustrations. In two large and impressive volumes, Lossing turned his readers into historical tourists. He provided no organizing principle other than plain geography; the narrative simply followed his journey from one place to the next. This conformed to the "antiquarian" approach to history prevalent at the time: the past survived in the present through physical relics and the stories of individual lives.

Such was the state of historical writing when George Bancroft, a prodigy who had graduated from Harvard at the age of sixteen, commenced his serious and comprehensive history of the British colonies in North America and their War for Independence. Bancroft combined the talents of scholar, writer, and political advocate. He drew on all traditions, written and oral, and geared his history to scholars and lay people alike. Gifted with a marvelous eye for detail, he could spin a yarn or eulogize a hero as well as any writer of his times—but he also believed in primary source documentation. Like Jared Sparks, with his biographical collections, and Peter Force, with his monumental compilation of newspaper accounts and official records,[39] Bancroft gathered a wealth of material from the colonial and Revolutionary eras; unlike Sparks and Force, he synthesized what he read into a coherent story with a definite perspective. Through 1,700,000 words Bancroft held fast a single perspective: that from the very beginning of colonial settlement, the colonists had moved toward independence. America was the promised land, and this was her age. European monarchies and aristocracies were old and corrupt; America, young and vital, represented humanity's best hope. Whatever Americans did to foster freedom and democratic values was commendable, while anyone who opposed America must be considered malevolent.[40]

Bancroft defined the American experience for the American people. His history, published serially between 1834 and 1875, told the story of our nation's founding from a passionately patriotic perspective. Later, learned professors would take him to task for his excesses, but the vibrant nationalism he espoused still permeates our popular culture today. Bancroft wove images of a perfect America into a rich mosaic with a strong narrative thread.

But there was some dissent. Richard Hildreth, a contemporary of Bancroft, took a different tack:

> Of centennial sermons and Fourth-of-July orations, whether professedly such or in the guise of history, there are more than enough. It is due to our fathers and ourselves, it is due to truth and philosophy, to present for once, on the historic stage, the founders of our American nation unbedaubed with patriotic rouge, wrapped up in no fine-spun cloaks of excuses and apology. . . . The result of their labors is eulogy enough; their best apology is to tell their story exactly as it was.[41]

Hildreth was not a commercial success. Precise but dry, his prose failed to excite. The public seemed to prefer history wrapped in "fine-spun cloaks." In scholarly circles, on the other hand, Hildreth received a warm response. Historians of the late-nineteenth-century's "scientific school" preferred Hildreth's tempered tone to Bancroft's hyperbole. The American Historical Association, founded in 1884, saw no need for "Fourth-of-July orations . . . in the guise of history." The history profession tried to remove itself from the peddling of patriotism. According to John Fiske, labeled the "Bancroft of his generation," the job of history, like that of science, was only "to emphasize relations of cause and effect that are often buried in the mass of details." [42]

Most common citizens, however, could not have cared less about cause and effect. They looked to history for different and more personal reasons: to connect with the past, often through tangible legacies, and to buttress the present with a sense of tradition. In 1876, triggered by the centennial celebrations, communities throughout the eastern states returned to Benson Lossing's physical, on-site approach. By consecrating particular locations, they claimed the Revolution as their own. During and after the centennial, almost every town with some stake in the Revolution formed its own historical society, dedicated to preserving the relics and traditions of the past. "George Washington slept here" had a more immediate ring than scholarly debates over abstract causes. The lay alternative to "scientific history" was clearly expressed in the first "objective" of the Daughters of the American Revolution, as stated in its by-laws of 1890:

To perpetuate the memory and spirit of the men and women who achieved American Independence; by the acquisition and protection of historic spots and the erection of monuments; . . . by the preservation of documents and relics, and of the records of individual services of Revolutionary soldiers and patriots; and by the promotion of celebrations of all patriotic anniversaries.[43]

Popular history and academic history were parting ways. Scholars dismissed popular history as "nostalgia"; lay people regarded academic works as irrelevant at best, irreverent at worst. The central scholarly debate during this time—whether the Revolution had been caused by the wrongdoing of select individuals or by a fundamental flaw in the concept of empire—played to deaf ears outside academia. Recently divided by the Civil War and Reconstruction, Americans now needed to remind themselves that South and North had fought side by side at our nation's inception. It was time to gather inspiration from the "Heroic Age" of the founders, "one equaling in interest and grandeur any similar period in the annals of Greece and Rome." The Revolution, according to a magazine editorial, was characterized by "a strange elevation of feeling and dignity of action" which furnished "a treasury of glorious reminiscences wherewith to reinvigorate . . . the national virtue." The editor continued:

> What political utility can there be in discovering, even if it were so, that Washington was not so wise, or Warren so brave, or Putnam so adventurous, or Bunker Hill not so heroically contested, as has been believed? Away with such skepticism, we say; and the mousing criticism by which it is sometimes attempted to be supported. Such beliefs have at all events become real for us by entering into the very soul of our history and forming the style of our national thought. To take them away would now be a baneful disorganizing of the national mind.[44]

THE REVOLUTION TRANSFORMED

By the end of the nineteenth century, romantic stories of the nation's founding had been fine-tuned and firmly implanted in the mainstream of American culture. Revolutionary mythologies, including but not limited to those featured in this book, helped create and support jingoistic attitudes. These stories portrayed war as a noble experience, and they praised Revolutionary soldiers as particularly valorous. Patrick Henry's "Liberty or Death" speech, conjured long after his death, made young Americans feel good about fighting for their country. Patriots had looked into the whites of the eyes of their foreign foe. They had suffered patiently at Valley Forge, remaining true to their cause and their leader. Tales of the Revolutionary War, reconstituted to reflect military values, taught Americans the logic and language of expansive nationalism: you fight a war, win it, and thereby become more powerful.

While these stories touted militarism and glorified war, they failed to acknowledge the revolutionary nature of the American Revolution. In fact, revolutions are the work of groups, not individuals, and ours was no exception. The dominant mode of the original patriots was collaborative action, and the ultimate end was to place government in the hands of a collectivity, the "body of the people." Yet the tales that emerged, with the notable exception of the Boston Tea Party, ignored that. Instead, they romanticized deeds of individual achievement. The story of the Massachusetts Revolution of 1774, in which ordinary farmers overthrew British rule, was replaced by the tale of Paul Revere, the lone rider who rousted farmers from their slumber. Rather than revealing the intricate web of patriotic resistance organizations in Boston, the tales showcased a charismatic mastermind, Sam Adams. Instead of unveiling the rash of state and local declarations of independence, which demonstrated a revolutionary groundswell, they bestowed all attention on Thomas Jefferson, the creative genius who allegedly conjured the ideas for the nation's sacred scripture "from deep within himself."

We owe our very existence, the stories said, to the wisdom and courage of a few special men. This elite group constituted something of a junta. Americans never used this term, but that's how the founders were (and still are) portrayed: a small cadre of leaders who worked closely together, as a separate and distinct group, to determine the fate of the nation. In fact, these men did not act in a vacuum. Outside official chambers a host of local activists, working in committees, tended unrelentingly to the business of the new nation. Meanwhile, poor men and boys of the Continental Army, together with countless local militiamen, repulsed British advances. The so-called founders *reflected* the fervor of the people—they did not create it. By ignoring or downplaying the widespread participation of ordinary people in Revolutionary affairs, stories that claimed to be patriotic subverted the very essence of popular sovereignty—the explicit reason for the nation's existence. Worse yet, by encouraging veneration of a handful of revered personalities, these tales promoted a passive civic model. They taught Americans to rally behind their leaders, not to participate actively in self-governance, as they did during the Revolution.

However mistaken or misleading, these tales survive to this day. They continue to anchor the telling of the American Revolution, despite advances in historical research that show them to be contrived, and despite their blatant promotion of nineteenth-century nationalism. Our nostalgic yearnings notwithstanding, America in the twenty-first century resembles the world of nineteenth-century nationalists more closely than that of Revolutionary patriots.

Revolutionary Americans were frightened by concentrations of power. Patriots viewed the presence of a standing army, which presided over a civilian population during times of peace, as the hallmark of oppression. They resented the favors that big government granted to big business: the official sanctioning of the East India Company's monopoly on tea provided the impetus for the Boston Tea Party, and that, in turn, was the spark that ignited the Revolution. In the state and local declarations of independence that preceded the document signed by Congress, patriots insisted that any national government be given no control over "internal" affairs of the states. Military, economic, and political concentrations of power were all seen as anathema to the basic aim of the Revolution: that people should control their own destinies. Standing armies, monopolistic corporations, or intrusive central governments all presented obstacles to the practice of popular sovereignty.

In the nineteenth century, however, these notions were turned on end. The United States developed its own standing army. Both economic and political power became increasingly concentrated. The many Americans who resisted these developments were branded, ironically, as "un-American," and by the end of the century, immigrants, union activists, or advocates of racial equality were portrayed as threats to the American way of life. Meanwhile, a revised script based on hero worship and jingoism removed any challenge to the concentration of military, corporate, and political power. Supporters of the status quo effectively suppressed any remembrance of the radical actions that had actually characterized the American Revolution.[45]

Today, most Americans implicitly accept what once was considered objectionable: the presence of a standing army, the economic dominance of corporations, and the authority of a strong central government. The official narrative of our nation's founding, transformed and reconfigured, presents no menace to these institutions. The stories we tell inspire no radical views; they do no more than instill reverence for leaders and allegiance to the United States. These conjured tales, watered down and whitewashed, argue against any recurrence of an event such as the American Revolution. We take comfort in our storybook nation.

HOW STORIES CHEAT THE TRUTH: LANGUAGE THAT DECEIVES

Irrespective of politics or patriotism, the various tales featured in this book endure because they work as stories. Based on important elements of traditional Western storytelling, they engage and excite and please. They portray America's birth as a fanciful affair, not a serious threat to established authority. This is important to understand, for a story, if good enough, will generally trump the truth.

Many of our stories of national creation feature heroes and heroines who personify the values we hold dear and exemplify the attributes we would like to possess. These tales, when masquerading as history, are bound to deceive. Heroes and heroines, selected for their uncommon features, are marshaled forth to represent people who are common, not special. History is supposedly revealed through the stories of people who were not really typical of the times. We assume we are learning about the many through the experiences of the select few, yet the language we use belies our intent. We describe our heroes as "giants" or "larger than life." Their exploits are "amazing" or "unbelievable." "Never before or since," we like to say, "has there been such a man or woman"—and yet, strangely, we present these people as "representative" of historical movements. George Washington, Benjamin Franklin, Thomas Jefferson—we speak of these illustrious individuals as *the* Revolutionaries, and we use them to represent all the other Revolutionaries, although we have just proclaimed they are not like the others.

The construction of our sentences, like the structure of our stories, leads to individualistic misinterpretations of history. Sentences written in the active voice require subjects, just as stories require protagonists. The problem is, we don't always know the exact identities of the subjects of our sentences. Composites will suffice for a while, but this gets old. So when we tire of saying "Republicans opposed" or "rebels demanded," we turn to a slightly more personalized alternative: "Republican spokesmen opposed" or "rebel leaders demanded." These subjects are still generic, but at least they refer to individual *people* rather than abstract *groups*. We like that, and we revert to it unconsciously. It's a default mode in the writing of history. "Rebels" and "rebel leaders" are used interchangeably, as if there were no difference between them.

But the casual use of the term "leaders" has a perilous side-effect: if some are leaders, all the others become followers. A few important individuals make things happen, the rest only tag along; a few write the scripts, the rest just deliver their lines. Adopting and extending this default grammar, history writers cast about for "leaders" to serve as subjects for their sentences and protagonists for their narratives.[46]

By a twist of linguistic convenience, storytellers turn history on its head. Since each sentence needs a subject and each tale a protagonist, groups are signified and subsumed by their alleged leaders. In reality, so-called leaders emerge from the people—they gain influence by expressing views that others espouse. In the telling of history, however, the genesis of leadership is easily forgotten. Historical narratives, distorted by quirks of language and the structure of stories, fail to portray the great mass of humanity as active players, as agents on their own behalf.

In popular narratives, only leaders function as agents of history. They provide the motive force; without them, nothing would happen. The famous founders, we are told, *made* the American Revolution. They dreamed up the ideas, spoke and wrote incessantly, and finally convinced others to follow their lead. But honoring these people as the architects of our nation's independence is like honoring Lyndon Johnson as the architect of civil rights. In both cases, powerful men finalized the deal, but others placed the deal on the table and pushed it forward.

In trickle-down history, as in trickle-down economics, the concerns of the people at the bottom are supposed to be addressed by mysterious processes that are not usually delineated. When they do get spelled out, these processes fail to convince. One model has a few men in Boston stirring up the urban crowd, then reaching out to the countryside to foment unrest there as well: thirty-seven men, with Sam Adams at their head, are said to have started the American Revolution.[47] By this reading of history, hundreds of thousands of Revolutionaries risked their lives on behalf of independence simply because they had been told by others to do so.

Another model breaks down all of humanity into six groups: Great Thinkers, Great Disciples, Great Disseminators, Lesser Disseminators, Participating Citizens, and the Politically Inert. Ideas filter down from one group to the next until they finally reach the bottom. In the American Revolution, the Great Thinkers were the philosophers of the European Enlightenment; Great Disciples included men like Thomas Jefferson, Benjamin Franklin, and Tom Paine; Great Disseminators were regional political organizers like Samuel Adams and Patrick Henry; Lesser Disseminators were the leaders of politically active groups such as the local Committees of Correspondence; Participating Citizens were the members of those groups; the Politically Inert were all the people who started out as neither patriots nor Loyalists. Ideas, like military orders, supposedly drifted down this chain of command until enough people were willing to engage in revolution.[48] There is no provision in this model for any movement *up* the ladder. Common citizens are perceived as no more than passive receptors. The model itself contradicts the avowed aim of the Revolutionaries: government must proceed from the bottom up, from citizens to their chosen representatives.

In both these dissemination models, a handful of special individuals, like prophets or seers, conjure ideas from the ether—there are no social, political, or economic influences emanating from people of the lower orders. With a deft sleight-of-hand, writers who believe that history always proceeds from the top down manage to dismiss the overwhelming majority of humanity as historically irrelevant.

Although dissemination theories, when laid bare, appear rather ludicrous, they too serve as a default mode in the writing of history. Authors of textbooks and popular histories do not think twice before telling us how one of the famous Revolutionaries—Samuel Adams, Tom Paine, or Thomas Jefferson—"convinced" others to do his bidding. These men, they are telling us, were head and shoulders above the rest. Writers make their stories flow by featuring a handful of active agents, but they do not present a very democratic view of the founding of our nation, and they do not accurately depict the way historical movements actually function.

THROUGH THE EYES OF A CHILD

This simplistic model—that a few individuals make history happen—works well with children. Fortuitously, that is the primary audience for stories of our nation's founding. What most Americans know about the Revolution they learned in the fifth grade, for at no later time do students undertake a serious study of the subject in the majority of public schools. Because most middle school and high school curricula focus on more recent events, they require no more than a cursory review of revolutionary history.

This quirk in curriculum is fortunate in some ways, unfortunate in others. On the one hand, since fifth graders are at the peak of their learning curve, the Revolution enjoys prime-time programming. Ten-year-olds have their basic learning skills intact. They read and converse intelligently, they are delightfully curious, and they are not yet distracted by the trials of pubescence. Take a ten-year-old to Valley Forge or the Minuteman National Historical Park, and he or she will most likely tune right in; take a sixteen-year-old, and he or she will probably evidence, or at least feign, a profound sense of boredom. In educational circles, everyone knows that fifth grade is as good as it gets.

On the other hand, fifth graders are not very sophisticated. However astute, they haven't amassed much in the way of worldly knowledge, and they are still weak in abstract reasoning. Few will be able to compare the American Revolution, the French Revolution, and the Russian Revolution. For better and worse, they have little experience in understanding the complex struggles for power which dominate political affairs, past and present.

So how do we purvey the American Revolution to these ten-year-olds? We enlist the basic elements of successful storytelling: heroes and heroines, with an emphasis on wise men; battles that pit good against evil and David against Goliath; and, of course, happy endings.

History aimed at children, however multicultural and politically correct, is still dominated by the study of particular men and women who are portrayed as "special." Although fifth grade texts include a narrative thread, they manage to leave their young readers with a sense that history is some sort of amalgamation of the lives of memorable personalities. This is by design, not chance. Since stories without protagonists would result in flat, unappealing texts, and since text-books are flat enough in any case, authors insert as many minibiographies as space will permit.

States with established "content standards" invariably require their students to learn about "key" individuals of the Revolution. The Nevada History Standards mention only George Washington and Benjamin Franklin by name; the Georgia Quality Core Curriculum Standards cast a wider net that includes eight famous patriots, three British leaders, one Frenchmen, one African American, one traitor, one real woman, and one imaginary woman. In Pennsylvania, children are expected to learn about two political leaders, John Adams and Thomas Jefferson; two military leaders, George Washington and Henry Knox; and two "cultural and commercial leaders," Paul Revere and Phyllis Wheatley. Although Revere did not achieve fame for his cultural or commercial achievements, and Phyllis Wheatley can scarcely be classified as one of the major "leaders" of the Revolutionary era, professional educators have concluded that the history of the American Revolution cannot be revealed without studying the lives of these particular individuals.[49]

George Washington and Benjamin Franklin, John Adams and Thomas Jefferson, Samuel Adams and Patrick Henry—these people, our Founding Fathers, are presented as very wise men. For children, the term "fathers" has a special ring: father knows best, and all is well. Just as children must have heroes, they want to know that some people have the answers. The founding of their nation, created and directed by great and venerable men, was in trustworthy hands.

History education, placed in the service of socialization, also requires an ethical component. The Founding Fathers were not only wise but good, while King George III, our enemy, personified evil. Consider this lesson plan, published by the Georgia Department of Education to accompany its Quality Core Curriculum Standards:

Students will learn about the causes of the Revolutionary War and how the King alienated the colonists with his laws and taxes.

They will examine the Declaration of Independence and participate in a mock court situation, formally charging the King of
England with "crimes." Finally, students will create wanted
posters for the King of England.

This lesson has a direct, concrete appeal to ten-year-olds, its intended
audience. Students experience hands-on learning. They participate in
simulated history. They learn to perceive history as a battle between
good and evil and to cast themselves on the appropriate side.

Battles, the most concrete manifestations of historical conflict, are
easy for children to comprehend. They have well-defined sides
("teams," as some children say) and definite winners and losers. Political tensions might appear abstract, but if they lead to war, kids can get
a grip on them. No textbook is complete without maps showing ar-
rows leading this way and that, each one accompanied by the name of
an American or British general.

Battles of the Revolutionary War have a particular appeal to children: the little guys beat out the bullies. Clever and dedicated to their
cause, the ragtag Americans outwitted and outfought their overconfi-
dent British rivals, all dressed up in fancy red uniforms. Invariably,
books aimed at children portray the American Revolution as a David
and Goliath tale: "Discover how a few brave patriots battled a great
empire," beckons the cover copy to *Eyewitness: The American Revolution*, published in 2002. All textbooks echo this theme.

Fortunately, the Americans won the war and lived happily ever
after. Resolution is important for children, and the Revolution had the
happiest of all possible endings: the birth of an independent nation,
our nation.

The traditional rendering of the American Revolution, first told to
a youthful audience, is periodically reinforced in our popular culture.
Stories told to adults continue to evidence the same forms and pat-
terns. No matter where or when we hear about the beginnings of our
nation, we still focus on wise men, we still see ourselves as David, and
we still assume that all ended well. Assumptions about the birth of our

nation all go back to those stories, and the stories themselves depend on structural components that insure their appeal. We've created perfect stories for a perfect America—but the stories are not driven by facts.

Although getting history wrong is bad enough in itself, it has further consequences. Our view of history shapes our perceptions of political processes, in the present as well as the past. It is through the study of history that young people first learn about politics and power. In California, students learn about state history in fourth grade, early United States history in fifth grade, ancient world history in sixth grade, not-so-ancient world history in seventh grade, and nineteenth-century United States history in eighth grade. After taking time off in ninth grade to learn how to drive, they return to modern world history in tenth grade and modern United States history in eleventh grade. Most other states follow a similar pattern. By the time seniors in high school finally get around to studying "politics and government," they have been reading and hearing stories for seven years about individuals and social groups who struggled for power. They have already learned and internalized a "grammar" they will use to decipher political events.

So what has their study of history taught them about politics and power? To the extent that their curriculum has been based on stories with traditional narrative structures, students will have developed a political grammar that is individualistic and linear. They will have learned that historical actors function as autonomous bundles of free will, devoid of context. The History and Social Science Standards for the California Public Schools require teachers to "describe the views, lives, and impact of key individuals," while the state of Arizona wants its teachers to "describe the influence of key personalities." Students are required to learn that individuals have an impact on events, but they are not told that events have an impact on individuals. The lines of influence are all in one direction. People magically conjure ideas with little help from their friends, then use these ideas to make history happen.

When political dynamics are personalized and simplified in this manner, future citizens do not learn to understand the real workings of power. They are not encouraged to explore some very important questions: How do certain individuals manage to determine the fates of others? How do people come together to resist domination and stand up for their own interests? History abounds in appropriate lessons that would shed light on these matters, but the lessons cannot be learned when the forces that drive politics are kept secret, hidden by stories designed to tout and promote individual achievement.

In the top-down approach to history, the experiences of a select few are made to stand for the many. But they do not and cannot. The choice of protagonists will always be biased, but even more important, the achievements of these people will never adequately reflect the dynamics of group processes. History happens because various people communicate and interact with each other. Working together, playing off their various ideas and energies, they develop agendas and programs, which they push in the political arena. Focusing on individuals who emerge from this process as "leaders" cannot do justice to the spirit of political life, which is by definition public and shared.

The way we learn about the birth of our nation is a case in point. Stories tell us that a few special people forged American freedom, and for their efforts, we should be forever grateful. This misrepresents, and even contradicts, the spirit of the American Revolution. Our country owes its existence to the political activities of groups of dedicated patriots who acted in concert. Throughout the rebellious colonies, citizens organized themselves into an array of local committees, congresses, and militia units that unseated British authority and assumed the reins of government. These revolutionary efforts could serve as models for the collective, political participation of ordinary citizens. Stories that focus on these models would confirm the original meaning of American patriotism: government must be based on the will of the people. They would also show some of the dangers inherent in majoritarian democracy, particularly the suppression of dissent and the use of jingoism to mobilize support and secure power. They would reflect what really happened, and they would reveal rather than conceal the dynamics of political struggle.

Instead, the democratic nature of our nation's creation is hidden from view by stories fashioned in a different mold. Individual heroics trump collective action; the few take the place of the many. Both real history and the meaning of American democracy are lost in the translation.

A NEVER-ENDING STORY

History can never adequately re-create the past. Back then, people didn't know how things would turn out; now, we do. Try as we might, since we already know the outcome, we will always be reading history backward. This in itself places an impenetrable barrier between past and present. There are other barriers as well, differences in culture and circumstance. Added to all this, the sheer multiplicity of events, always chaotic, belies our attempts at neat packaging.

It is little wonder, in light of our inevitable befuddlement, that we like to reduce history to a series of simple, comprehensible stories with tidy beginnings and endings. We might not be able to comprehend the subtleties and complexities of previous times, but we can still place the dead in service of the living. As we search for ideals to live by today, we can and do turn historical characters into symbolic icons.

This is not only understandable—it is part of being human. People in all cultures tell stories about events of the past, and these stories feature heroes and heroines who embody virtues and represent ideals deemed worthy of celebration. The problem lies not in the act of conjuring stories, but in failing to acknowledge their purpose and limitations. They are designed for us, the living. We tell tales for our own reasons, not necessarily because they correspond to historical happenings or serve as realistic depictions of what actually happened.

To tell historical tales uncritically, believing them to be literal representations of real events, is like treating paintings on a museum wall
as photographic reproductions. Unless we acknowledge the hand and
mind of the artist, we mistake fiction for fact. This can be dangerously
self-serving. By choosing stories specifically tailored to make us feel
good, we turn people who once lived and breathed, with their richly
textured lives, into stick figures. We pay a high price for the illusion
that we can bring the past to bay.

Sometimes, this illusion is put to political uses. The hero-worship
that passed as history in the early nineteenth century served the interests of a developing nationalism. The telling of history was itself of
historical import: shared stories of the Revolution helped people feel
like "Americans."

This still happens today. Now more than ever, reshaping the public
record is consciously conceived and politically motivated. Professional marketers use sophisticated techniques to give every event a desired "spin." Storytelling has become a science, not just an art, and it is
used audaciously to manipulate public opinion. The overarching
reach of mass media makes these marketing strategies particularly in-
sidious. Contrived stories, self-serving interpretations of public
events, are not just quaint or incidental—they are anathema to the
functioning of democracy, which depends on the free flow of accurate
and often complex information.

Although we must always remain apprehensive, some stories are
more suspect than others. As a rule of thumb, the better the story, the
more we should be on guard. Certain tales play so well they demand
to be told, regardless of the evidence. Stories this good are told so
often that they appear immune to critical complaint. For these especially, we must beware.

If and when we do decide to tell more honest stories, we must do so
in ways that invite discussion and critique. Contentious debate is more
appropriate to the functioning of a democratic society than rote
recitation. In Revolutionary times, common folk deliberated the crucial questions of the day in every tavern and meetinghouse in the land.

Today, the way we tell history should reflect this rich, rambunctious heritage.

Whoever controls the narrative controls history. This is a powerful message. Those who ignore it will remain blind to the manipulation of others, but those who get it, like the people of the American Revolution, will be able to challenge abusive authority and take control of their destinies.

A NOTE FOR TEACHERS

Although this book may be too advanced for many younger students, the ideas can still be made accessible at any grade level. To help introduce a more grounded approach to our nation's founding, a number of classroom teachers participating in one of the nation's "Teaching American History" programs have volunteered to construct sample lesson plans based on each chapter of *Founding Myths*. The plans are geared to fifth, eighth, and eleventh grade levels, in conformity with both the California State Standards and the National Standards for History. These lesson plans have been reviewed by Gayle Olson-Raymer, a professor in the History and Education Departments at Humboldt State University, and by the author. The Teaching American History program is administered through Humboldt State University and the Northern Humboldt Union High School District, but any views expressed in the lesson plans or the book are not officially endorsed by any organization or program.

The lesson plans are hosted on the Northern Humboldt Union High School District Webpage. Teachers can either do a Google search for "northern humboldt union high school district" or type in: http://www.nohum.k12.ca.us/nhuhsd/nhuhsd.htm. On this Webpage, they will find a link to the "Teaching American History" Website, and this will have the link to the lesson plans for *Founding Myths*.

Teachers are also welcome to contact Ray Raphael (e-mail: raphael@asis.com), Gayle Olson-Raymer (e-mail: gol@humboldt. edu), or Jack Bareilles (e-mail: humboldtcountyhistory@hotmail. com) if they wish to comment on the lesson plans or add others to the site.

NOTES

Introduction

1. Thomson quotations cited in Benjamin Rush to John Adams, February 12, 1812, *The Spur of Fame: Dialogues of John Adams and Benjamin Rush, 1805–1813*, John A. Schutz and Douglas Adair, eds. (San Marino, CA: Huntington Library, 1966), 210; Benjamin Rush, *Autobiography of Benjamin Rush*, ed. George W. Corner (Princeton: Princeton University Press, 1948), 155, cited in J. Edwin Hendricks, *Charles Thomson and the Making of a New Nation, 1729–1824* (Rutherford, NJ: Fairleigh Dickinson University Press, 1979), 189. Thomson extended his idea of voluntary censorship to others: on one occasion, he urged David Ramsay, who was writing a history of the Revolution, to delete a story that was "too low for history" and to change some phrases "which did not please" and seemed "too common to comport with the dignity of history" (Hendricks, *Charles Thomson*, 164).

2. Noah Webster, *A Collection of Essays and Fugitiv Writings* (Boston: I. Thomas and E. T. Andrews, 1790; reprint edition, Scholars' Facsimiles and Reprints, 1977), 23.

3. The text that includes virtually all of the tales is Joy Hakim's *A History of US* (New York: Oxford University Press, 2003). This is no accident, for Hakim, in undertaking the task of making history fun, has chosen stories for their appeal rather than their veracity. In her keen desire to make history inclusive, however, she has managed to tell the story of African Americans and Native Americans at the time of our nation's founding much more extensively and accurately than in most other texts.

4. I do not mean, however, to include professional scholars within the "we" who still take these tales at face value. The academic profession sees its task as reading history correctly, not simply creating images that promote a sense of belonging. Some scholars have done an excellent job in deconstructing the traditional tales, and I draw on their work liberally, but I also extend their scope by examining not just one tale at a time but the entire

rubric. We are dealing here not just with the ear of the elephant or its tail, but with the creature itself. The telling of history has been seriously skewed—more so, I think, than even most scholars have imagined.

5. I use the term "patriots" with some hesitation. At the time, Loyalists as well as rebels would have considered themselves "patriots," for they too thought they were defending their country. But since the term has long denoted a particular group—those who opposed British policies and eventually the British army—I cede to common usage and call the rebels "patriots."

6. Ray Raphael, *The First American Revolution: Before Lexington and Concord* (New York: The New Press, 2002), 168.

1: Paul Revere's Ride

1. The tug-of-war between Unionists and slaveholding Southerners over the nation's founders reached its zenith when Lincoln tried to usurp the prestige of Jefferson, master of some 300 slaves, in support of the Union. (See chapter 6, pp. 119–122.) Even the nineteenth-century Know-Nothings, nativists who opposed any further immigration, claimed Washington as their hero. "Put none but natives on watch tonight," Washington had once said—and that became the rallying cry for a political party that marshaled many votes from 1844 to 1860. (See Boleslaw and Marie-Louise D'Otrange Mastai, *The Stars and the Stripes: The American Flag as Art and History* [New York: Alfred A. Knopf, 1973], 27.)

2. David Hackett Fischer, *Paul Revere's Ride* (New York: Oxford University Press, 1994), 331. This chapter draws extensively on Fischer's research.

3. The poem is reprinted in Edmund S. Morgan, ed., *Paul Revere's Three Accounts of His Famous Ride* (Boston: Massachusetts Historical Society, 1961).

4. Copley's portrait, in the Boston Museum of Fine Arts, is dated 1768–1770.

5. William E. Lincoln, ed., *The Journals of Each Provincial Congress of Massachusetts in 1774 and 1775, with an Appendix Containing the Proceedings of the Country Conventions* (Boston: Dutton and Wentworth, 1838), 148.

6. Morgan, *Paul Revere's Three Accounts,* np.

7. *Pennsylvania Gazette,* June 7, 1775. Later in his article Gordon mentioned Revere by name, but only as a witness to the firing of the first shots at Lexington.

8. William Gordon, *The History of the Rise, Progress, and Establishment of the Independence of the United States of America* (Freeport, NY: Books for Libraries Press, 1969; first published in 1788), 1: 477.

9. David Ramsay, *The History of the American Revolution* (Philadelphia: R. Aitken and Son, 1789; reprinted by Liberty Classics in 1990), 1: 187.

10. John Marshall, *The Life of George Washington* (New York: AMS Press, 1969; first published 1804–1807), 2: 211.

11. Mercy Otis Warren, *History of the Rise, Progress and Termination of the American Revolution, Interspersed with Biographical, Political and Moral Observations* (Boston: E. Larkin,

1805; reprinted by Liberty Classics in 1988), 1: 184. Warren's book has been transcribed for the Internet by Richard Seltzer, 2002, at www.samizdat.com/warren/.

12. Fischer, *Paul Revere's Ride*, 328.

13. Ibid.

14. Morgan, *Paul Revere's Three Accounts*, np.

15. Fischer, *Paul Revere's Ride*, 329.

16. Morgan, *Paul Revere's Three Accounts*, np.

17. Richard Frothingham, *History of the Siege of Boston, and of the Battles of Lexington, Concord, and Bunker Hill* (Boston: Little, Brown and Company, 1903; reprint edition, Da Capo Press, 1970; first published in 1849), 57–61.

18. Benson J. Lossing, *Pictorial Field-Book of the Revolution* (New York: Harper and Brothers, 1851), 1: 523.

19. George Bancroft, *History of the United States of America, from the Discovery of the Continent* (Boston: Little, Brown and Company, 1879; first published 1834–1874), 4: 517.

20. For the treatment of history-as-anecdote in the antebellum nineteenth century, see chapter 14.

21. Bancroft and Lossing wrote approximately 1,500 pages each on the Revolution. Bancroft, who spins a coherent narrative, weaves in about one good ministory per page, while Lossing, who uses an entirely anecdotal approach, works in several per page. Lossing published 1,095 visual images, including several hundred portraits and signatures of famous revolutionaries, but he offered no image of Revere or his ride.

22. Although Longfellow believed strongly in abolitionism, he did not actively participate in any of the reform movements of the mid-nineteenth century. Instead of engaging with others toward common goals, he wrote poems and told stories. In 1842 he published a book, *Poems on Slavery,* that reflected his abolitionist sentiments.

23. Fischer, *Paul Revere's Ride*, 90–112, 124–148.

24. Edward Eggleston, *A History of the United States and Its People, for the Use of Schools* (New York: D. Appleton and Co., 1888), 168.

25. Reuben Post Halleck, *History of Our Country, for Higher Grades* (New York: American Book Co., 1923), 179.

26. Ruth West and Willis Mason West, *The Story of Our Country* (Boston: Allyn and Bacon, 1935), 152; Gertrude Hartman, *America: Land of Freedom* (Boston: D. C. Heath and Co., 1946), 154–155.

27. John Fiske, *The American Revolution* (Boston and New York: Houghton Mifflin, 1891), 1: 121. For Fiske as "the Bancroft of his generation," see Michael Kraus and Davis D. Joyce, *The Writing of American History* (Norman: University of Oklahoma Press, 1985), 181.

28. Fischer, *Paul Revere's Ride*, 337.

29. Esther Forbes, *Paul Revere and the World He Lived In* (Boston: Houghton Mifflin, 1942); Fischer, *Paul Revere's Ride*, 338.

30. Joy Hakim, *A History of US* (New York: Oxford University Press, 2003), 3: 71–73. Although Hakim does include Dawes and Prescott, she passes on the signal light tale pre-

cisely as Longfellow conjured it: "Someone had to get a warning to those towns—and fast. It would help to know which way the redcoats would march. Would they go by the land route over the Boston Neck? Or would they take the shorter route—by boat across the water to Charlestown and then on foot from there? . . . Paul Revere sent someone to spy on the British. 'Find out which way the redcoats will march,' the spy was told. 'Then climb into the high bell tower of the North Church and send a signal. Light one lantern if they go by land. Hang two lanterns if they go by sea.' Revere got in a boat and quietly rowed out into the Charles River. A horse was ready for him on the Charlestown shore. He waited—silently." At this point, Hakim shifts to Longfellow himself: "And lo! As he looks, on the belfry's height / A glimmer, and then a gleam of light! / He springs to the saddle, the bridle he turns, / But lingers and gazes, till full on his sight / A second lamp in the belfry burns!" Hakim then continues: "Now he knew! The redcoats would take the water route across the Charles River, just as Paul Revere was doing."

31. Michael J. Berson, ed., *United States History: Beginnings* (Orlando: Harcourt, 2003), 291.

32. Jesus Garcia et al., *Creating America: A History of the United States, Beginnings through Reconstruction* (Evanston: McDougal Littell, 2002), 156–157. Emphasis in the original.

33. The thirteen texts surveyed were displayed at the 2002 annual conference of the National Council for Social Studies in Phoenix, Arizona. They included six elementary and middle school texts: Sterling Stuckey and Linda Kerrigan Salvucci, *Call to Freedom* (Austin: Holt, Rinehart and Winston, 2003); Joyce Appleby et al., *The American Republic to 1877* (New York: Glencoe McGraw-Hill, 2003); Berson, *United States History: Beginnings*; James West Davidson, *The American Nation: Beginnings through 1877* (Upper Saddle River, NJ: Prentice Hall, 2003); Garcia, *Creating America: A History of the United States*; and Hakim, *A History of US*. The seven secondary school texts are: Joyce Appleby et al., *The American Vision* (New York: Glencoe McGraw-Hill, 2003); Gerald A. Danzer et al., *The Americans* (Evanston: McDougal Littell, 2003); Daniel J. Boorstin and Brooks Mather Kelley, *A History of the United States* (Upper Saddle River, NJ: Prentice Hall, 2002); David Goodfield et al, *The American Journey: A History of the United States* (Upper Saddle River, NJ: Prentice Hall, 2001); John Mack Faragher et al, *Out of Many: A History of the American People* (Upper Saddle River, NJ: Prentice Hall, 2003); Robert A. Divine et al., *America: Past and Present* (New York: Longman, 2003); and Paul Boyer, *American Nation* (Austin: Holt, Rinehart and Winston, 2003).

34. Howard H. Peckham, *The Toll of Independence: Engagements and Battle Casualties of the American Revolution* (Chicago: University of Chicago Press, 1974), 3.

2: Molly Pitcher

1. See Karin Wolf's entry for Betsy Ross in *American National Biography,* John A. Garraty and Mark C. Carnes, eds. (New York: Oxford University Press, 1999), 18: 900–901.

2. Thomas Fleming, in his companion volume to the PBS program *Liberty!* includes Abigail Adams's image as one of five key "portraits" of the American Revolution (Thomas Fleming, *Liberty! The American Revolution* [New York: Viking, 1997], 1–7). Joseph Ellis features Abigail Adams as one of his eight "Founding Brothers," despite the obvious

gender incongruity. She was "one of the eight most prominent political leaders of the early republic," he claims. (Joseph Ellis, *Founding Brothers: The Revolutionary Generation* [New York: Alfred A. Knopf, 2001], 17, 162–205.)

3. Holly A. Mayer, *Belonging to the Army: Camp Followers and Community during the American Revolution* (Columbia: University of South Carolina Press, 1996), 20. For the most recent and thorough treatment of Deborah Sampson, see Alfred Young, *Masquerade: The Life and Times of Deborah Sampson, Continental Soldier* (New York: Alfred A. Knopf, 2004).

4. Sterling Stuckey and Linda Kerrigan Salvucci, *Call to Freedom* (Austin: Holt, Rinehart and Winston, 2003), 168.

5. Gerald A. Danzer et al, *The Americans* (Evanston: McDougal Littell, 2003), 117.

6. Joyce Applyby et al, *The American Republic to 1877* (New York: Glencoe McGraw-Hill, 2003), 164.

7. The six elementary and middle school texts surveyed were all displayed at the annual convention of the National Council for Social Studies at Phoenix in November 2002. Those containing the Molly Pitcher story are Stuckey and Salvucci, *Call to Freedom;* Appleby, *The American Republic to 1877*; Michael J. Berson, ed., *United States History: Beginnings* (Orlando: Harcourt, 2003); James West Davidson, *The American Nation: Beginnings through 1877* (Upper Saddle River, NJ: Prentice Hall, 2003); and Joy Hakim, *A History of US* (New York: Oxford University Press, 2003). The one that made no mention of Molly Pitcher is Jesus Garcia et al, *Creating America: A History of the United States, Beginnings through Reconstruction* (Evanston: McDougal Littell, 2002). Four secondary texts displayed at the NCSS conference also include the Molly Pitcher story: Joyce Appleby et al, *The American Vision* (New York: Glencoe McGraw-Hill, 2003); Danzer, *The Americans;* Daniel J. Boorstin and Brooks Mather Kelley, *A History of the United States* (Upper Saddle River: Prentice Hall, 2002); and David Goldfield, et al, *The American Journey: A History of the United States* (Upper Saddle River, NJ: Prentice Hall, 2001). Only *The American Journey* refers to Molly Pitcher as a legend; the others portray her as flesh and blood.

8. In the paperback edition of my own *People's History of the American Revolution* (New York: HarperCollins, 2002), which states that Molly Pitcher never really lived, her dramatic presence on the front cover, leading the men into battle, belies my quibbles inside.

9. Augusta Stevenson, *Molly Pitcher: Young Patriot* (New York: Macmillan, 1986; originally published in 1960), 184–191.

10. Howard H. Peckham, *The Toll of Independence, Engagements & Battle Casualties of the American Revolution* (Chicago: University of Chicago Press, 1974), 52.

11. Advocates of John point to the marriage between Casper Hays and Mary Ludwig in 1769, although it remains unclear how "Casper" turned into "John." Advocates of Mary point to tax records for 1783, which show William and Mary Hays living with a three-year-old boy (ironically, his name was John). Probate records confirm that young John was the son of William and Mary. If John (Casper) Hays lived in Carlisle after the war, he left no traces. For almost a century, most historians believed John was the husband in question. (John B. Landis, "Investigation into American Tradition of Woman Known as

Molly Pitcher," *Journal of American History* 5 [1911]: 83–94.) This view was challenged in 1989 by local historian and genealogist D. W. Thompson ("Goodbye, Molly Pitcher," *Cumberland County History* 6 [1989]: 3–26). In the revised *American National Biography*, published in 1999, John K. Alexander favors John over William, although he fails to explain John's mysterious disappearance after the war and the fact that subsequent records indicate that William was the father of Mary's son. Could there have been two women named Mary Hays, each married to a soldier? Might Mary have left her husband, John Casper Hays, to live with another Hays named William—and then named her son after her "ex"? Did John Casper leave her, or die? Perhaps John really did die while firing a cannon at Monmouth, leaving Mary to take up with his namesake after performing her exploits on the field. To investigate the matter further, contact the Cumberland County Historical Society in Carlisle, Pennsylvania.

12. I use McCauly, in keeping with the quote on page 29 of this chapter.

13. Her pension amounted to a soldier's half-pay. The first draft of the bill that approved her petition read "widow of a soldier"; the revised version read "for services rendered." The specific nature of those services was not stipulated. See D. W. Thompson and Merri Lou Schaumann, "Goodbye, Molly Pitcher," *Cumberland County History* 6 (1989): 18–20.

14. Ibid., 20.

15. Ibid., 21–22.

16. Here is Waldo's full account: "One of the camp women I must give a little praise to. Her gallant, whom she attended in battle, being shot down, she immediately took up his gun and cartridges and like a Spartan heroine fought with astonishing bravery, discharging the piece with as much regularity as any soldier present. This a wounded officer, whom I dressed, told me he did see himself, she being in his platoon, and assured me I might depend on its truth." (William S. Stryker, *The Battle of Monmouth* [Princeton: Princeton University Press, 1927], 189.)

17. Since Martin showed no surprise at a woman firing a cannon, this might well have been commonplace. He told the story only for its petticoat punch line. Here is Martin's complete story: "One little incident happened, during the heat of the cannonade, which I was eye-witness to, and which I think would be unpardonable not to mention. A woman whose husband belonged to the Artillery, and who was then attached to a piece in the engagement, attended with her husband at the piece the whole time; while in the act of reaching a cartridge and having one of her feet as far before the other as she could step, a cannon shot from the enemy passed directly between her legs without doing any other damage than carrying away all the lower part of her petticoat,—looking at it with apparent unconcern, she observed, that it was lucky it did not pass a little higher, for in that case it might have carried away something else, and ended her and her occupation." (Joseph Plumb Martin, *A Narrative of a Revolutionary Soldier* [New York: Signet, 2001; originally published in 1830], 115. I cite this edition because it is most readily available.)

18. Edward Hagaman Hall, *Margaret Corbin: Heroine of the Battle of Fort Washington, 16 November 1776* (New York: American Scenic and Historic Preservation Society, 1932), 14–15.

19. Thompson and Schaumann, "Goodbye, Molly Pitcher," 15–16. Numerous Internet sites give additional references to Moll Pitcher of Lynn.

20. For two different references, one from an oral tradition and the other printed in the *Pennsylvania Archives*, see Hall, *Margaret Corbin*, 34–35. A poem cited in 1905 uses "Moll" and "Molly" interchangeably (Carol Klaver, "An Introduction into the Legend of Molly Pitcher," *Minerva: Quarterly Report on Women and the Military* 12 (1994): 52). As recently as 1978, Michael Kammen confused the protagonist of the play with the heroine of Monmouth (Michael Kammen, *A Season of Youth: The American Revolution and the Historical Imagination* [New York: Alfred A. Knopf, 1978], 11, 121, 132).

21. John Laffin, *Women in Battle* (London and New York: Abelard-Schuman, 1967), 38–43.

22. Custis began publishing his "recollections" of Washington serially in the 1820s. In 1840 these were gathered in the *National Intelligencer,* and in 1859, after his death, they appeared in book form. This is from the book edition, quoted in Thompson and Schaumann, "Goodbye, Molly Pitcher," 11. It appeared in the *National Intelligencer,* February 22, 1840, and possibly in the *United States Gazette* in the late 1820s. Custis included a prologue to the story that has since been dropped: "At one of the guns of Proctor's battery, six men had been killed or wounded. It was deemed an unlucky gun and murmurs arose that it should be drawn back and abandoned." This was the cannon that Captain Molly would fire. After she had saved the day, Custis wrote, "the doomed gun was no longer deemed unlucky." Thompson and Schaumann argue that this prologue is improbable on two counts: the lion's share of casualties among the artillery at Monmouth would have occurred at this one location, and the Americans rarely abandoned any of their cannons. ("Goodbye, Molly Pitcher," 12.)

23. Benson J. Lossing, *Pictorial Field-Book of the Revolution* (New York: Harper & Brothers, 1852), 2: 361–2.

24. The informants were Alexander Hamilton's aging widow, a Mrs. Beverly Garrison, and a Mrs. Rebecca Rose. Hamilton described Molly as "a stout, red-haired, freckled-face young Irish woman, with a handsome, piercing eye." Garrison recalled, "She generally dressed in the petticoats of her sex, with an artilleryman's coat over." Rose painted a less idyllic picture: "Mrs. Rose remembers her as *Dirty Kate*, living between Fort Montgomery and Buttermilk Falls, at the close of the war, where she died a horrible death from the effects of syphilitic disease." (Lossing, *Pictorial Field-Book*, 2: 164.)

25. Documentation comes from the "Waste Book for the Quartermaster Stores" and the "Letter Books of Captain William Price, Commissary of Ordinance and Military Stores," in the library at West Point. The numerous tents she received were possibly turned into clothing. See Hall, *Margaret Corbin*, 24–30.

26. Hall, *Margaret Corbin*, 22. Brandywine figures in another account. In 1822, following Mary Hays McCauly's successful pension application, the *National Advocate* of New York published a note of praise: "She was called Sgt. McCauly, and was wounded at some battle, supposed to be the Brandywine, where her sex was discovered. It was a common practice for her to swing her sabre over her head, and huzza for 'Mad Anthony' as she termed General Wayne." Was the woman who would later become Molly Pitcher really a cross-dresser, like Deborah Sampson? The myths, like their locations, become

confused and intertwined. Later in the article, the author pays tribute to the heroine of Fort Washington, telling the story of Margaret Corbin correctly but using a different name: "Elizabeth Canning was at a gun at Fort Washington when her husband was killed and she took his place immediately, loaded, primed and fired the cannon with which he was entrusted. She was wounded in the breast by grapeshot." (*National Advocate*, March 7, 1822, quoted in Thompson and Schaumann, "Goodbye, Molly Pitcher," 21.)

27. Lossing, *Pictorial Field-Book*, 2: 164.

28. Historian John Todd White has observed, "Because the artillery was immobile and removed from direct fire, access to it was relatively easy for the women camp followers." (John Todd White, "The Truth about Molly Pitcher," in James Kirby Martin and Karen R. Stubaus, eds., *The American Revolution: Whose Revolution?* (Huntington, NY: Robert E. Krieger, 1977), 104.)

29. Lossing, *Pictorial Field-Book of the Revolution*, 2: 164.

30. Elizabeth Ellet, *The Women of the American Revolution* (New York: Haskell House, 1969; originally published in 1850).

31. "Searching for Molly Pitcher Exhibit, 2001," Monmouth County Archives Internet site, accessed February 3, 2004. www.visitmonmouth.com/archives/. Ironically, the most powerful woman in America during the Revolutionary Era was probably a different Molly, totally unrelated to "Captain Molly" or the fictive "Molly Pitcher": Molly Brant, who held much sway among the Iroquois.

32. *Carlisle Herald*, May 18, 1876, quoted in Linda Grant De Pauw, *Battle Cries and Lullabies: Women in War from Prehistory to the Present* (Norman, OK: University of Oklahoma Press, 1998), 128. There is no indication from Mary Hays McCauly's obituaries that she was buried with military honors.

33. Stryker, *Battle of Monmouth*, 192. *The Cumberland Valley Chronicle: Writings about Colonial Times and People*, in a packet of information put out by the Cumberland County Historical Society, states that the spelling on this headstone was actually "McCauly."

34. Klaver, "Legend of Molly Pitcher," 49.

35. John B. Landis, *A Short History of Molly Pitcher, the Heroine of Monmouth* (Carlisle, PA: Patriotic Sons of America, 1905); Thompson and Schaumann, "Goodbye, Molly Pitcher," 24; Klaver, "Legend of Molly Pitcher," 42.

36. Landis, *A Short History of Molly Pitcher*, 15. Quoted in Klaver, "Legend of Molly Pitcher," 41.

37. Landis, "Investigation into American Tradition of Woman Known as Molly Pitcher," 83–96. This was not the first time recovered memory was ushered forth on behalf of Mary Hays McCauly. In 1856, when Captain Molly was turning into Molly Pitcher and acquiring far-reaching fame, Mary's son died. According to his obituary, "The deceased was a son of the ever-to-be remembered heroine, the celebrated 'Molly Pitcher' whose deeds of daring are recorded in the annals of the Revolution and over whose remains a monument ought to be erected. The writer of this [could it have been Wesley Miles?] recollects well to have frequently seen her in the streets of Carlisle, pointed out by admiring friends thus: 'There goes the woman who fired the cannon at the British when her husband was killed.' " (*American Volunteer*, March 27, 1856, quoted in Thompson and

Schaumann, "Goodbye, Molly Pitcher," 22.) It is curious that none of her "admiring friends" had come forth at the time of Molly's death, before the story had gained currency in writing.

38. This was not necessarily "the very same pitcher carried by Molly Pitcher at the battle of Monmouth," the descendent admitted, but she claimed before a notary that the pitcher had belonged to her great-great-grandmother. A picture of the pitcher, along with a newspaper article announcing the gift to the Hamilton Library and the Cumberland County Historical Association, is included in the packet on Molly Pitcher currently available through the Cumberland County Historical Society. This packet also includes the article by D. W. Thompson and Merri Lou Schaumann, "Goodbye, Molly Pitcher."

39. Klaver, "Legend of Molly Pitcher," 49.

40. Stryker, *Battle of Monmouth*, 192.

41. Jeremiah Zeamer, "Molly McCauley Monument," *Carlisle Herald*, April 5, 1905, and "Molly Pitcher Story Analyzed," *Carlisle Volunteer*, February 20, 1907. The first is included in the Cumberland County Historical Society's Molly Pitcher packet; the second is cited in Klaver, "Legend of Molly Pitcher," 41–42.

42. Molly Pitcher packet, Cumberland County Historical Society.

43. Hall, *Margaret Corbin*, 38–43.

44. For a full century following the nation's centennial celebration in Carlisle, Mary Hays McCauly reigned supreme as Molly Pitcher. Henry Steele Commager and Richard B. Morris, in their classic compilation of primary sources published in 1958, told the story of Mary Hays's heroic deeds at Monmouth. By way of documentation, they included Joseph Plumb Martin's recollections under the title " 'Molly Pitcher' Mans a Gun at Monmouth"—even though Martin mentions neither Molly Pitcher nor Mary Hays, and his heroine neither lost her husband nor served water to thirsty men. (Henry Steele Commager and Richard B. Morris, *The Spirit of 'Seventy-Six: The Story of the American Revolution as Told by Participants* [Indianapolis and New York: Bobbs-Merrill, 1958], 710, 714, 714–715.) Other than the glancing blows delivered by the prudish Zeamer, the only serious threat she received came in the early 1960s. At issue then was not her identity or her good name, but her body. The Friendly Sons of Molly Pitcher, based in Monmouth County, threatened to steal the heroine's bones from their resting place in Carlisle and place them at the scene of the battle. (Klaver, "Legend of Molly Pitcher," 49.)

Not until the U.S. bicentennial was the veracity of the story seriously questioned. John Todd White in 1975 and Linda Grant De Pauw and Conover Hunt in 1976 suggested that the "Molly Pitcher" story was more folklore than fact, and that Molly herself should be treated as a compilation of camp followers. (White, "Truth about Molly Pitcher," 99–105; Linda Grant De Pauw and Conover Hunt, *Remember the Ladies: Women in America, 1750–1815* [New York: Viking, 1976], 90. De Pauw elaborated in "Women in Combat: The Revolutionary Experience," *Armed Forces and Society 7* [1981]: 215, and *Battle Cries and Lullabies*, 126–131.) In 1989 Merri Lou Schaumann published the work of the late D. W. Thompson, who pointed out the weaknesses in John Landis's documentation and genealogy. Mary Hays, Thompson claimed, was not the woman

Landis took her to be—she even had a different husband. (Thompson and Schaumann, "Goodbye, Molly Pitcher," 16–22.) Unlike Landis, however, Scribner and Thompson did not achieve national publication. Like the earlier quibbles of Jeremiah Zeamer, these new critiques have scarcely made a dent in Molly's armor.

45. Dumas Malone, ed., *Dictionary of American Biography* (New York: Scribner's, 1948), 11: 574.

46. John A. Garraty and Mark C. Carnes, eds., *American National Biography* (New York: Oxford University Press, 1999), 17: 564–565. All deeds ever attributed to "Molly Pitcher" are now attributed to Mary Hays as well. Benson Bobrick, in his 1997 *Angel in the Whirlwind: The Triumph of the American Revolution* (New York: Simon & Schuster, 1997), follows folkloric accounts picked up in the mid-nineteenth century when he writes, without citation, that "Mary Ludwig Hayes . . . had done equally brave service at Fort Clinton, where, in October 1777, she had actually fired the last shot before the fortress fell" (346). There is no evidence, nor even any indication, that this native of Carlisle had been present at the fall of Fort Clinton.

47. Website for the Military History Research Center in Virginia, accessed February 3, 2004. www.mlarc_va.com/molly_pitcher_poem.html.

48. For a discussion of women in the wagons, and Washington's general distaste for women in the army, see Ray Raphael, *A People's History of the American Revolution* (New York: The New Press, 2001, 121–123; reprinted by HarperCollins, 2002, 153–155).

49. The 1840 pension application of Rebecca Clendenen, for instance, included a mention of "Captain Molly," who had just made her way into print. Clendenen's husband John, then deceased, had "often mentioned to this respondent the toils and fatigues which he underwent and related particularly that he was at the Battle of Monmouth and suffered greatly with the heat and thirst, that a woman who was called by the troops Captain Molly was busily engaged in carrying canteens of water to the famished [and presumably thirsty] soldiers." (*Cumberland Valley Chronicle*, 17.)

3: The Man Who Made a Revolution

1. A. J. Langguth, *Patriots: The Men Who Started the American Revolution* (New York: Simon and Schuster, 1988), 35, 57, 63, 89, 93.

2. Thomas Fleming, *Liberty! The American Revolution* (New York: Viking, 1997), 83.

3. Dennis B. Fradin, *The Signers: The Fifty-six Stories Behind the Declaration of Independence* (New York: Walker and Company, 2002), 2.

4. Pauline Maier, *The Old Revolutionaries: Political Lives in the Age of Samuel Adams* (New York: Alfred A. Knopf, 1980), 7.

5. Peter Oliver, *Origin and Progress of the American Rebellion*, Douglass Adair and John A. Schutz, eds. (Stanford: Stanford University Press, 1961), 65, 75.

6. Oliver, *Origin and Progress*, 28.

7. Thomas Hutchinson, *The History of the Colony and Province of Massachusetts-Bay* (Cambridge: Harvard University Press, 1936; first published, 1828), 3: 63.

8. Oliver, *Origin and Progress*, 39–41. Again, Hutchinson had a similar view of Adams, but

he expressed this view less flamboyantly (see Hutchinson, *History of Massachusetts-Bay*, 3: 212).

9. John Andrews to William Barrell, August 11, 1774, in Massachusetts Historical Society, "Letters of John Andrews of Boston, 1772–1776," *Proceedings* 8 (1864–1865), 340.

10. The entire affidavit is reprinted in James K. Hosmer, *Samuel Adams* (Boston and New York: Houghton Mifflin, 1885), 117–119.

11. Stewart Beach, *Samuel Adams: The Fateful Years, 1764–1776* (New York: Dodd, Mead, and Co., 1965), 171–172. We do not know exactly why the charges were dismissed, but the attempt to frame Samuel Adams does not ring true: Adams's tone is uncharacteristic of all his known words; there is no evidence that he knew anyone named Sylvester; and it is implausible to think that Adams would have been visiting such a man frequently at his home. Sylvester attributed identical words to Benjamin Church, whom he was also trying to implicate as treasonous, and who would have been even less likely to say anything of the kind.

12. George Bancroft, *History of the United States of America, from the Discovery of the Continent* (Boston: Little, Brown, 1879; first published, 1834–1874), 4: 109–110.

13. William Hallahan, *The Day the American Revolution Began* (New York: William Morrow, 2000), 65.

14. Samuel Adams to John Smith, Dec. 20, 1765, in Harry Alonzo Cushing, ed., *The Writings of Samuel Adams*, (New York: G. P. Putnam's Sons, 1904), 1: 60.

15. Louis Birnbaum, *Red Dawn at Lexington* (Boston: Houghton Mifflin, 1986), 25.

16. Hutchinson, *History of Massachusetts-Bay*, 3: 198–199.

17. Birnbaum, *Red Dawn at Lexington*, 29. See also Langguth, *Patriots*, 179.

18. Although the author remains unknown, this account, from the Sewall papers in Ottawa, is accepted by scholars as an authentic remembrance of the meeting at Old South. After Francis Rotch, one of the ship owners, reported that the governor would not let him return the tea to England, "Mr. Adams said that he could think of nothing further to be done." "About 10 or 15 minutes later," the account continues, "I heard a hideous yelling in the Street at the S. West Corner of the Meeting House and in the Porch, as of an Hundred People, some imitating the Powaws of Indians and other the Whistle of a Boatswain, which was answered by some few in the House; on which Numbers hastened out as fast as possible while Mr. Adams, Mr. Hancock, Dr. Young with several others called out to the People to stay, for they said they had not quite done. . . . Mr. Adams addressed the Moderator in these Words, 'Mr. Moderator, I move that Dr. Young make (or be desired to make) a Speech'—which being approved of, Dr. Young made one accordingly of about 15 or 20 Minutes Length. . . . [W]hen he had done, the Audience paid him the usual Tribute of Bursts of Applause, Clapping, etc. and immediately Mr. Savage (the Moderator) dissolved the Meeting." (L. F. S. Upton, ed., "Proceeding of Ye Body Respecting the Tea," *William and Mary Quarterly,* Third Series, 22 [1965]: 297–298.)

19. "Samuel Adams rose and gave the word: 'This meeting can do nothing more to save the country.' On the instant, a cry was heard at the porch; the war-whoop resounded; a body of men, forty or fifty in number, disguised and clad in blankets as Indians, each holding a hatchet, passed by the door; and encouraged by Samuel Adams, Hancock, and others,

and increased on the way to near two hundred, marched two by two to Griffin's Wharf." (Bancroft, *History of the United States*, 4: 280.)

20. William V. Wells, *The Life and Public Services of Samuel Adams* (Freeport, NY: Books for Libraries Press, 1969; first published, 1865–1888), 2: iv, and 2: 122.

21. William Gordon, *The History of the Rise, Progress, and Establishment of the Independence, of the United State of America* (Freeport, NY: Books for Libraries Press, 1969; first published in 1788), 1: 479.

22. Even the critical and astute David Hackett Fischer accepts Gordon's account as viable, because it was supposedly based "on personal interviews immediately after the battle." (David Hackett Fischer, *Paul Revere's Ride* [New York: Oxford University Press, 1994], 399.) But we have no indication that Gordon made use of these sources for this story, since he failed to include them in his extensive report of the interviews he conducted at the time.

23. Edmund S. Morgan, ed, *Paul Revere's Three Accounts of his Famous Ride* (Boston: Massachusetts Historical Society, 1961). Although Revere had accompanied Adams and Hancock when they left Lexington, he returned to town after traveling two miles. When the shots were fired, Adams and Hancock, without Revere, were at least two miles away.

24. Gordon's letter of May 17, 1775, was reprinted in several newspapers, including the *Pennsylvania Gazette*, June 7, 1775.

25. John Alexander, Adams's most recent biographer, supports the notion that Adams rejoiced in the bloodbath with an unspecified quotation (Alexander provides no references) written the following month: "I rejoyce that my Countrymen had adhered punctually to the Direction of the General Congress, and were at length driven to Resistance through Necessity. I think they may now justly claim the Support of the confederated Colonies." (John K. Alexander, *Samuel Adams: America's Revolutionary Politician* [Lanham, Boulder, and New York: Rowman and Littlefield, 2002], 146.) The context here is all off, however. Ever since the previous fall, Adams had been counseling the people of Massachusetts, many of whom wanted to start a war by attacking Boston, to hold back. He played the role of the moderate, not the hawkish radical, for he feared that if Massachusetts patriots became the aggressors, they would lose the support of other colonies. (See Ray Raphael, *The First American Revolution: Before Lexington and Concord* [New York: New Press, 2002], 171–196.) In the passage cited by Alexander, Adams could "rejoyce" because Massachusetts patriots had followed the cautionary "Direction of the General Congress," waiting patiently until "Necessity" (a British offensive) drove them to "Resistance." By doing so, they could "justly claim the Support of the confederated Colonies." Writing from Congress to Joseph Warren months earlier, Samuel Adams had stated specifically that people in other colonies would give support only "if you should be driven to the necessity of acting in the defence of your lives or liberty." This clarifies Adams's use of "necessity" in the passage cited by Alexander. (Cushing, *Writings of Samuel Adams*, 3: 159; Raphael, *First American Revolution*, 172.)

Alexander's misinterpretation, a standard one, is significant. In the traditional telling of history, Congress, led by Sam Adams, is placed in a hawkish role, with the people lagging behind—but at least in Massachusetts, these roles were reversed. Both Samuel and John Adams were urging their radical constituents back home to take a more defensive posture so as not to alienate other colonists.

26. Sources suggesting that Adams advocated independence long before anyone else need to be examined critically. The most direct "evidence" comes from Joseph Galloway, a moderate at the First Continental Congress who turned Tory when his views did not prevail. According to Galloway, when independence was declared, Adams boasted that "he had laboured upwards of twenty years to accomplish the measure." (Galloway, *Historical and Political Reflections on the Rise and Progress of the American Revolution* [London: G. Wilkie, 1780], 109–110. Cited in Ralph Volney Harlow, *Samuel Adams: Promoter of the American Revolution* [New York: Farrar, Straus and Giroux, 1975; first published in 1923], 288.) Galloway, who blamed his defeat on Adams, claimed also that Adams directed the "faction" at the Continental Congress as well as in Boston. (*Historical and Political Reflections*, 67.)

Undoubtedly, declaring independence caused Samuel Adams to rejoice—just as it caused all ardent patriots to rejoice. Adams probably claimed some credit for the historic event, as did others; fueled by hindsight, he might have uttered some sort of "I-told-you-so," which Galloway naturally embellished. But even if Adams himself, glancing backward, saw his prior activities in a different light, we don't read history backward—what counts is what happened at the time. However Adams felt in 1776, he had not preached the merits of independence back in the 1760s.

An Internet reference site, ABC-CLIO, www.abc-clio.com, includes in its list of famous quotations, "The country shall be independent, and we shall be satisfied with nothing short of it." These words, attributed to Samuel Adams on March 9, 1774, will doubtless be repeated in countless student papers, complete with name and date. The oft-cited quotation comes from William Gordon's early history, written in 1788. As a stylistic device, Gordon wrote in the present tense to simulate a contemporary narrative, and this passage appears under a conjured "entry" for March 9, 1774: "But there are a few in this colony who hanker after independency, and will be likely to bend their whole influence for the obtaining of it, whenever there is the least opening to encourage their efforts. At the head of these we must place Mr. Samuel Adams, who has long since said in small confidential companies—'the country shall be independent, and we will be satisfied with nothing short of it.' " (Gordon, *Rise, Progress, and Establishment of Independence*, 1: 347.) This artistic fabrication, combined with after-the-fact folklore, now passes for historical authenticity. In 1788 William Gordon said that other people had said in 1774 that Adams had said these words in private, at some undisclosed time in the past. There is no possible way of verifying Gordon's reporting of private conversations supposedly held "long since" 1774, presumably back in the 1760s—two decades before Gordon set them to paper. Although Adams himself left no writings dated March 9, 1774, this "source" has been accepted as valid simply because it was "contemporary."

27. Maier, *Old Revolutionaries*, 21–26. Maier's entry for Samuel Adams in the updated (1999) *American National Biography* serves as a corrective for many of the traditional myths.

28. Adams to Reverend G. W., November 11, 1765, and Adams to John Smith, December 19,

1765, Cushing , *Writings*, 1: 28, 45. These sentiments are echoed in all his writings from 1765.

29. Adams, under the name of "Vindex," *Boston Gazette*, December 5, 1768, in Cushing, *Writings*, 1: 259.

30. Adams to Dennys De Berdt, October 3, 1768, in Cushing, *Writings*, 1: 249. Emphasis in original.

31. Adams, under the name of "Valerius Poplicola," *Boston Gazette*, October 28, 1771, in Cushing, *Writings*, 2: 262. By this time it was true that Samuel Adams was beginning to wonder: Will the rights of colonists ever be granted? In despair, he envisaged that "in some hereafter," when all appeals to reason had failed, "America herself under God must finally work out her own Salvations." (Adams to Arthur Lee, October 31, 1771, and Adams to Henry Merchant, January 7, 1772, in Cushing, *Writings*, 2: 267 and 309.) But in the words of historian Pauline Maier, this apocalyptic prediction, born of frustration, "fell short of advocacy." (Maier, *Old Revolutionaries*, 23.)

32. Adams to Arthur Lee, June 21, 1773, in Cushing, *Writings*, 3: 44.

33. Adams to Joseph Warren, September 25, 1774, in Cushing, *Writings*, 3: 158–159.

34. Adams to Samuel Cooper, April 3 and April 30, 1776; Adams to Joseph Hawley, April 15, 1776; in Cushing, *Writings*, 3: 276–285.

35. Adams to John Smith, December 20, 1765, in Cushing, *Writings*, 1: 60.

36. Adams, under the name "Determinatus," *Boston Gazette*, August 8, 1768, in Cushing, *Writings*, 1: 240. Emphasis in original.

37. Adams, under the name "Vindex," *Boston Gazette*, December 5, 1768, in Cushing, *Writings*, 1: 259. Emphasis in original.

38. Adams to Darius Sessions, January 2, 1773, in Cushing, *Writings*, 2: 398.

39. Adams to James Warren, May 21, 1774, *The Warren-Adams Letters* (Boston: Massachusetts Historical Society, 1917–1925), 1: 26. Pauline Maier states that this letter is misdated. (Maier, *Old Revolutionaries*, 28.)

40. Adams to Benjamin Kent, July 27, 1776, in Cushing, *Writings*, 3: 304.

41. Alexander, *Samuel Adams: America's Revolutionary Politician*, 185.

42. For the less revolutionary meaning of "revolution" which prevailed before the turmoil of the French Revolution, see Garry Wills, *Inventing America: Jefferson's Declaration of Independence* (New York: Doubleday, 1978), 51–52.

43. John C. Miller, *Sam Adams: Pioneer in Propaganda* (Stanford: Stanford University Press, 1936), 53, 136–138, 141, 144–145.

44. As cited in note 2, this quote comes not from the works of Hutchinson or Oliver but from Thomas Fleming's volume which accompanied the recent PBS series *Liberty!*

45. George Bancroft, for all his professed belief in democracy, certainly followed this way of thinking. " 'Make way for the committee!' was the shout of the multitude, as Adams came out from the council chamber, and baring his head, which was already becoming gray, moved through their ranks, inspiring confidence. . . . On ordinary occasions he seemed like ordinary men; but in moments of crisis, he rose naturally and unaffectedly to the highest dignity, and spoke as if the hopes of humanity hung on his words." (Bancroft, *History of the United States*, 4:192.)

46. John W. Tyler, *Smugglers and Patriots: Boston Merchants and the Advent of the American Revolution* (Boston: Northeastern University Press, 1986), 17.

47. Gordon, *Rise, Progress, and Establishment of Independence*, 1: 178.

48. Wills, *Inventing America*, 20–24.

49. See Richard D. Brown, *Revolutionary Politics in Massachusetts: The Boston Committee of Correspondence and the Towns, 1772–1774* (New York: W. W. Norton, 1970), 48, 62–64.

50. Alfred Young, "Liberty Tree: Made in America?" Newberry Library Seminar in Early American History, September 25, 2003 (to be included in a forthcoming collection of Alfred Young's essays).

51. For a recent treatment that places Adams's effectiveness within this political rubric, see Alexander, *Samuel Adams: America's Revolutionary Politician*.

52. Mercy Otis Warren, *History of the Rise, Progress and Termination of the American Revolution, interspersed with Biographical, Political and Moral Observations* (Boston: E. Larkin, 1805; reprinted by Liberty Classics in 1988), 1: 211.

4: The Shot Heard 'Round the World

1. David Hackett Fischer, *Paul Revere's Ride* (New York and Oxford: Oxford University Press 1994), 327.

2. A. J. Langguth, *Patriots: The Men Who Started the American Revolution* (New York: Simon and Schuster, 1988), 240. Joy Hakim, even as she quotes the "Concord Hymn" verbatim, says Emerson applied "the shot heard 'round the world" to Lexington. (*A History of US* [New York: Oxford University Press, 2003], 3: 73.)

3. Alfred F. Young, *The Shoemaker and the Tea Party* (Boston: Beacon Press, 1999), 108–133.

4. The story of the 1774 overthrow of British authority throughout Massachusetts, outlined in the subsequent paragraphs, is told in Ray Raphael, *The First American Revolution: Before Lexington and Concord* (New York: The New Press, 2002).

5. Joseph Clarke to unknown recipient, August 30, 1774, in James R. Trumbull, *History of Northampton, Massachusetts, from its Settlement in 1654* (Northampton: Gazette Printing Co., 1902), 346–348; reprinted in Raphael, *First American Revolution*, 98–101.

6. Raphael, *First American Revolution*, 112–130.

7. Raphael, *First American Revolution*, 130–138.

8. John Andrews to William Barrell, October 6, 1774, in Massachusetts Historical Society, "Letters of John Andrews of Boston, 1772–1776," *Proceedings* 8 (1864–1865), 373–374; Raphael, *First American Revolution*, 155–156.

9. Andrews to Barrell, August 29, 1774, Massachusetts Historical Society, "Letters," 348; Raphael, *First American Revolution*, 94.

10. Jonathan Judd, Jr., Diary, v. 2 (1773–1782), Forbes Library, Northampton, entry for September 7, 1774; Raphael, *First American Revolution*, 168.

11. Much is made in many narratives about the "Day of Prayer and Fasting" held in Virginia, the most populous colony, on June 1, 1774. Supposedly, this revealed how devoted the Virginians were to the people of Massachusetts, since it caused the British to disband

the Virginia House of Burgesses. In fact, many Virginians were acting in self-interest, not charity, when they decided on this course. The previous year, growers of tobacco (the basis of Virginia's economy) had announced that by 1775 they would withhold their crops from the market. They hoped that British merchants would then buy tobacco at higher prices, anticipating the shortage to come. Since many tobacco planters were in debt, however, they feared that creditors would take them to court in retaliation, and if their scheme failed, the courts could seize their property. Supporting Boston with a "Day of Prayer and Fasting" and a pledge to boycott British trade solved all their problems. Not only did these actions give their market manipulation a patriotic cover, but they also caused the British government to dissolve the legislature—and since the legislature had not yet authorized the court fees, that meant the courts would have to close as well. The planters' plan worked like a charm: tobacco prices soared in anticipation of future shortages while growers sold out their crops before nonexportation was scheduled to take effect. Meanwhile, no British merchants could take any Virginians to court for unpaid bills.

Boston had asked other colonies to withdraw trade from both Britain and the West Indies. For the reasons already mentioned, Virginia planters were more than willing to comply with respect to Britain, but they refused to end their lucrative trade with the Indies. Similarly, South Carolina went along with much of the boycott but insisted on an exemption for rice, its main moneymaker. These actions, traditionally touted as sympathetic gestures of support, had decidedly self-serving overtones. (Woody Holton, *Forced Founders: Indians, Debtors, Slaves and the Making of the American Revolution in Virginia* [Chapel Hill: University of North Carolina Press, 1999], 115–129.)

12. A "revolution," according to the *Random House Webster's College Dictionary*, is "a complete and forcible overthrow and replacement of an established government or political system by the people governed." By this definition, the people of Massachusetts staged a textbook example of a revolution.

13. Quoted in Thomas A. Bailey and David M. Kennedy, eds., *The American Spirit: United States History as Seen by Contemporaries* (Lexington, MA: D. C. Heath and Co., 1994), 1: 143.

14. American Political Society, Records, American Antiquarian Society, Worcester, MA.

15. Proceedings, Worcester County Convention, August 30–31, 1774, in William E. Lincoln, ed., *The Journals of Each Provincial Congress of Massachusetts in 1774 and 1775, with an Appendix Containing the Proceedings of the County Conventions* (Boston: Dutton and Wentworth, 1838), 634.

16. Proceedings, Worcester County Convention, September 20–21, 1774, in Lincoln, *Journals of Each Provincial Congress*, 642–643.

17. Lincoln, *Journals of Each Provincial Congress*, 30.

18. A good account of the storming of Fort William and Mary appears in Fischer, *Paul Revere's Ride*, 52–58. Documentary sources are reprinted in Charles L. Parsons, "The Capture of Fort William and Mary, December 14 and 15, 1774," *New Hampshire Historical Society Proceedings* 4 (1890–1905), 18–47.

19. *Providence Gazette*, December 23, 1774; Fischer, *Paul Revere's Ride*, 57; J. L. Bell, "Be-

hold, the Guns Were Gone!" presented in the Boston Area Early American History Summer Seminars, Massachusetts Historical Society, July 26, 2001.

20. *The Annual Register for the Year 1775* (London: J. Dodsley, 1776), 2–3, 16–17.

21. David Ramsay, *The History of the American Revolution* (Philadelphia: R. Aitken and Son, 1789; reprinted by Liberty Classics in 1990), 1: 106–107.

22. William Gordon, *The History of the Rise, Progress, and Establishment of the Independence of the United States of America,* reprint edition (Freeport, NY: Books for Libraries Press, 1969; first published in 1788), 1: 382, 380, 377.

23. Mercy Otis Warren, *History of the Rise, Progress and Termination of the American Revolution, interspersed with Biographical, Political and Moral Observations* (Boston: E. Larkin, 1805; reprinted by Liberty Classics in 1988), 1: 145–146. In 1776 Samuel Adams himself took note of the dramatic turn of events "since the stopping of the Courts in Berkshire." In this context, he seemed to marking the beginning of the Revolution by this event. (Samuel Adams to Joseph Hawley, April 15, 1776, in Cushing, *Writings of Samuel Adams,* 3: 281.)

24. Paul Allen, *A History of the American Revolution: Comprising All the Principal Events Both in the Field and in the Cabinet* (Baltimore: John Hopkins, 1819) 1: 180–198.

25. Salma Hale, *History of the United States, from their First Settlement as Colonies, to the Close of the War with Great Britain in 1815* (New York: Collins and Hannay, 1830; first published in 1822), 142–144.

26. Charles A. Goodrich, *A History of the United States of America* (Hartford: Barber and Robinson, 1823), 154.

27. Richard Snowden, *The American Revolution Written in the Style of Ancient History* (Philadelphia: Jones, Hoff and Derrick, 1793), 1: 14.

28. George Bancroft, *History of the United States of America* (Boston: Little, Brown, and Co., 1879; first published in 1854), 4: 379, 389, 390.

29. William V. Wells, *The Life and Public Services of Samuel Adams* (Freeport, NY: Books for Libraries Press, 1969; first published in 1865).

30. Lord Dartmouth to Thomas Gage, January 27, 1775, in *Correspondence of General Thomas Gage,* Clarence E. Carter, ed. (New Haven: Yale University Press, 1931), 2: 179.

31. Henry Steele Commager and Richard B. Morris, *The Spirit of Seventy-Six, The Story of the Revolution as Told by it Participants* (Indianapolis and New York: Bobbs-Merrill Co., 1958), 31–38, 45–56, 66–97.

32. The texts surveyed were all displayed at the annual convention of the National Council for Social Studies in Phoenix in November 2002: *Call to Freedom* (Austin: Holt, Rinehart and Winston, 2003; *The American Republic to 1877* (New York: Glencoe McGraw-Hill, 2003); *United States History: Beginnings* (Orlando: Harcourt, 2003); *The American Nation: Beginnings through 1877* (Upper Saddle River, NJ: Prentice Hall, 2003); *Creating America: A History of the United States, Beginnings through Reconstruction* (Evanston: McDougal Littell, 2002); and Joy Hakim's *A History of US* (New York: Oxford University Press, 2003).

33. These were also featured at the 2002 NCSS convention. The eight that ignore the Revolution of 1774 are: Gerald A. Ranzer et al, *The Americans* (Evanston: McDougal Littell,

2003); Daniel J. Boorstin and Brooks Mather Kelley, *A History of the United States* (Upper Saddle River: Prentice Hall, 2002); David Goodfield et al, *The American Journey* (Upper Saddle River: Prentice Hall, 2001); Mary Beth Norton et al, *A People and a Nation* (Boston: Houghton Mifflin, 2000); Paul Boyer, *The American Nation* (Austin: Holt, Rinehart and Winston, 2003); John Mack Faragher et al, *Out of Many* (Upper Saddle River: Prentice Hall, 2003); James L. Roark et al, *The American Promise* (Boston: Bedford/ St. Martins, 2002); and Robert A. Divine et al, *America: Past and Present* (New York: Longman, 2003).

34. Gary B. Nash and Julie Roy Jeffrey, *The American People* (New York: Addison-Wesley, 2001), 149.

35. Joyce Appleby et al, *The American Vision* (New York: Glencoe McGraw-Hill, 2003), 129.

36. Langguth, *Patriots*, 188–203.

37. Thomas Fleming, *Liberty! The American Revolution* (New York: Viking, 1997), 98.

38. Benson Bobrick, *Angel in the Whirlwind: The Triumph of the American Revolution* (New York: Simon and Schuster, 1997), 103. The Suffolk Resolves did play a key role in gaining acceptance for the Massachusetts revolution in other colonies, for it was endorsed by the Continental Congress of September 17. But it was only one of many radical documents stemming from the county conventions across Massachusetts, and Suffolk, which included Boston, was the only county in contiguous, mainland Massachusetts that did not overthrow British authority. Joseph Warren, meanwhile, was hardly the most radical Revolutionary. In fact, he did what he could to slow the Revolution down. (Raphael, *First American Revolution*, 117–119, 149–151, 172.)

39. Even serious scholars who undertake survey histories fail to give this democratic revolution its due. Robert Middlehauff highlights the Suffolk Resolves, which he attributes to "Dr. Joseph Warren, Sam Adams's henchman." He also cites the wrong dates for the court closures in western Massachusetts and the delivery of the Suffolk Resolves to Congress, and he belittles the 1774 revolution by his choice of words: it was "small-scale," he pronounces, and the First Provincial Congress, which in fact was a radical act of defiance, merely "eased into . . . place." (Robert Middlekauff, *The Glorious Cause: The American Revolution, 1763–1789* [New York: Oxford University Press, 1982], 246, 252–254.) Gordon Wood, likewise, makes the actions of the 1774 revolutionaries seem less than they were. Although Wood says nothing about the Massachusetts revolution specifically, he does acknowledge that "the Coercive Acts of 1774 produced open rebellion in America." But the syntax Wood uses in describing this rebellion undervalues the unheralded revolutionaries of rural Massachusetts. "Mass meetings that sometimes *attracted* thousands of aroused colonists *endorsed* resolutions and *called for* new political organizations [emphases added]." These verbs are either passive or tentative. In fact, the aroused colonists *organized* meetings, *wrote* resolutions, and *created* new political organizations. (Gordon Wood, *The American Revolution: A History* [New York: Modern Library, 2002], 47.) The only survey of the American Revolution in almost a century and a half to highlight the Massachusetts Revolution of 1774 is Merrill Jensen's *The Founding of a Nation: A History of the American Revolution, 1763–1776* (New York: Oxford University Press, 1968), 553–567.

5: The Winter at Valley Forge

1. F. Van Wyck Mason, *The Winter at Valley Forge* (New York: Random House, 1953), 1, 6, 7, 8.

2. Howard Peckham, in his tabulation of battlefield casualties, lists only fifteen American deaths during the three winter months that the Continental Army was camped at Valley Forge—and not a single one of these occurred in Pennsylvania. The deadliest skirmish in this period was an Indian attack at Dunkard Creek, in western Virginia. (Peckham, *The Toll of Independence* [Chicago: University of Chicago Press, 1974], 46–48.)

3. Washington to John Hancock, September 24, 1776, in *The Writings of George Washington from the Original Manuscript Sources,* John C. Fitzpatrick, ed. (Washington, DC: United States Government Printing Office, 1931–1944), 6: 107–108.

4. John Shy, *A People Numerous and Armed: Reflections on the Military Struggle for American Independence* (Ann Arbor: University of Michigan Press, 1990), 173.

5. Soldiers John Brooks and Isaac Gibbs, cited in Wayne Bodle, *The Valley Forge Winter: Civilians and Soldiers in War* (University Park: Pennsylvania State University Press, 2002), 127, 202.

6. Cited from the diary of Albigence Waldo in Charles Royster, *A Revolutionary People at War: The Continental Army and the American Character, 1775–1783* (Chapel Hill: University of North Carolina Press, 1979), 191.

7. Bodle, *Valley Forge Winter,* 134.

8. Joseph Plumb Martin, *Narrative of a Revolutionary Soldier* (New York: Signet, 2001; originally published in 1830), 245.

9. Bodle, *Valley Forge Winter,* 165–169; Washington to Nathanael Greene, February 12, 1778, in Fitzpatrick, *Writings of George Washington,* 10: 454–455.

10. Martin, *Narrative,* 90.

11. Royster, *A Revolutionary People at War,* 196.

12. Bodle, *Valley Forge Winter,* 180; Washington to Thomas Wharton, February 12, 1778, in Fitzpatrick, *Writings of George Washington,* 10: 452–453.

13. Washington to the president of Congress, December 23, 1777, in Fitzpatrick, *Writings of George Washington,* 10: 193.

14. Washington to William Smallwood, February 16, 1778, and Washington to George Clinton, February 16, 1778, in Fitzpatrick, *Writings of George Washington,* 10: 467, 469.

15. Washington to John Banister, April 21, 1778, in Fitzpatrick, *Writings of George Washington,* 11: 285.

16. Thomas Fleming, *Liberty! The American Revolution* (New York: Viking, 1997), 280.

17. Edmund Lindop, *Birth of the Constitution* (Hillside, NJ: Enslow Publishers, 1987), 16.

18. Martin, *Narrative,* 157.

19. Ibid.

20. Ibid., 161–162.

21. David M. Ludlum, *The Weather Factor* (Boston: Houghton Mifflin, 1984), 50–51.

22. Temperatures for the winter of 1777–1778 come from Thomas Coombe, who resided in

what is now West Philadelphia, near Sixty-third Street and Market Street, about seventeen miles southeast of Valley Forge. Coombe took at least two readings every day from an outdoor thermometer, one at 8:00 A.M. and one at 2:00 or 3:00 P.M., roughly corresponding to the low and high temperatures of the day. Most evenings, he also recorded temperatures at 9:00 or 10:00. The vast majority of the "low" temperatures tabulated in this chart are from the 8:00 A.M. readings. (David M. Ludlum, *Early American Winters, 1604–1820* (Boston: American Meteorological Society, 1966), 1: 101.) The historic average comes from the low daily temperatures reported on the Internet by CityRatings. com.

23. Ludlum, *Weather Factor*, 57.

24. Joseph Lee Boyle, "The Weather and the Continental Army, August 1777–June 1778," unpublished manuscript, available electronically by contacting the Valley Forge National Historical Park, www.nps.gov/vafo/. Boyle's masterful work is a chronological compilation of primary sources that mention the weather and its impact on the army, for both the winter of 1777–1778 and the winter of 1779–1780. Because the manuscript is transmitted electronically, pagination is not reliable. Boyle's entries appear in chronological order, however, so citation below should be easy to locate. The section on the 1779–1780 winter at Morristown appears at the end of the manuscript.

25. Boyle, "Weather and the Continental Army." In Elizabethtown, near Morristown, the *indoor* temperature in the morning never rose above freezing for the entire month. (See "The Hard Winter of 1779–1780," available electronically from the Morristown National Historical Park. www.nps.gov/morr/.)

26. Ludlum, *Weather Factor*, 57.

27. Ludlum, *Early American Winters*, 1: 115.

28. Ludlum, *Weather Factor*, 56.

29. Ludlum, *Early American Winters*, 1: 114–116; Ludlum, *Weather Factor*, 56–58; Boyle, "Weather and the Continental Army."

30. Martin, *Narrative*, 147–148.

31. Boyle, "Weather and the Continental Army."

32. Ibid.

33. Washington to magistrates of Virginia, January 8, 1780, in Fitzpatrick, *Writings of George Washington*, 17: 362–363; cited in Boyle, "Weather and the Continental Army."

34. Boyle, "Weather and the Continental Army."

35. Ibid.

36. Washington to Lafayette, March 18, 1780, in Fitzpatrick, *Writings of George Washington*, 18: 124–125. Cited in Ludlum, *The Weather Factor*, 59, and Boyle, "Weather and the Continental Army."

37. Eric P. Olsen, park ranger and historian at Morristown National Historical Park, writes:

> Parts of the Continental Army spent four winters around Morristown during the Revolutionary War. The first two winters featured General Washington and the bulk of the "main" Continental Army. The later two winters did not include Washington and featured only small parts of the Continental Army.

1. January 1777 to May 1777—Washington stays at Arnold's Tavern in Morristown [building no longer exists]. The troops stay in private homes and public buildings spread out from Princeton through Morristown to the Hudson Highlands.
2. December 1779 to June 1780—Washington stays at the Ford Mansion [part of Morristown NHP] and up to 13,000 soldiers camp 5 miles south of Morristown in Jockey Hollow [also part of Morristown NHP].
3. November 1780 to January 1781—The Pennsylvania Line camps in Jockey Hollow while Washington is in New Windsor, NY. The Pennsylvania Line mutinies on January 1, 1780, and most of them leave Jockey Hollow. Later in January/ February 1781 the Pennsylvania Line is replaced in Jockey Hollow by the New Jersey Brigade. The NJ Brigade had been camped further north in New Jersey and had also mutinied but their mutiny, unlike the PA Line mutiny, was suppressed. The NJ Brigade stays in Jockey Hollow until sometime in the Spring/Summer of 1781.
4. Winter 1781–1782. The New Jersey Brigade returns to Jockey Hollow for this winter. (Personal correspondence with author; September 2003.)

38. According to military historian Howard Peckham, about 7,000 American soldiers lost their lives in battle, while 10,000 American soldiers perished from disease. (Peckham, *Toll of Independence,* 130.)
39. Washington to Congress, December 22 and 23, 1777, in Fitzpatrick, *Writings of George Washington,* 10: 183, 195–196.
40. Washington to Congress, December 22, 1777, in Fitzpatrick, *Writings of George Washington,* 10: 183. Washington also was the source of the defining metaphor of the soldiers' plight. On April 21, 1778, he wrote that because the soldiers had no shoes, "their Marches might be traced by the blood from their feet." (Washington to John Banister, April 21, 1778, in Fitzpatrick, *Writings of George Washington,* 11: 291.) William Gordon, in his 1788 history of the Revolution, claimed that Washington had told the story to him personally at a dinner party after the war: "Through the want of shoes and stockings, and the hard frozen ground, you might have tracked the army from White Marsh to Valley-forge by the blood of their feet." (William Gordon, *The History of the Rise, Progress, and Establishment of Independence, of the United States of America,* reprint edition [Freeport, NY: Books for Libraries Press, 1969, first published in 1788], 3: 11–12.) Writers for over two centuries have followed Gordon's lead, using this catchy image to sum up the experience of Valley Forge. Lost in the translation has been a practical aspect of this quaint remark: tracking footprints in those days was a matter of supreme military importance.
41. John Marshall, *Life of George Washington* (London and Philadelphia: Richard Phillips, 1804–1807), 3: 279–282.
42. Mercy Otis Warren, *History of the Rise, Progress and Termination of the American Revolution, interspersed with Biographical, Political and Moral Observations* (Boston: E. Larkin, 1805; reprinted by Liberty Classics in 1988), 1: 389; 3: 268–269.
43. In John Resch, *Suffering Soldiers: Revolutionary War Veterans, Moral Sentiment, and Political Culture in the Early Republic* (Amherst: University of Massachusetts Press, 1999), 72.

44. Mason L. Weems, *The Life of Washington* (Cambridge: Belknap Press, 1962; reprint of ninth edition, 1809), 181–182.

45. Resch, *Suffering Soldiers*, 75.

46. Ibid., 73–74.

47. Salma Hale, *History of the United States, from their first Settlement as Colonies, to the Close of the War with Great Britain in 1815* (New York: Cothins and Hannay, 1830; first published in 1822), 188–189.

48. Charles A. Goodrich, *A History of the United States of America* (Hartford: Barber and Robinson, 1823), 193.

49. From the *Tri-Weekly Post*, Springfield, MA, March 7, 1848. Cited in Boyle, "Weather at Valley Forge," Introduction.

50. Benson Lossing, *The Pictorial Field-Book, of the Revolution* (New York: Harper & Brothers, 1851), 2: 331. George Bancroft, writing in the same era, cemented a place for Valley Forge in America's collective memory. Bancroft devoted a full chapter to "Winter-Quarters at Valley Forge," but only half a paragraph to the winter camp of 1779–1780, without even mentioning Morristown by name. For Bancroft, the secret to the soldier's success at Valley Forge was filial piety: "Washington's unsleeping vigilance . . . secured them against surprise; love of country and attachment to their general sustained them under their unparalleled hardships; with any other leader, the army would have dissolved and vanished." Bancroft played heavily on the contrast between the British and American armies: while Continental soldiers at Valley Forge starved and froze, the Redcoats in Philadelphia danced, gambled, and attended theatrical productions. (George Bancroft, *History of the United States of America, from the Discovery of the Continent* [Boston: Little, Brown, 1879; first published 1834–1874], 6: 41, 46.) Richard Hildreth, writing concurrently with Lossing and Bancroft, gave a more matter-of-fact rendering of the winter at Valley Forge, in keeping with his usual style. Although he detailed the shortages and bemoaned the need for soldiers to forage for their food, he did not glorify their suffering or use it to indulge in effusive displays of patriotism. (Richard Hildreth, *The History of the United States of America* [New York: Harper & Brothers, 1849; Augustus Kelly reprint of 1880 edition, 1969], 3: 231–232.)

51. Lorett Treese, *Valley Forge: Making and Remaking a National Symbol*, published on the Internet site for the Valley Forge National Historical Park, www.nps.gov/vafo/.

52. Allen Bowman, *The Morale of the American Revolutionary Army* (Port Washington, NY: Kennikat Press, 1943), 30; Broadus Mitchell, *The Price of Independence: A Realistic View of the American Revolution* (New York: Oxford University Press, 1974), 117–118.

6: Jefferson's Declaration of Independence

1. Thomas Fleming, *Liberty! The American Revolution* (New York: Viking, 1997), 170–171.

2. Joseph Ellis, *American Sphinx: The Character of Thomas Jefferson* (New York: Alfred A. Knopf, 1997), 56–57.

3. Ibid., 58.

5. Locke was read by the more educated classes. Copies of the *Second Treatise on Government*, which patriots called "Liberty Books," circulated particularly among preachers, who contributed to the spread of Lockean ideas.

6. Franklin P. Rice, ed., *Worchester Town Records from 1753 to 1783* (Worchester: Worchester Society of Antiquity 1882), 244; Ray Raphael, *The First American Revolution, Before Lexington and Concord* (New York: New Press, 2002), 159.

7. Samuel Adams to Joseph Warren, September 25, 1774, Harry Alonzo Cushing, ed., *Writings of Samuel Adams* (New York: G. P. Putnam & Sons, 1907), 3: 159.

8. John Adams to Joseph Palmer, September 26, 1774, and John Adams to William Tudor, October 7, 1774, in Robert J. Taylor, ed., *Papers of John Adams* (Cambridge: Harvard University Press, 1977), 2: 173 and 2: 187.

9. Woody Holton, *Forced Founders: Indians, Debtors, Slaves, and the Making of the American Revolution in Virginia* (Chapel Hill: University of North Carolina Press, 1999), 106–129, 191–205.

10. Holton, *Forced Founders*, 200–205. The turnover in the Virginia Convention was 38 percent, compared with only 10 percent the previous term. (Holton cites Michael A. McDonnell, "The Politics of Mobilization in Revolutionary Virginia: Military Culture and Political and Social Relations, 1774–1783" [D. Phil. thesis, Balliol College, Oxford University, 1995], 95–96.)

11. Charles Lee to Patrick Henry, May 7, 1776, in Holton, *Forced Founders*, 199.

12. Jefferson to Thomas Nelson, May 16, 1776, in Julian P. Boyd, ed., *Papers of Thomas Jefferson* (Princeton: Princeton University Press, 1950), 1: 292.

13. Mason's draft from *Pennsylvania Gazette*, June 12, 1776; Jefferson's draft from Pauline Maier, *American Scripture: Making the Declaration of Independence* (New York: Vintage, 1998; first published 1997) 236–246. At the time, Jefferson thought the work of the Virginia Convention in setting up a new constitution was even more important than that of the Continental Congress, and he suggested Virginia recall its congressional delegates. (Jefferson to Thomas Nelson, May 16, 1776, in Lyman H. Butterfield and Mina R. Bryan, eds., *Papers of Thomas Jefferson* [Princeton: Princeton University Press, 1950], 1: 292.) Jefferson would certainly have scrutinized all the reports emanating from the Virginia Convention, particularly any matter relating to the issue of independence.

14. A list of these documents appears in Maier, *American Scripture*, 217–223.

15. Peter Force, ed., *American Archives, Fourth Series: A Documentary History of the English Colonies in North America from the King's Message to Parliament of March 7, 1774, to the Declaration of Independence by the United States* (New York: Johnson Reprint Corporation, 1972; first published 1833–1846), 6: 933.

16. From the Congress of North Carolina, April 12, 1776, in Force, *American Archives, Fourth Series*, 5: 860.

17. Ibid., 6: 933.

18. Ibid., 5: 1208–1209.

19. Here, for instance, is a list of grievances from the "Declaration of the Delegates of Maryland":

The Parliament of Great Britain has of late claimed an uncontrollable right of binding these Colonies in all cases whatsoever. To enforce an unconditional submission to this claim, the Legislative and Executive powers of that state have invariably pursued for these ten years past a studied system of oppression, by passing many impolitick, severe, and cruel acts for raising a revenue from the Colonists; by depriving them in many cases of the trial by Jury; by altering the chartered Constitution of one Colony, and the entire stoppage of the trade of its Capital; by cutting off all intercourse between the Colonies; by restraining them from fishing on their own coasts; by extending the limits of, and erecting an arbitrary Government in the Province of Quebeck; by confiscating the property of the Colonists taken on the seas, and compelling the crews of their vessels, under the pain of death, to act against their native country and dearest friends; by declaring all seizures, detention, or destruction, of the persons or property of the Colonists, to be legal and just. (Force, *American Archives, Fourth Series,* 6: 1506.)

20. Force, *American Archives, Fourth Series,* 6: 557, 603. Although the other declarations varied in style and length, they were similar in their intent: the time had come for the United States to make a clean break. One example will stand for the rest:

> To the Honourable Representatives of the Province of New-York, in Provincial Congress convened. The humble Address of the General Committee of Mechanicks in union, of the City and County of New-York, in behalf of themselves and their constituents:
>
> GENTLEMAN: We, as a part of your constituents, and devoted friends to our bleeding country, beg leave, in a dutiful manner, at this time to approach unto you, our Representatives, and request your kind attention to this our humble address.
>
> When we cast a glance upon our beloved continent, where fair freedom, civil and religious, we have long enjoyed, whose fruitful fields have made the world glad, and whose trade has filled with plenty of all things, sorrow fills our hearts to behold her now struggling under the heavy load of oppression, tyranny, and death. But when we extend our sight a little farther, and view the iron hand that is lifted up against us, behold it is our King; he who by his oath and station, is bound to support and defend us in the quiet enjoyment of all our glorious rights as freemen, and whose dominions have been supported and made rich by our commerce. Shall we any longer sit silent, and contentedly continue the subjects of such a Prince, who is deaf to our petitions for interposing his Royal authority in our behalf, and for redressing our grievances, but, on the contrary, seems to take pleasure in our destruction? When we see that one whole year is not enough to satisfy the rage of a cruel Ministry, in burning our towns, seizing our vessels, and murdering our precious sons of liberty; making weeping widows for the loss of those who were dearer to them than life, and helpless orphans to bemoan the death of an affectionate father; but who are still carrying on the same bloody pur-

suit; and for no other reason than this, that we will not become their slaves, and be taxed by them without our consent,—therefore, as we would rather choose to be separate from, than to continue any longer in connection with such oppressors, We, the Committee of Mechanicks in union, do, for ourselves and our constituents, hereby publickly declare that, should you, gentlemen of the honourable Provincial Congress, think proper to instruct our most honourable Delegates in Continental Congress to use their utmost endeavors in that august assembly to cause these United Colonies to become independent of Great Britain, it would give us the highest satisfaction; and we hereby sincerely promise to endeavour to support the same with our lives and fortunes.

    Signed by order of the Committee,

Lewis Thibou, Chairman.

Mechanick-Hall, New York, May 29, 1776.

(Force, *American Archives, Fourth Series,* 6: 614–615.)

21. Philip F. Detweiler, "The Changing Reputation of the Declaration of Independence: The First Fifty Years," *William and Mary Quarterly,* Third Series, 19 (1962): 559–561.

22. Maier, *American Scripture,* 165–167; Detweiler, "Changing Reputation," 561.

23. Detweiler, "Changing Reputation," 562.

24. David Ramsay, *The History of the American Revolution* (Philadelphia: R. Aitken & Son, 1789; reprinted by Liberty Classics in 1990), 1: 340–346; William Gordon, *The History of the Rise, Progress, and Establishment of Independence, of the United State of America* (Freeport, NY: Books for Libraries Press, 1969; first published in 1788), 2: 274–297.

25. Charles Warren, "Fourth of July Myths," *William and Mary Quarterly,* Third Series, 2 (1945): 263.

26. John Marshall, *The Life of George Washington* (New York, AMS Press, 1969; first published 1804–1807), 2: 405.

27. Ironically, Marshall described the declaring of independence with a populist slant. "American independence became the general theme of conversation, and, more and more, the general wish," this leading Federalist wrote. "The measures in Congress took their complexion from the temper of the people." Marshall, *Life of George Washington,* 2: 396–404.

28. Mercy Otis Warren, *History of the Rise, Progress and Termination of the American Revolution, interspersed with Biographical, Political and Moral Observations* (Boston: E. Larkin, 1805; reprinted by Liberty Classics in 1988), 3: 307–308. This appears in her concluding remarks. Earlier in the text, Warren wrote that the Declaration was "drawn by the ingenious and philosophic pen of Thomas Jefferson, Esquire." (1: 309.)

29. Irma B. Jaffe, *Trumbull: The Declaration of Independence* (New York: Viking, 1976), 69.

30. Maier, *American Scripture,* 175–176; Detweiler, "Changing Reputation," 572.

31. Jaffe, *Trumbull,* 62–66.

32. Maier, *American Scripture,* 186.

33. Jefferson to Dr. James Mease, September 26, 1825, in Paul Leicester Ford, ed., *Writings of Thomas Jefferson* (New York: G. P. Putnam's Sons, 1899), 10: 346.

34. John Adams to Benjamin Rush, June 21, 1811, in John A. Schutz and Douglass Adair, eds., *The Spur of Fame: Dialogues of John Adams and Benjamin Rush, 1805–1813* (San Marino, CA: Huntington Library, 1966), 182.

35. For Adams's most forceful statements of this argument, see his *Autobiography* and the accompanying letter to Timothy Pickering, August 6, 1822, in Charles Francis Adams, ed., *The Works of John Adams* (Boston: Charles Little and James Brown, 1850), 2: 510–515. Although Adams's memory of the committee was indeed flawed, the fact that the committee met, and that individual members made revisions, is suggested by Jefferson's own correspondence at the time. (See Robert E. McGlone, "Deciphering Memory: John Adams and the Authorship of the Declaration of Independence," *Journal of American History* 85 [1998]: 411–438; and Maier, *American Scripture*, 101–102.) Here is the key piece of contemporary evidence: "Th: J. to Doctr. Franklyn. Friday morn. The inclosed paper has been read and with some small alterations approved of by the committee. Will Doctr. Franklyn be so good as to peruse it and suggest such alterations as his more enlarged view of the subject will dictate? The paper having been returned to me to change a particular sentiment or two, I propose laying it again before the committee tomorrow morning, if Doctr. Franklyn can think of it before that time." (Boyd, *Papers of Jefferson*, 1: 404.) There is no definitive proof that Jefferson's note to Franklin refers to the Declaration of Independence, but according to Julian Boyd, the editor, other possibilities are implausible, while all circumstantial and corroborating evidence points to the Declaration.

36. Boyd, *Papers of Jefferson*, 1: 414.

37. Jefferson to James Madison, August 30, 1823, in Ford, *Writings of Thomas Jefferson*, 10: 266–268.

38. Maier, *American Scripture*, 203–204.

39. Quoted in Garry Wills, *Inventing America: Jefferson's Declaration of Independence* (New York: Doubleday, 1978), xix–xx.

40. Maier, *American Scripture*, 202.

41. Wilson's pamphlet, *Considerations on the Nature and Extent of the Legislative Authority of the British Parliament*, was written in response to the Townshend duties, but since these were repealed in 1770, Wilson did not see fit to publish it until 1774. One paragraph shows a remarkable resemblance to Jefferson's draft of the Declaration of Independence: "All men are, by nature, equal and free: no one has a right to any authority over another without his consent: all lawful government is founded in the consent of those who are subject to it: such consent was given with a view to ensure and to increase the happiness of the governed, above what they would enjoy in an independent and unconnected state of nature." (Wills, *Inventing America*, 248; Carl Becker, *The Declaration of Independence: A Study in the History of Political Ideas* [New York: Alfred A. Knopf, 1948; first published 1922], 108.)

42. Force, *American Archives, Fourth Series*, 6: 514.

43. Ibid., 5: 1206.

44. Wills, *Inventing America*, xxi. Lincoln's argument would have been stronger had Jefferson stayed with Mason's phrase "equally free and independent," instead of paraphrasing the words of James Wilson, who had argued several years before that "all men are, by

nature, equal and free." To Lincoln's contemporary critics, the vague and undefined notion of "equality" was preposterous: people were obviously not equal with respect to all sorts of physical attributes, let alone social position or political standing. Mason's terminology would have eliminated this glib rebuttal: "equally free and independent" makes it clear that people are to be considered equal precisely because they are free and independent. This would have provided a much more forceful argument against slavery, although Mason, like Jefferson, probably had not intended his words to be used to this end. Mason's Declaration of Rights, however, had lost its luster—not because of inferior wording, but because the congressional Declaration had supplanted it in the public mind.

45. For Jefferson's attitudes on miscegenation, see his *Notes on the State of Virginia* (Chapel Hill: University of North Carolina Press, 1955; written in 1781), 138–140. Jefferson's breeding of slaves for profit can be deduced from his letters. On January 17, 1819, Jefferson wrote to his plantation overseer: "I consider the labor of a breeding woman as no object, and that a child raised every 2 years is of more profit than the crop of the best laboring man." The following year he reiterated this little piece of fiscal philosophy: "I consider a woman who brings a child every two years as more profitable than the best man of the farm. What she produces is an addition to capital, while his labors disappear in mere consumption." (Jefferson to Joel Yancy, January 17, 1819, and Jefferson to John W. Eppes, June 30, 1820, in Edwin Morris Betts, ed., *Thomas Jefferson's Farm Book* [University Press of Virginia, 1976] 43, 46. Whenever Jefferson ran into debt, which was often, he could and did sell slaves to meet the demands of his creditors. (Betts, *Jefferson's Farm Book*, 5.) Compromised ethically and politically, Jefferson tried to conceal these embarrassing transactions in human flesh: "I do not (while in public life) like to have my name annexed in the public papers to the sale of property," he wrote—the "property," in this case, being a euphemism for slaves. (Jefferson to Bowling Clarke, September 21, 1792, in Betts, *Jefferson's Farm Book*, 13.)

46. For a discussion of the relation of Lincoln to others who made this argument before him, see Maier, *American Scripture*, xix–xx, 202–203.

47. Vivian Bernstein, *America's History: Land of Liberty—Beginning to 1877* (Austin: Steck-Vaughn, 1997), 81.

48. Joy Hakim, *A History of US*, (New York: Oxford University Press, 2003) 3: 98–100. This is the cornerstone of Hakim's treatment of the American Revolution. The cover copy for volume 3, *From Colonies to Country*, reads: "Read all about it! How the people in thirteen small colonies beat a great and very powerful nation, became free, and went on to write some astounding words that inspired the whole world."

49. See James West Davidson, *The American Nation* (Upper Saddle River: Prentice Hall, 2003), 173; Michael J. Berson, ed., *United States History: Beginnings* (Orlando: Harcourt, 2003), 302; Sterling Stuckey and Linda Kerrigan Salvucci, *Call to Freedom* (Austin: Holt, Rinehart and Winston, 2003), 158. *Common Sense* was indeed popular, selling over 100,000 copies in the winter and spring of 1776. How strange that this staggering figure—one book for every four households—is not deemed sufficient.

50. Jefferson to Henry Lee, May 8, 1825, in Ford, *Writings of Thomas Jefferson*, 10: 343. See

also Jefferson to James Madison, August 30, 1823, in Ford, *Writings of Thomas Jefferson,*
10: 268.

51. Jefferson to Dr. James Mease, September 26, 1825, in Ford, *Writings of Thomas Jefferson,*
10: 346.

7: Founding Fathers: The Greatest Generation

1. Gordon Wood, "The Greatest Generation," *New York Review of Books,* March 29, 2001.
2. David McCullough, "The Argonauts of 1776," *New York Times,* July 4, 2002.
3. Joseph Ellis, *Founding Brothers: The Revolutionary Generation* (New York: Alfred A. Knopf, 2001), 13, 17.
4. Gordon Wood, the nation's most esteemed scholar of the American Revolution, perceives the need to apply some sort of standard. In his essay entitled "The Greatest Generation," he first attests to the founders' foibles:

> Certainly they were not immune to temptations of self-interest that attracted most ordinary human beings. They wanted wealth and position and often speculated heavily in order to realize their aims. They were not democrats, certainly not democrats in any modern manner. They were never embarrassed by talk of their being an elite, and they never hid their superiority to ordinary folk.

So what makes these acquisitive snobs, in Woods's estimation, "the greatest generation"?

> They struggled to internalize the new liberal man-made standards that had come to define what it meant to be truly civilized—politeness, taste, sociability, learning, compassion, and benevolence—and what it meant to be good political leaders—virtue, disinterestedness, and an aversion to corruption and courtier-like behavior.
> Of course, they often did not live up to such standards; but once internalized, these enlightened and classically republican ideals and values to some degree circumscribed and controlled their behavior. Members of this revolutionary generation sought, often unsuccessfully, to be what Jefferson called "natural aristocrats"—aristocrats who measured their status not by birth or family but by enlightened values and benevolent behavior. It meant, in short, having all the characteristics that we today sum up in the idea of a liberal arts education. ("The Greatest Generation," *New York Review of Books,* March 29, 2001.)

Woods's standards are minimal: the founders were "great" because they internalized the values of a liberal arts education and externalized the manners of a finishing school. The thrill is gone. Do members of "the greatest generation" deserve our adulation simply because they tried (but often failed) to be virtuous?

5. Charles Murray, in *Human Accomplishment: The Pursuit of Excellence in the Arts and Sci-*

ences, 800 B.C. to 1950 (New York: HarperCollins, 2003), attempts to quantify and rank people who "have achieved great things." By examining how many times people are mentioned in standard reference works and indexes, Murray claims to distinguish "great accomplishment from lesser achievement." Only by equating "greatness" with "influence" could this method claim any objective validity. It is no accident that Murray does not extend his analysis to the political arena. If he did, Hitler would certainly emerge as one of the greatest humans ever to walk the earth.

6. American Heritage, *Great Minds of History: Interviews with Roger Mudd* (New York: Wiley, 1999).
7. Ellis, *Founding Brothers*, 13.
8. Burr's career was fading, and Hamilton was out of power. Hamilton's ideas had indeed shaped history in very meaningful ways, but whether he would have influenced public policy had he lived into old age is highly conjectural. It is also conjectural whether Alexander Hamilton, who fired the first shot in the duel, meant to hit or miss Aaron Burr. Ellis delves into this subject at great length—an interesting but certainly peripheral question in the annals of American history.
9. Ellis, *Founding Brothers*, 51.
10. Ellis specifically designates the experiences of slaves as peripheral. He takes to task scholars who focus on Revolutionary era slaves like Venture Smith, while "ignoring mainstream politics." Ironically, by claiming primacy for his own style of political history, as opposed to the social history of "marginal or peripheral" slaves, he portrays people "at the center of the national story" who talk *about* slavery as the only significant players in the history of slavery. (Ellis, *Founding Brothers*, 12–13.)
11. David McCullough, *John Adams* (New York: Simon and Schuster, 2001), 129.
12. McCullough, *John Adams*, jacket copy (written by McCullough).
13. John Ferling, *Setting the World Ablaze: Washington, Adams, Jefferson, and the American Revolution* (New York: Oxford University Press, 2000), 306. Here is the entire quotation, the closing paragraph of Ferling's book: "Washington and Adams achieved historical greatness in the American Revolution. In some ways, Adams's achievement was the more impressive. His was the more lonely struggle. Before 1778 he battled for unpopular, but necessary, ends against a recalcitrant Congress. Later, when faced with a menacing isolation in Europe, he struggled against America's most popular diplomat and citizen and refused to quail before an imperious ally in whose clutches the very survival of the American Revolution seemed to rest. He was a 'bold spirit,' as Daniel Webster stated in an address at Faneuil Hall in Boston shortly after Adams's death, a 'manly and energetic' leader who possessed the qualities of 'natural talent and natural temperament' which the Revolutionary crisis demanded. The Revolutionary generation was indeed fortunate to have had Washington and Adams as its greatest stewards and shepherds."
14. McCullough, *John Adams*, 78.
15. Ibid., 90. McCullough also notes that delegates for six states in the Continental Congress "were under specific instructions not to vote for independence." This was true in the early spring of 1776, but over the course of the next few months, all states except New York either instructed their delegates to vote for independence or permitted them to do

so. These changed instructions were not due to debates within Congress, but to pressure from without.

16. John Adams to Benjamin Rush, March 19, 1812, in the Rare Books and Manuscripts Department, ms no. 229 (44), Boston Public Library.

17. John Adams, with his handy breakdown of one-third, one-third, and one-third, is often cited as the definitive source on the strength of Tories, patriots, and neutrals during the American Revolution. In 1815, writing to James Lloyd, he stated that a "full one third were averse to the Revolution. . . . An opposite third conceived a hatred of the English. . . . The middle third . . . were rather lukewarm." (Charles Francis Adams, ed., *The Works of John Adams* [Boston: Charles Little and James Brown, 1850], 10: 110.) Here, however, Adams was speaking not about the American Revolution but about the attitudes of American toward the French Revolution in 1797. Adams showed a penchant for breaking down the population into thirds; writers of history texts, in turn, have shown a penchant for accepting as fact these quick-and-easy assessments, set to paper several decades later by an aging man and taken totally out of context.

18. John Adams to Abigail Adams, July 3, 1776, in Charles Francis Adams, ed., *Familiar Letters of John Adams and his Wife Abigail Adams, during the Revolution* (Boston: Houghton Mifflin, 1875), 193.

19. John Adams to Joseph Palmer, September 26, 1774, and John Adams to William Tudor, October 7, 1774, in Robert J. Taylor, ed., *Papers of John Adams* (Cambridge: Belknap Press, 1977), 2: 173, 187.

20. Samuel Adams to Joseph Warren, September 25, 1774, in *Writings of Samuel Adams,* Harry Alonzo Cushing, ed. (New York: G. P. Putnam's Sons, 1904), 3: 158–159.

21. Abigail Adams to John Adams, October 16, 1774, in Adams, *Familiar Letters of John and Abigail Adams,* 48.

22. McCullough, "Argonauts of 1776," July 4, 2002.

23. Ellis, *Founding Brothers,* 18.

24. Ibid., 16.

8: "Give Me Liberty or Give Me Death"

1. William Wirt, *Sketches of the Life and Character of Patrick Henry* (Philadelphia: James Webster, 1818), 121–123. Paragraph delineations added, and Wirt's descriptive interludes omitted. Emphasis in original.

2. Richard R. Beeman, *Patrick Henry: A Biography* (New York: McGraw-Hill, 1974), xi; Andrew Burstein, *America's Jubilee* (New York: Alfred A. Knopf, 2001), 35, 39. Wirt continued: "[T]he style of the narrative, fettered by a scrupulous regard to real facts, is to me the most difficult in the world. It is like attempting to run, tied up in a bag. My pen wants perpetually to career and frolic it away."

3. Wirt to Adams, January 12, 1818, in Burstein, *America's Jubilee,* 46.

4. Citations here are based on the third edition, published in 1818 by James Webster in Philadelphia.

5. A list of several of these editions appears in Judy Hample, "The Textual and Cultural

Authenticity of Patrick Henry's 'Liberty or Death' Speech," *Quarterly Journal of Speech* 63 (1977): 299. The speech itself was actually exerpted a few months prior to publication of the book in *Port Folio*, December 1816.

6. Wirt to Tucker, August 16, 1815, *William and Mary Quarterly*, First Series, 22 (1914), 252. Cited in Hample, "Textual Authenticity," 300. Unfortunately, the term "verbatim" in this sentence is unclear: does it refer to the speech itself, or merely to the effect it had on Tucker, which Wirt did in fact include in a footnote to his biography? (Wirt, *Patrick Henry*, 122.)

7. Hample, "Textual Authenticity," 298–310; Stephen T. Olsen, "A Study in Disputed Authorship: the 'Liberty or Death' Speech," Ph.D. dissertation, Pennsylvania State University, 1976; Charles I. Cohen, "The 'Liberty or Death' Speech: A Note on Religion and Revolutionary Rhetoric," *William and Mary Quarterly*, Third Series, 38 (1981), 702–717; David A. McCants, "The Authenticity of William Wirt's Version of Patrick Henry's 'Liberty or Death' Speech," *Virginia Magazine of History and Biography* 87 (1979), 387–402.

8. Moses Coit Tyler, *Patrick Henry* (Boston: Houghton, Mifflin, 1887), 126; Hample, "Textual Authenticity," 301.

9. Thanks to the written record (and in this case, the audio and visual record as well), we do know the exact words of Kennedy's exciting conclusion:

> My fellow citizens: let no one doubt that this is a difficult and dangerous effort which we have set out. No one can foresee precisely what course it will take or what costs or casualties will be incurred. Many months of sacrifice and self-discipline lie ahead—months in which both our patience and our will will be tested—months in which many threats and denunciations will keep us aware of our dangers. But the greatest danger of all would be to do nothing.
>
> The path we have chosen for the present is full of hazards, as all paths are—but it is the one most consistent with our character and courage as a nation and our commitments around the world. The cost of freedom is always high—but Americans have always paid it. And one path we shall never choose, and that's the path of surrender or submission.
>
> Our goal is not the victory of might, but the vindication of right—not peace at the expense of freedom, but both peace and freedom, here in this hemisphere, and we hope, around the world. God willing, that goal will be achieved. Thank you and good night.

10. Hample, "Textual Authenticity," 308. The letter was originally published in *Magazine of History*, March 1906, 158.

11. From the *South Carolina Gazette and Country Journal*, June 6, 1775, cited in Woody Holton, "Rebel Against Rebel: Enslaved Vigrinians and the Coming of the American Revolution," *Virginia Magazine of History and Biography* 105 (1997): 171, 176; Woody Holton, *Forced Founders: Indians, Debtors, Slaves, and the Making of the American Revolution in Virginia* (Chapel Hill: University of North Carolina Press, 1999), 149–151;

312 NOTES

Peter Wood, " 'Taking Care of Business' in Revolutionary South Carolina: Republican-
ism and the Slave Society," in Jeffrey J. Crow and Larry E. Tise, eds., *Southern Experience in the American Revolution* (Chapel Hill: University of North Carolina Press, 1978),
282; Ray Raphael, *People's History of the American Revolution: How Common People
Shaped the Fight for Independence* (New York: New Press, 2001), 246.

12. William J. Van Schreeven, Robert L. Scribner, and Brent Tarter, eds., *Revolutionary Virginia: The Road to Independence, a Documentary Record* (Charlottesville: University Press
of Virginia, 1973–1983), 3: 6.

13. Holton, "Rebel Against Rebel," 174.

14. According to the 1787 and 1788 tax records, Patrick Henry owned sixty-six slaves in the
years following the Revolution. This was modest, however, by statewide standards:
George Washington owned 390. (Jackson T. Main, "The One Hundred," *William and
Mary Quarterly,* Third Series, 11 (1954), 376 and 383.)

15. Holton, "Rebel Against Rebel," 174; Beeman, *Patrick Henry,* 70.

16. A photocopy of Henry's warning is reprinted in Beeman, *Patrick Henry,* insert between
pp. 57 and 59. Some historians portray Henry as being soft on slavery, based on a single
letter he wrote in 1773: "Is it not amazing, that at a time, when ye Rights of Humanity are
defined & understood with precision, in a Country above all others fond of Liberty, that
in such an Age, & such a Country we find Men, professing a Religion ye most humane,
mild, meek, gentle & generous; adopting a Principle as repugnant to humanity as it is in-
consistent with the Bible and destructive to Liberty? . . . Would any one believe that I
am Master of Slaves of my own purchase! I am drawn by ye general inconvenience of
living without them, I will not, I cannot justify it. However culpable my Conduct, I will
so far pay my devoir to Virtue, as to own the excellence & rectitude of her Precepts, & to
lament my want of conforming to them." (Robert D. Meade, *Patrick Henry: Patriot in the
Making* [Philadelphia and New York: J. B. Lippincott Co., 1957], 299–300.)

Clearly, Henry understood the inherent evils of slavery, but over the course of three
decades of public service—as a state legislator, governor, and representative to the Continental Congress—he made no moves to further the sentiments he voiced in 1773, while
he did take actions to defend the institution of slavery. In May 1776, Henry served on the
committee that drafted the Virginia Declaration of Rights, which stated in its first article
that "all men are born equally free and independent." Some of the more astute delegates
were distressed by these dangerous words, which they feared could be used in the future
to justify the abolition of slavery. The bill was sent back to committee "to vary the language, as not to involve the necessity of emancipating the slaves." The committee soon
reported back: although all men are born free and independent, they can claim their
rights only "when they enter into a state of society"—and slaves, of course, were not
"part of the society to which the declaration applied." Apparently, this bit of sophistry
quieted the dissent. (Henry Mayer, *Son of Thunder* [New York: Franklin Watts, 1986],
300–301; Beeman, *Patrick Henry,* 101–102.)

Henry did oppose the African slave trade, but this position, supported by most Virginia slaveholders, served their economic interests: since Virginia was the primary sup-
plier of slaves to the rest of the states, they naturally opposed foreign competition. In

1785 Patrick Henry supported a bill prohibiting slave importation; this bill, passed by and for the Virginia gentry, included one provision which prevented slaves from testifying in court and another which allowed them to be punished "with stripes" for gathering in groups or leaving home without a pass. The net effect was to tighten control over the slaves that were already there.

In 1788, during the ratification debates, Henry complained that the proposed Constitution did not provide adequate safeguards against emancipation. Slavery, he insisted, was strictly a local issue, yet the Constitution failed to guarantee that it would be treated that way. Under the "necessary and proper" clause, he feared, Congress could tax slavery so heavily that masters would be forced to free their slaves.

In his will, Henry allowed his wife Dolly, "if she chooses," to "set free one or two of my slaves"—cautious words indeed from such a flamboyant defender of freedom (Henry Mayer, *Son of Thunder,* 473.) By contrast, Patrick's sister Elizabeth stated as her last wishes: "Whereas by the wrongdoing of man it hath been the unfortunate lot of the following negroes to be Slaves for life, to wit, Nina, Adam, Nancy senr, Nancy, Kitty and Selah. And whereas believing the same have come unto my possession by the direction of providence, and conceiving from the clearest conviction of my conscience aided by the power of a good and just God, that it is both sinful and unjust, as they are by nature equally free with myself, to continue them in Slavery I do therefore by these presents, under the influence of a duty I not only owe my own conscience, but the just God who made us all, make free the said Negros, hoping while they are free of man they will faithfully serve their MAKER through the merits of CHRIST." (Meade, *Patrick Henry,* 312–313.) Here was some fire, the sort of passion that her brother managed to muster only for the "liberty" of free whites.

17. Holton, "Rebel Against Rebel," 173.
18. Beeman, *Patrick Henry,* 25–28; Holton, *Forced Founders,* 10, 32, 37; Alan Taylor, " 'To Man Their Rights': The Frontier Revolution," in Ronald Hoffman and Peter J. Albert, eds., *The Transforming Hand of Revolution: Reconsidering the American Revolution as a Social Movement* (Charlottesville: University Press of Virginia, 1995), 238.
19. Randolph C. Downes, *Council Fires on the Upper Ohio: A Narrative of Indian Affairs in the Upper Ohio Valley until 1795* (Pittsburgh: University of Pittsburgh Press, 1968), 209; Louise P. Kellogg, ed., *Frontier Advance on the Upper Ohio, 1778–1779* (Madison: State Historical Society of Wisconsin, 1916), 100.
20. Colin C. Calloway, *The American Revolution in Indian Country* (New York: Cambridge University Press, 1995), 202.
21. Beeman, *Patrick Henry,* 123.
22. Wirt, *Patrick Henry,* 65.
23. McCants, *Patrick Henry,* 121–122.
24. Joy Hakim, *A History of US* (New York: Oxford University Press, 2003), 3: 62. Hakim's dramatic rendering is based on a secondhand account, a conversation with a man over ninety years of age, who allegedly recalled the event fifty-nine years after the fact. Hakim and many others have accepted this account, at face value, as trustworthy and accurate. By 1834, when the conversation was reported, Wirt had successfully established

an official "memory" of the speech, which clearly influenced the informant, John Roane. (Tyler, *Patrick Henry,* 129–133; Hample, "Textual Authenticity," 301–302.)

9: "Do Not Fire Till You See the Whites of Their Eyes"

1. Richard Frothingham, *History of the Siege of Boston, and of the Battles of Lexington, Concord, and Bunker Hill* (Boston: Little, Brown, and Company, 1903; reprint edition, Da Capo Press, 1970; first published in 1849), 140.

2. Paul F. Boller Jr. and John George, *They Never Said It* (New York: Oxford University Press, 1989), 106; Tom Burnham, *Dictionary of Misinformation* (New York: Crowell, 1975), 69–70; Lyman C. Draper, *King's Mountain and Its Heroes* (Cincinnati: Peter G. Thomson, 1881), 107.

3. Howard H. Peckham, *Toll of Independence: Engagements & Battle Casualties of the American Revolution* (Chicago: University of Chicago Press, 1974), 130–134.

4. Charles Royster, *A Revolutionary People at War: The Continental Army and American Character, 1775–1783* (Chapel Hill: University of North Carolina Press, 1979), 225.

5. William Moultrie, *Memoirs of the American Revolution* (New York: David Longworth, 1802), 2: 96–97; quoted in John Buchanan, *The Road to Guillford Courthouse: The American Revolution in the Carolinas* (New York: John Wiley and Sons, 1997), 69.

6. Joseph Plumb Martin, *A Narrative of a Revolutionary Soldier* (New York: Signet, 2001; originally published in 1830), 79–80.

7. John Chester to Joseph Fish, July 22, 1775, in Frothingham, *Siege of Boston,* 391.

8. Peter Brown to his mother, June 25, 1775, in Frothingham, *Siege of Boston,* 392.

9. William Prescott to John Adams, August 25, 1775, in Frothingham, *Siege of Boston,* 395.

10. William Tudor to John Adams, June 26, 1775, in Frothingham, *Siege of Boston,* 396.

11. Issachar Bates, *The Revolutionary War* (Old Chatham, NY: Shaker Museum Foundation, 1960; originally published in 1833), np.

12. Ray Raphael, *A People's History of the American Revolution: How Common People Shaped the Fight for Independence* (New York: New Press, 2001), 161.

13. Bates, *The Revolutionary War,* np.

14. "Lieut. Dana tells me he was the first man that fired, and that he did it singly, and with a view to draw the enemy's fire, and he obtained his end fully, without any damage to our party." (John Chester to Joseph Fish, July 22, 1775, in Frothingham, *Siege of Boston,* 390.)

15. Peter Brown to his mother, June 25, 1775, in Frothingham, *Siege of Boston,* 393.

16. These figures are from the official British returns. See Frothingham, *Siege of Boston,* 389.

17. Ibid., 382–384.

18. John Marshall, *The Life of George Washington* (New York: AMS Press, 1969, first published 1804–1807), 2: 239.

19. David Humphreys, *An Essay on the Life of the Honorable Major Israel Putnam* (Hartford:

Hudson and Goodwin, 1788). Putnam, at the time, was almost as renowned as Washington. This was the first biography of an American written by an American.

20. Humphreys, *Israel Putnam*, 103.

21. Mason L. Weems, *The Life of George Washington* (Cambridge: Belknap Press, 1962; reprint of ninth edition, published in 1809), 74–75. Emphasis in original. Weems did not have to invent this story; very likely, it was already part of folkloric tradition. Major General Israel Putnam, the protagonist, was a legendary hero, one of the most famous men in America. Not only had "Old Put" served with distinction in the French and Indian War, but he had also been shipwrecked near Havana, held prisoner by the French, and nearly burned at the stake by Indians.

22. Paul Allen, *A History of the American Revolution, Comprising all the Principle Events both in the Field and the Cabinet* (Baltimore: John Hopkins, 1819), I: 259; Charles A. Goodrich, *History of the United States of America* (Hartford: Barber and Robinson, 1823), 158; Salma Hale, *History of the United States, from their First Settlement as Colonies, to the Close of the War with Great Britain in 1815* (New York: Collins and Hannay, 1822), 151; Noah Webster, *History of the United States* (New Haven: Durric & Peck, 1833).

23. Richard Hildreth, *The History of the United States of America* (New York: Harper & Brothers, 1880, first published 1849), 3: 83.

24. George Bancroft, *History of the United States of America, from the Discovery of the Continent* (Boston: Little, Brown, and Company, 1879; first published 1834–1874), 4: 615.

25. Frothingham, *Siege of Boston*, 154–164.

26. David Saville Muzzey, *The United States of America* (Boston: Ginn and Co., 1933) 1: 111. Muzzey was the most widely read textbook writer of his, or perhaps any, generation.

27. Louis Birnbaum, *Red Dawn at Lexington* (Boston: Houghton Mifflin, 1986), 241.

28. Robert Lieke, *George Washington's War: The Saga of the American Revolution* (New York: HarperCollins, 1992), 159.

29. A. J. Langguth, *Patriots: The Men Who Started the American Revolution* (New York: Simon and Schuster, 1988), 281; Fleming, *Liberty!*, 140. Both Langguth and Fleming note that the command had been used in the past.

30. Benson Bobrick, *Angel in the Whirlwind: The Triumph of the American Revolution* (New York: Simon and Schuster, 1997), 141.

31. George Canning Hill, *American Biography: General Israel Putnam* (Boston: E. O. Libby and Co., 1858), 148.

32. John A. Garraty and Mark C. Carnes, *American National Biography* (New York: Oxford University Press, 1999), 18: 11–12 and 17: 564–564. The quotation cited in the entry for Putnam is based on a footnote in Frothingham: "Philip Johnson states of Putnam: 'I distinctly heard him say, "Men, you are all marksmen—don't one of you fire until you see the white of their eyes." ' " (Frothingham, *Siege of Boston*, 140.)

33. Writers during the second half of the twentieth century who have stated the distance generally shortened it greatly. Richard Ketchum and Francis Russell, for instance, listed it at 50 feet, or 3 rods—down considerably from the 10–12 rods of the Committee of Safety. (Ketchum and Russell, *Lexington, Concord, and Bunker Hill* [New York: Harper

and Row, 1963], 108.) Even at 50 feet, however, patriots could not have seen the whites of the eyes of the advancing Redcoats.

34. Promotional copy from Amazon.com.

10: Patriotic Slaves

1. For a discussion of Dunmore proclamation, see Ray Raphael, *A People's History of the American Revolution: How Common People Shaped the Fight for Independence* (New York: New Press, 2001), 254–261.

2. For a discussion of Clinton's offer and the response it triggered, see Raphael, *People's History of the American Revolution,* 261–270.

3. Contemporary estimates place the "loss" of slaves in South Carolina at 20,000–25,000. See Abbott Hall, Custom House Report, December 31, 1784, *Papers of Thomas Jefferson,* Julian P. Boyd, ed. (Princeton: Princeton University Press, 1950), 8: 199; David Ramsay, *History of the Revolution in South Carolina* (Trenton: Isaac Collins, 1785), 2: 382. These figures are probably exaggerated. For more realistic estimates, see note 30.

4. W. W. Abbot and Dorothy Twohig, eds., *Papers of George Washington* (Charlottesville: University Press of Virginia, 1983–), Revolutionary War Series, 2: 125, 354.

5. George D. Massay, "The Limits of Antislavery Thought in the Revolutionary Lower South: John Laurens and Henry Laurens," *Journal of Southern History* 63 (1997): 517.

6. The average term for blacks who served was actually four and a half years, not the single year implied by this notice. (Robert Ewell Greene, *Black Courage, 1775–1783: Documentation of Black Participation in the American Revolution* [Washington, DC: Daughters of the American Revolution, 1984], 2, cited in Charles Patrick Neimeyer, *America Goes to War: A Social History of the Continental Army* [New York: New York University Press, 1996], 82.)

7. For the names and ages of seventeen slaves who fled from Washington's plantation in 1781, see Raphael, *People's History of the American Revolution,* 262, 361. In addition, three slaves were known to have fled to the British in 1776. See Casandra Pybus, "Negotiating Freedom in the Revolutionary South," conference on "Class and Class Struggles in North America and the Atlantic World, 1500–1820," Montana State University September 2003; Charles Lincoln, ed., *Naval Documents of the American Revolution* (Washington, D.C.: Government Printing Office, 1906), 5: 1250–1251. For the number of slaves Washington owned, see Jackson T. Main, "The One Hundred," *William and Mary Quarterly,* Third Series, 11 (1954).

8. Benson Lossing, *Pictorial Field-Book of the Revolution* (New York: Harper Brothers, 1851), 2: 779. See also Ramsay, *History of the Revolution in South Carolina,* 2: 382.

9. William C. Nell, *Colored Patriots of the American Revolution* (Boston: Robert F. Wallcut, 1855; Arno Press and New York Times reprint edition, 1968), 7–8. Phillips's remarks were written as an introduction to an earlier draft of Nell's work, published as a pamphlet in 1852.

10. Nell, *Colored Patriots,* 5–6.

11. Ibid., 236–237.

12. The views of staunch abolitionists were echoed by George Bancroft, who always gave a northern slant to his history of the Revolution. Bancroft reported that "more than seven hundred black Americans fought side by side with the white" at Monmouth, and he made a special point of including blacks in his treatment of Bunker Hill: "Nor should history forget to record that, as in the army at Cambridge, so also in this gallant band, the free negroes of the colony had their representatives; for the right of free negroes to bear arms in the public defence was, at that day, as little disputed in New England as their other rights. They took their place not in a separate corps, but in the ranks with the white men; and their names may be read on the pension roles of the country, side by side with those of other soldiers of the revolution." (George Bancroft, *History of the United States of America, from the Discovery of the Continent* [Boston: Little, Brown, and Company, 1879; first published 1834–1874], 6: 142, and 4: 614. Bancroft probably based his Monmouth numbers on the returns of Alexander Scammell, adjutant general of the Continental Army, for August 24, 1778, which identified 755 black soldiers. [Neimeyer, *America Goes to War*, 83].) Bancroft's regional pride was unabashed: while slavery prevailed in the South, the rights of "free negroes" were never questioned in his native New England. But Bancroft failed to mention the next chapter in this saga: within a month of the heroic performance of African-American soldiers at Bunker Hill, Horatio Gates, the adjutant general for the rebel forces, prohibited the recruitment of "any stroller, Negro, or vagabond." (Benjamin Quarles, *The Negro in the American Revolution* [Chapel Hill: University of North Carolina Press], 15.)

13. John Fiske, *The American Revolution* (Boston: Houghton Mifflin, 1891), 1: 178.

14. Edward Eggleston, *The Ultimate Solution of the American Negro Problem* (Boston: Gorham Press, 1913), 127–128.

15. Edward Eggleston, *A History of the United States and its People* (New York: D. Appleton, 1888) and *The New Century History of the United States* (New York: American Book Company, 1904).

16. These are the texts available at the University of California's Northern Regional Library Facility in Richmond: D. H. Montgomery, *The Leading Fact of American History* (Boston: Ginn and Co., 1891); D. H. Montgomery, *The Student's American History* (Boston: Ginn and Co., 1897); D. H. Montgomery, *The Beginner's American History* (Boston: Ginn and Co., 1899); Roscoe Lewis Ashley, *American History, for Use in Secondary Schools* (New York: Macmillan, 1907); David Saville Muzzey, *An American History* (Ginn and Co., 1911); Willis Mason West, *American History and Government* (Boston: Allyn and Bacon, 1913); Henry Eldridge Bourne, and Elbert Jay Benton, *A History of the United States* (Boston: D. C. Heath and Co., 1913); William Backus Guitteau, *Our United States: A History* (New York: Silver, Burdett and Co., 1919); Reuben Post Halleck, *History of Our Country for Higher Grades* (New York: American Book Company, 1923); Rolla Tryon and Charles R. Lingley, *The American People and Nation* (Boston: Ginn and Co., 1927); William A. Hamm, Henry Eldridge Bourne, and Elbert Jay Benton, *A Unit History of the United States* (Boston: D. C. Heath and Co., 1932); David Saville Muzzey, *The United States of America* (Boston: Ginn and Co., 1933); David Saville Muzzey, *An American History* (Boston: Ginn and Co., 1933); David Saville Muzzey, *History of the American People*

(Boston: Ginn and Co., 1934); Harold Underwood Faulkner and Tyler Kepner, *America: Its History and People* (New York: Harper and Brothers, 1934); Ruth West and Willis Mason West, *The Story of Our Country* (Boston: Allyn and Bacon, 1935); James Truslow Adams and Charles Garrett Vannest, *The Record of America* (New York: Charles Scribner's Sons, 1935); Harold Rugg and Louise Krueger, *The Building of America* (Boston: Ginn and Co., 1936); William A. Hamm, *The American People* (Boston: D. C. Heath and Co., 1942); George Earl Freeland and James Truslow Adams, *America's Progress in Civilization* (New York: Charles Scribner's Sons, 1942); Gertrude Hartman, *America: Land of Freedom* (Boston: D. C. Heath and Co., 1946); Robert E. Riegel and Helen Haugh, *United States of America: A History* (New York: Charles Scribner's Sons, 1953).

17. The lack of attention given to blacks during the early years of Jim Crow comes as no surprise, but it is astonishing that the silence continued in the subsequent writings of the Progressives. Despite their interest in the social "revolution" fought on the home front, historians such as Carl Becker, Charles and Mary Beard, and John Franklin Jameson paid little attention to the most fundamental class conflict of all: that between slaves and masters. The Beards chronicled the "desperate struggle" in Virginia "between planters on the seaboard and small farmers of the interior, a struggle which involved nothing less than a revolution in the social order of the Old Dominion"—but the slaves must have sat that revolution out, for they are not included in the tale. The fact that the institution of slavery rigidified in the South ran counter to the Beards' thesis that the American Revolution had brought about "the opening of a new humane epoch." (Charles A. Beard and Mary R. Beard, *The Rise of American Civilization* [New York: Macmillan, 1927] 1: 267, 296.) In a similar vein, Jameson stated that "very substantial progress was made" during the Revolution toward "the removal or amelioration of slavery." (J. Franklin Jameson, *The American Revolution Considered as a Social Movement* [Princeton: Princeton University Press, 1940; first published in 1926], 26.) The flight of slaves to the British was not included as part of the "amelioration" of slavery or the "new human epoch." Although the northern version of the black Revolutionary tale made occasional cameo appearances, the Southern version was entirely left out.

18. George W. Williams, *History of the Negro Race in America, from 1619 to 1880* (New York: G. P. Putnam's Sons, 1883; reprint edition, Arno Press, 1968), 326. Between Nell and Williams, there was one other black historian who gained some readership. In 1867 William Wells Brown recapitulated Nell's work in a book titled *The Negro in the American Rebellion: His Heroism and His Fidelity* (Boston: Lee and Shepard, 1867). Like Nell, Brown ingratiated himself to a white audience by pointing to the patriotic service of blacks; his only major change was to use the term "Negro" instead of "colored."

19. Williams, *History of Negro Race*, 1: 355–359. Although he did include David Ramsay's statement that 25,000 slaves had fled to the British in South Carolina and Thomas Jefferson's claim that 30,000 had escaped in Virginia, Williams accepted at face value Jefferson's version of the story: those who escaped had been cruelly mistreated.

20. Ibid., 1: 384.

21. Carter G. Woodson, *The Negro in Our History* (Washington: Associated Publishers, 1922), 60–61.

22. Ibid., 71.

23. W. E. B. Du Bois, *The Gift of Black Folk: The Negroes in the Making of America* (Boston: Stratford Co., 1924; reprint edition, 1975), 82.

24. John Hope Franklin, *From Slavery to Freedom: A History of American Negroes* (New York: Alfred A. Knopf, 1947), 132–134.

25. Benjamin Quarles, *The Negro in the American Revolution* (Chapel Hill: University of North Carolina Press, 1961).

26. Gary Nash, personal communication, November 2003. For the importance of Quarles's book, see Nash's introduction to the 1996 reprint, published by University of North Carolina Press.

27. Thomas Fleming, *Liberty! The American Revolution* (New York: Viking, 1997), 1–2, 6.

28. For more on the Black Revolutionary War Patriots Memorial Project, see their Website at www.blackpatriots.org.

29. The thirteen texts surveyed were displayed at the 2002 annual conference of the National Council for Social Studies in Phoenix, Arizona. They included six elementary and middle school texts: Sterling Stuckey and Linda Kerrigan Salvucci, *Call to Freedom* (Austin: Holt, Rinehart and Winston, 2003); Joyce Appleby et al., *The American Republic to 1877* (New York: Glencoe McGraw-Hill, 2003); Michael J. Berson, *United States History: Beginnings* (Orlando: Harcourt, 2003); James West Davidson, *The American Nation: Beginnings through 1877* (Upper Saddle River, NJ: Prentice Hall, 2003); Jesus Garcia, *Creating America: A History of the United States* (Evanston: McDougal Littell, 2003); and Hakim, *A History of US*. The seven secondary school texts are: Joyce Appleby, et al., *The American Vision* (New York, Glencoe McGraw-Hill, 2003); Gerald A. Danzer et al., *The Americans* (Evanston: McDougal Littell, 2003); Daniel J. Boorstin and Brooks Mather Kelley, *A History of the United States* (Upper Saddle River, NJ: Prentice Hall, 2002); David Goodfield et al, *The American Journey: A History of the United States* (Upper Saddle River, NJ: Prentice Hall, 2001); John Mack Faragher et al, *Out of Many: A History of the American People* (Upper Saddle River, NJ: Prentice Hall, 2003); Robert A. Divine et al., *America: Past and Present* (New York: Longman, 2003); and Paul Boyer, *American Nation* (Austin: Holt, Rinehart and Winston, 2003).

30. In the late 1780s Jefferson recalled that thirty of his slaves had escaped. (Boyd, *Papers of Thomas Jefferson*, 9: 388–390, 11:16, and 13: 362–364.) Historian Cassandra Pybus has carefully documented twenty-three. (Pybus, "Negotiating Freedom in the Revolutionary South.") Gary Nash states that thirty-five fled to the British. (Gary Nash, personal communication and forthcoming book, tentatively titled *The Unknown American Revolution*.) Lucia Stanton, in *Free Some Day: The African American Families of Monticello* [Chapel Hill: University of North Carolina Press, 2002] reproduces a page from Jefferson's Farm Book that lists twenty-three who escaped. (Three names are blotted out, and ten more are said to have died from smallpox.) We know by a report from Washington's foreman that seventeen slaves ran from Washington's plantation in 1781 and that three others fled in 1776. (See note 7.) According to estimates by patriots after the war, 60,000 slaves fled to the British from three states, but these figures were undoubtedly exaggerated to highlight the losses of their masters, who were trying to avoid payment of debts

to British merchants by claiming that the British had "stolen" their property. The estimates were also very rough: Jefferson, for instance, recalled that thirty slaves had ran from his own plantation, and twenty-seven of these had died of smallpox; by adding the appropriate number of zeroes, this led him to conjecture that in Virginia as a whole, 30,000 had fled and 27,000 had died. (Boyd, *Papers of Thomas Jefferson*, 13: 363; Raphael, *People's History of the American Revolution*, 261–262; Pybus, "Negotiating Freedom in the Revolutionary South.") Despite these gross exaggerations, even the most conservative estimates by modern scholars suggest that well over 10,000 slaves fled to the British in search of freedom, while the total number of blacks who served in the Continental army was only about 5,000—and many of these, perhaps most, were freeman, not slaves. (Pybus, "Negotiating Freedom in the Revolutionary South"; Allan Kulikoff, "Uprooted Peoples: Black Migrants in the Age of the American Revolution, 1790–1820," in Ira Berlin and Ronald Hoffman, eds., *Slavery and Freedom in the Age of the American Revolution* [Charlottesville: University Press of Virginia, 1983], 143–145.) For patriots who were sent back into slavery at war's end, see Raphael, *People's History of the American Revolution*, 284–292.

31. Berson, *United States History: Beginnings*, 310; Hakim, *History of US*, 3: 121; Davidson, *American Nation*, 188. The figure 300 comes either from the estimate of Andrew Sprowel five days after the proclamation or from the number of those who left with Lord Dunmore after the "Ethiopian regiment" had been decimated by disease. Dunmore himself stated that 2,000 came his way. (Raphael, *People's History of the American Revolution*, 256–260.) The mass exodus of tens of thousands occurred later in the war, when slaves found it more viable to escape, but none of the texts mentions the exodus at this later period.

32. Hakim, *History of US*, 3: 121.

33. Raphael, *People's History of the American Revolution*, 293–295. The makers of *The Patriot* were so taken with the Northern version of the African-American saga that they used it in South Carolina, where it has no place. They did not wish to tell the Southern story, even if their movie was set in the South.

34. Thirty-seventh Congress, Second Session, Executive Document 116, *Preliminary Report of the Eighth Census, 1860* (Washington: Government Printing Office, 1862), 12, 137. These figures were reported by slaveowners.

35. See notes 3 and 30.

36. Gary B. Nash, *Race and Revolution* (Madison: Madison House, 1990), 57.

37. Boston King's narrative, which originally appeared in 1798, is reprinted in Vincent Carretta, ed., *Unchained Voices: An Anthology of Black Authors in the English-Speaking World of the Eighteenth Century* (Lexington: University of Kentucky Press, 1996), 351–366. Sections dealing specifically with the American Revolution are reprinted in Raphael, *People's History of the American Revolution*, 272–276.

38. David George's narrative, which originally appeared in 1793, is also reprinted in Carretta, *Unchained Voices*, 333–346. Sections dealing specifically with the American Revolution are reprinted in Raphael, *People's History of the American Revolution*, 276–280.

Raphael includes primary source citations for both the Boston King and David George narratives.

39. For an in-depth treatment of Thomas Peters, see Gary B. Nash, "Thomas Peters: Millwright and Deliverer," in David G. Sweet and Gary B. Nash, eds., *Struggle and Survival in Colonial America* (Berkeley: University of California Press, 1981), 69–85; reprinted in Gary B. Nash, *Race, Class, and Politics: Essays on American Colonial and Revolutionary Society* (Urbana: University of Illinois Press, 1986), 269–282. Nash bases his story on two studies of blacks who sided with Britain: Ellen Gibson Wilson, *The Loyal Blacks* (New York: Capricorn, 1976), and James W. St. G. Walker, *The Black Loyalists: The Search for a Promised Land in Nova Scotia and Sierra Leone, 1783–1870* (New York: Africana, 1976).

11: Brutal British

1. John Buchanan, *The Road to Guilford Courthouse: The American Revolution in the Carolinas* (New York: John Wiley and Sons, 1997), 60, 81–84.

2. Robert M. Weir, " 'The Violent Spirit,' The Reestablishment of Order, and the Continuity of Leadership in Post-Revolutionary South Carolina," in Ronald Hoffman, Thad W. Tate, and Peter J. Albert, eds., *An Uncivil War: The Southern Backcountry during the American Revolution* (Charlottesville: University Press of Virginia, 1985), 74. Tarleton later explained the butchery at the Waxhaws by the fact that he had gone down when his horse was shot from under him, "which stimulated the soldiers to a vindictive asperity not easily restrained." (Buchanan, *Road to Guilford Courthouse*, 85.)

3. Kevin Phillips, *The Cousins' Wars: Religion, Politics, and the Triumph of Anglo-America* (New York: Basic Books, 1999), 162, 638.

4. A. Roger Ekirch, "Whig Authority and Public Order in Backcountry North Carolina," in Hoffman, Tate, and Albert, *Uncivil War*, 107–108.

5. William Pierce to St. George Tucker, July 20, 1781, in Sylvia R. Frey, *Water from the Rock: Black Resistance in a Revolutionary Age* (Princeton: Princeton University Press, 1991), 133.

6. John C. Dann, ed., *The Revolution Remembered: Eyewitness Accounts of the War of Independence* (Ann Arbor: University of Michigan Press, 1990), 188–9. This punishment, called "spicketing," was a brutal variation of the common practice of "picketing," in which the prisoner, like a horse, was merely tied to a stake in the ground.

7. Edward J. Cashin, *The King's Ranger: Thomas Brown and the American Revolution on the Southern Frontier* (Athens: University of Georgia Press, 1989), 27–28.

8. Dann, *Revolution Remembered*, 202–3.

9. Buchanan, *Road to Guilford Courthouse*, 237.

10. Shelby's statement, taken from conversations in 1815 and 1819, appears in Lyman C. Draper, *King's Mountain and its Heroes* (Cincinnati: Peter G. Thomson, 1881), 545. Draper reprints Shelby's complete narrative, as well as the diary of a Huguenot Tory from New York, Lieutenant Anthony Allaire, who recorded the hanging and the trampled prisoners. (Draper, *King's Mountain*, 511–513.)

11. William Gordon, *The History of the Rise, Progress, and Establishment of the Independence, of the United State of America* (Freeport, NY: Books for Libraries Press, 1969; first published in 1788), 3: 231, 456.

12. Ibid., 4: 27, 99–100, 174.

13. David Ramsay, *History of the Revolution in South Carolina* (Trenton: Isaac Collins, 1785).

14. Cashin, *The King's Ranger*, 120, 127, 219.

15. David Ramsay, *The History of the American Revolution* (Philadelphia: R. Aitken & Son, 1789; reprinted by Liberty Classics in 1990), 2: 249.

16. Ibid., 2: 293, 324.

17. Mercy Otis Warren, *History of the Rise, Progress and Termination of the American Revolution, interspersed with Biographical, Political and Moral Observations* (Boston: E. Larkin, 1805; reprinted by Liberty Classics in 1988), 3: 428–429. For a discussion of Warren's treatment of barbarities, with additional citations, see William Raymond Smith, *History as Argument: Three Patriot Historians of the American Revolution* (The Hague: Mouton and Co., 1966), 87–88.

18. Salma Hale, *History of the United States, from their First Settlement as Colonies, to the Close of the War with Great Britain in 1815* (New York: Collins and Hannay, 1830; first published in 1822), 210.

19. John Frost, *History of the United States of North America* (London: Charles Tilt, 1838), 261.

20. George Bancroft, *History of the United States of America, from the Discovery of the Continent* (Boston: Little, Brown, and Company, 1879; first published 1834–1874), 6: 458, 427, 295, 289, 293.

21. Richard Hildreth, *The History of the United States of America* (New York: Harper & Brothers, 1880; first published in 1849), 3: 329.

22. John Fiske, *The American Revolution* (Boston: Houghton-Mifflin, 1891), 2: 182.

23. Claude Halstead Van Tyne, *The American Revolution, 1776–1783* (New York: Harper and Brothers, 1905), 255. This is volume 9 of a 27-volume series titled *The American Nation*, edited by Albert Bushnell Hart.

24. Cited in Gary B. Nash, "The Concept of Inevitability in the History of European-Indian Relations," in Carla Gardina Pestana and Sharon V. Salinger, eds., *Inequality in Early America* (Hanover: University Press of New England, 1999), 280.

25. David Hackett Fischer, "*The Patriot* is to History as Godzilla Was to Biology," *Minneapolis Star Tribune*, July 4, 2000. Originally published in the *New York Times*.

26. Thomas Fleming, *Liberty! The American Revolution* (New York: Viking, 1997), 311. As in *The Patriot*, Fleming focuses much of his attention on Banastre Tarleton, whom he refers to as Britain's most potent "weapon."

27. For a deconstruction of this and other Thomas Brown mythologies, see Cashin, *The King's Ranger*, 120–121, 127, 219–228.

28. Robert Leckie, *George Washington's War: The Saga of the American Revolution* (New York: HarperCollins, 1992), 587–588.

29. Ibid., 583–584.

30. Michael Norris, "Army Awards Veterans Who Stopped My Lai Massacre," Army News Service, March 11, 1998.

12: The Final Battle at Yorktown

1. Joy Hakim, *A History of US* (New York: Oxford University Press, 2003), 3: 146.
2. A. J. Langguth, *Patriots: The Men Who Started the American Revolution* (New York: Simon and Schuster, 1988), 544. Emphasis added.
3. Robert Harvey, *A Few Bloody Noses: The American War of Independence* (London: John Murray, 2001), 412.
4. Washington to president of Congress, October 27, 1781 in John C. Fitzpatrick, ed., *The Writings of George Washington, from the Original Manuscript Sources* (Washington: United States Government Printing Office, 1931–1944), 23: 297.
5. Fitzpatrick, *Writings of George Washington*, 23: 271, 297, 302, 347, 352, 359, 361, 365, 367, 390, 443, 447, 477.
6. Washington to Nathanael Greene, November 16, 1781, in Fitzpatrick, *Writings of George Washington*, 23: 347.
7. Douglas Southall Freeman, *George Washington: A Biography* (New York: Charles Scribner's Sons, 1952), 5: 405, 415.
8. Ibid., 415.
9. Fitzpatrick, *Writings of George Washington*, 24: 315.
10. On August 10, 1782, Washington wrote to Chevalier de Chastellux, "The enemy talk loudly, and very confidently of Peace; but whether they are in earnest, or whether it is to amuse and while away the time till they can prepare for a more vigorous prosecution of the War, time will evince." (Fitzpatrick, *Writings of George Washington*, 24: 496.)
11. Ibid., 25: 42.
12. Washington to James McHenry, September 12, 1782, in Fitzpatrick, *Writings of George Washington*, 25: 151. Four days later he wrote again, "I have no doubt on my Mind of the Kings wishes to prosecute the War . . . as long as the Nation will vote Men or Money to carry it on." (Washington to John Mitchell, September 16, 1782, in Fitzpatrick, *Writings of George Washington*, 25: 166.)
13. Ibid., 25: 265.
14. Freeman, *George Washington*, 438; Washington to Chevalier de la Luzerne, March 19, 1783, in Fitzpatrick, *Writings of George Washington*, 26: 236; Washington to president of Congress, March 19, 1783, Fitzpatrick, *Writings of George Washington*, 26: 238.
15. Freeman, *George Washington*, 5: 513; Piers Mackesy, *The War for America, 1775–1783* (Cambridge: Harvard University Press, 1965), 524–25.
16. Mackesy, *War for America*, 404; Washington to Marquis de Lafayette, November 15, 1781, in Fitzpatrick, *Writings of George Washington*, 23: 341.
17. Mackesy, *War for America*, 461.
18. Howard H. Peckham, *The Toll of Independence: Engagements and Battle Casualties of the American Revolution* (Chicago: University of Chicago Press, 1974), 3–16, 91–92.

19. William Gordon, *The History of the Rise, Progress, and Establishment of Independence, of the United State of America* (Freeport, NY: Books for Libraries Press, 1969; first published in 1788), 4: 196–392.

20. David Ramsay, *The History of the American Revolution* (Philadelphia: R. Aitken & Son, 1789; reprinted by Liberty Classics in 1990), 2: 290, 293.

21. Mercy Otis Warren, *History of the Rise, Progress and Termination of the American Revolution, interspersed with Biographical, Political and Moral Observations* (Boston: E. Larkin, 1805; reprinted by Liberty Classics in 1988), 3: 42–436.

22. John Marshall, *The Life of George Washington* (New York: AMS Press, 1969; first published 1804–1807), 4: 532–537.

23. These four early historians understood well that what started as America's War for Independence had extended to the West Indies and even to Gibraltar, that it had come to involve the major powers of Europe, and that the conclusion to that war could only be understood in this wider context. Strangely, only Gordon, who published in England, included a running account of events in East India—that was simply too far away, even though it seriously impacted British policies with respect to the United States.

24. Mason L. Weems, *The Life of Washington* (Cambridge: Belknap Press, 1962; reprint of ninth edition, 1809), 113.

25. Noah Webster, *History of the United States* (Hew Haven: Durrie & Peck, 1833), 242.

26. John Frost, *History of the United States of North America* (London: Charles Tilt, 1838), 255–257. Although the book was published in London, Frost was an American from Philadelphia.

27. George Bancroft, *History of the United States of America, from the Discovery of the Continent* (Boston: Little, Brown, and Company, 1879; first published 1834–1874), 432–484.

28. I surveyed twenty-three textbooks, published between 1890 and 1955, available at the University of California's Northern Regional Library Facility in Richmond: D. H. Montgomery, *The Leading Fact of American History* (Boston: Ginn and Co., 1891); D. H. Montgomery, *The Student's American History* (Boston: Ginn and Co., 1897); D. H. Montgomery, *The Beginner's American History* (Boston: Ginn and Co., 1899); Edward Eggleston, *The New Century History of the United States* (New York: American Book Company, 1904); Roscoe Lewis Ashley, *American History, for Use in Secondary Schools* (New York: Macmillan, 1907); David Saville Muzzey, *An American History* (Boston: Ginn and Co., 1911); Willis Mason West, *American History and Government* (Boston: Allyn and Bacon, 1913); Henry Eldridge Bourne and Elbert Jay Benton, *A History of the United States* (Boston: D. C. Heath and Co., 1913); William Backus Guitteau, *Our United States: A History* (New York: Silver, Burdett and Co., 1919); Reuben Post Halleck, *History of Our Country for Higher Grades* (New York: American Book Company, 1923); Rolla Tryon and Charles R. Lingley, *The American People and Nation* (Boston: Ginn and Co., 1927); William A. Hamm, Henry Eldridge Bourne, and Elbert Jay Benton, *A Unit History of the United States* (Boston: D. C. Heath and Co., 1932); David Saville Muzzey, *The United States of America* (Boston: Ginn and Co., 1933); David Saville Muzzey, *An American History* (Boston: Ginn and Co., 1933); David Saville Muzzey, *History of the American People* (Boston: Ginn and Co., 1934); Harold Underwood Faulkner and Tyler

Kepner, *America: Its History and People* (New York: Harper and Brothers, 1934); Ruth West and Willis Mason West, *The Story of Our Country* (Boston: Allyn and Bacon, 1935); James Truslow Adams and Charles Garrett Vannest, *The Record of America* (New York: Charles Scribner's Sons, 1935); Harold Rugg and Louise Krueger, *The Building of America* (Boston: Ginn and Co., 1936); William A. Hamm, *The American People* (Boston: D. C. Heath and Co., 1942); George Earl Freeland and James Truslow Adams, *America's Progress in Civilization* (New York: Charles Scribner's Sons, 1942); Gertrude Hartman, *America: Land of Freedom* (Boston: D. C. Heath and Co., 1946); Robert E. Riegel and Helen Haugh, *United States of America: A History* (New York: Charles Scribner's Sons, 1953).

29. Bourne and Benton, *A History of the United States*, 220.

30. West and West, *The Story of Our Country*, 171.

31. The thirteen texts surveyed were displayed at the 2002 annual conference of the National Council for Social Studies in Phoenix, Arizona. They included six elementary and middle school texts: Sterling Stuckey and Linda Kerrigan Salvucci, *Call to Freedom* (Austin: Holt, Rinehart and Winston, 2003); Joyce Appleby et al., *The American Republic to 1877* (New York: Glencoe McGraw-Hill, 2003); Michael J. Berson, *United States History: Beginnings* (Orlando: Harcourt, 2003); James West Davidson, *The American Nation: Beginnings through 1877* (Upper Saddle River, NJ: Prentice Hall, 2003); Jesus Garcia, *Creating America: A History of the United States*; and Hakim, *A History of US*. The seven secondary school texts are: Joyce Appleby et al., *The American Vision* (New York: Glencoe McGraw-Hill, 2003); Gerald A. Danzer et al., *The Americans* (Evanston: McDougal Littell, 2003); Daniel J. Boorstin and Brooks Mather Kelley, *A History of the United States* (Upper Saddle River, NJ: Prentice Hall, 2002); David Goodfield et al, *The American Journey: A History of the United States* (Upper Saddle River, NJ: Prentice Hall, 2001); John Mack Faragher et al, *Out of Many: A History of the American People* (Upper Saddle River, NJ: Prentice Hall, 2003); Robert A. Divine et al., *America: Past and Present* (New York: Longman, 2003); and Paul Boyer, *American Nation* (Austin: Holt, Rinehart and Winston, 2003).

32. Boyer, *American Nation*, 129.

33. Boorstin and Kelley, *A History of the United States*, 97.

13: March of the American People

1. Henry S. Commager and Richard B. Morris, *The Spirit of Seventy-Six: The Story of the American Revolution as Told by the Participants* (Indianapolis and New York: Bobbs-Merrill, 1958), 1295.

2. This phrase comes from Daniel K. Richter, *Facing East from Indian Country* (Cambridge: Harvard University Press, 2001).

3. For a more complete treatment of the internal politics of the Iroquois during the Revolution, see Ray Raphael, *People's History of the American Revolution: How Common People Shaped the Fight for Independence* (New York: New Press, 2001), 193–209.

4. James H. Merrell, "Declarations of Independence: Indian-White Relations in the New

Nation," in Jack P. Greene, ed., *The American Revolution: Its Character and Limits* (New York: New York University Press, 1987), 198.

5. Frederick Cook, ed., *Journals of the Military Expedition of Major General John Sullivan against the Six Nations of Indians in 1779* (Auburn, NY: Knapp, Peck, and Thomson, 1887), 303. This volume contains several firsthand accounts against the "war on vegetables" staged by Sullivan's forces (112–113, 70–77, 172–175). Sullivan follows contemporary usage when he refers to the Iroquois as "the Five nations," ignoring the incorporation of the Tuscaroras in the early eighteenth century.

6. C. A. Weslager, *The Delaware Indians: A History* (New Brunswick, NJ: Rutgers University Press, 1972), 305. The full text of the treaty that offered this alluring suggestion is reprinted in Colin G. Calloway, ed., *The World Turned Upside Down: Indian Voices from Early America* (Boston: St. Martin's Press, 1994), 190–193.

7. Raphael, *People's History of the American Revolution*, 221–222.

8. Cited in Tom Hatley, *The Dividing Paths: Cherokees and South Carolinians through the Era of Revolution* (New York and Oxford: Oxford University Press, 1993), 199–200.

9. William Drayton to Francis Salvador, July 24, 1776, in R. W. Gibbes, ed., *Documentary History of the American Revolution* (New York: D. Appleton, 1857), 2: 29.

10. Williamson to Drayton, August 22, 1776, in Gibbes, *Documentary History*, 2: 32.

11. John W. Caughey, *McGillivray of the Creeks* (Norman: University of Oklahoma Press, 1938), 91–92.

12. The thirteen texts surveyed were displayed at the 2002 annual conference of the National Council for Social Studies in Phoenix, Arizona. They included six elementary and middle school texts: Sterling Stuckey and Linda Kerrigan Salvucci, *Call to Freedom* (Austin: Holt, Rinehart and Winston, 2003); Joyce Appleby et al., *The American Republic to 1877* (New York: Glencoe McGraw-Hill, 2003); Michael J. Berson, *United States History: Beginnings* (Orlando: Harcourt, 2003); James West Davidson, *The American Nation: Beginnings through 1877* (Upper Saddle River, NJ: Prentice Hall, 2003); Jesus Garcia, *Creating America: A History of the United States*; and Hakim, *A History of US*. The seven secondary school texts are: Joyce Appleby et al., *The American Vision* (New York, Glencoe McGraw-Hill, 2003); Gerald A. Danzer et al., *The Americans* (Evanston: McDougal Littell, 2003); Daniel J. Boorstin and Brooks Mather Kelley, *A History of the United States* (Upper Saddle River, NJ: Prentice Hall, 2002); David Goodfield et al, *The American Journey: A History of the United States* (Upper Saddle River, NJ: Prentice Hall, 2001); John Mack Faragher et al, *Out of Many: A History of the American People* (Upper Saddle River, NJ: Prentice Hall, 2003); Robert A. Divine et al., *America: Past and Present* (New York: Longman, 2003); and Paul Boyer, *American Nation* (Austin: Holt, Rinehart and Winston, 2003).

13. These are the texts available at the University of California's Northern Regional Library Facility in Richmond: D. H. Montgomery, *The Leading Fact of American History* (Boston: Ginn and Co., 1891); D. H. Montgomery, *The Student's American History* (Boston: Ginn and Co., 1897); D. H. Montgomery, *The Beginner's American History* (Boston: Ginn and Co., 1899); Edward Eggleston, *The New Century History of the United States* (New York: American Book Company, 1904); Roscoe Lewis Ashley, *American History, for Use in Sec-*

ondary Schools (New York: Macmillan, 1907); David Saville Muzzey, *An American History* (Ginn and Co., 1911); Willis Mason West, *American History and Government* (Boston: Allyn and Bacon, 1913); Henry Eldridge Bourne and Elbert Jay Benton, *A History of the United States* (Boston: D. C. Heath and Co., 1913); William Backus Guitteau, *Our United States: A History* (New York: Silver, Burdett and Co., 1919); Reuben Post Halleck, *History of Our Country for Higher Grades* (New York: American Book Company, 1923); Rolla Tryon and Charles R. Lingley, *The American People and Nation* (Boston: Ginn and Co., 1927); William A. Hamm, Henry Eldridge Bourne, and Elbert Jay Benton, *A Unit History of the United States* (Boston: D. C. Heath and Co., 1932); David Saville Muzzey, *The United States of America* (Boston: Ginn and Co., 1933); David Saville Muzzey, *An American History* (Boston: Ginn and Co., 1933); David Saville Muzzey, *History of the American People* (Boston: Ginn and Co., 1934); Harold Underwood Faulkner and Tyler Kepner, *America: Its History and People* (New York: Harper and Brothers, 1934); Ruth West and Willis Mason West, *The Story of Our Country* (Boston: Allyn and Bacon, 1935); James Truslow Adams and Charles Garrett Vannest, *The Record of America* (New York: Charles Scribner's Sons, 1935); Harold Rugg and Louise Krueger, *The Building of America* (Boston: Ginn and Co., 1936); William A. Hamm, *The American People* (Boston: D. C. Heath and Co., 1942); George Earl Freeland and James Truslow Adams, *America's Progress in Civilization* (New York: Charles Scribner's Sons, 1942); Gertrude Hartman, *America: Land of Freedom* (Boston: D. C. Heath and Co., 1946); Robert E. Riegel and Helen Haugh, *United States of America: A History* (New York: Charles Scribner's Sons, 1953). The three that mention Sullivan are Eggleston (1904), Guitteau (1919), and Halleck (1923). The latter two devote only a single sentence; only Eggleston describes the nature of Sullivan's campaign.

14. Halleck, *History of Our Country*, 206.
15. Muzzey, *History of the American People*, 145.
16. Freeland and Adams, *America's Progress in Civilization*, 189.
17. Guitteau, *Our United States*, 191.
18. These texts are listed in note 12.
19. Richard White, *The Middle Ground: Indians, Empires, and Republics in the Great Lakes Region, 1650–1815* (Cambridge and New York: Cambridge University Press, 1991), 376. Cited from Clark's *Memoir*. A slightly modified version of the *Memoir* has recently been published under the title *The Conquest of the Illinois*, Milo Milton Quaffe, ed. (Carbondale and Edwardsville: Southern Illinois University Press, 2001), 147.
20. Colin G. Calloway, *The American Revolution in Indian Country: Crisis and Diversity in Native American Communities* (Cambridge and New York: Cambridge University Press, 1995), 54.
21. Hakim, *History of US*, 3: 133.
22. The college texts are James L. Roark et al., *The American Promise: A History of the United States* (Boston: Bedford/St. Martin's, 2002); Gary B. Nash and Julie Roy Jeffrey, *The American People: Creating a Nation and a Society* (New York: Addison Wesley, 2001); and Mary Beth Norton et al., *A People and a Nation: A History of the United States* (Boston: Houghton Mifflin, 1990).

23. Roark, *American Promise*, 205.

24. Bourne and Benton, *History of the United States*, 211.

25. Montgomery, *Beginner's American History*, 131.

26. Appleby et al., *American Republic*, 196.

27. Hakim, *History of US*, 3: 151.

28. Technically, the act applied only to land "which has been purchased of the Indian inhabitants." This requirement was repeatedly and increasingly ignored. In 1851, for instance, when government agents in California negotiated eighteen treaties to purchase Indian land, the treaties were unanimously rejected by the Senate. The land already belonged to the government, opponents of the treaty argued, by a treaty with Mexico, which had supposedly relinquished territory it never settled or even controlled. Since government ownership was simply *assumed*, land could be divided and sold at will. (See Ray Raphael, *Little White Father: Redick McKee on the California Frontier* [Eureka, CA: Humboldt Country Historical Society, 1993].)

29. These are the texts from the 2002 NCSS conference, as listed in note 12. One, *The American Journey* (Prentice Hall), does mention Alexander McGillivray, but only as an ally of Spain. The authors engage in a lengthy discussion of the struggles between Spain and the United States over control of the Mississippi, but other than the brief mention of McGillivray, they make no mention of Indians or their attempts to keep their lands.

30. Washington to John Posey, June 24, 1767. W. W. Abbott and Dorothy Twohig, eds., *The Papers of George Washington* (Charlottesville: University Press of Virginia, 1993), Colonial Series, 8: 3. Cited in Woody Holton, *Forced Founders, Indians, Debtors, Slaves, and the Making of the American Revolution in Virginia* (Chapel Hill: University of North Carolina Press, 1999), 3.

31. Writing to Charles Washington on January 31, 1770, Washington gave detailed instructions concerning his secretive purchase of Western lands: "I should be glad if you woud (in a joking way, rather than in earnest at first) see what value they seem to set upon their Lands, and if you can buy any of the rights . . . at the rate of about five, Six, or Seven pounds a thousand acres I shall be obligd to you, & will pay the money upon demand." (Abbott and Twohig, *Papers of Washington*, 8: 301.) A detailed breakdown of Washington's stake in western lands appears in Abbott and Twohig, *Papers of Washington*, Confederation Series, 1: 91–100. For more on Washington's land interests, see Holton, *Forced Founders*, 8, 11.

32. Holton, *Forced Founders*, 3–13. For Henry's land acquisitions, see chapter 8.

33. Ruth Miller Elson, *Guardians of Tradition: American Schoolbooks of the Nineteenth Century* (Lincoln: University of Nebraska, 1964), 73.

34. Cited in Gary Nash, "The Concept of Inevitability in the History of European-Indian Relation," in Carla Gardina Pestana and Sharon V. Salinger, eds., *Inequality in Early America* (Hanover: University Press of New England, 1999) 275–276.

35. Cited in Nash, "Concept of Inevitability," 277.

Conclusion: Storybook Nation

1. See Michael McDonnell, "National Identity and the American War for Independence: A Reappraisal," *Australasian Journal of American Studies* 20 (2001), 3–17.

2. John Shy, *A People Numerous and Armed: Reflections on the Military Struggle for American Independence* (Ann Arbor: University of Michigan Press, 1990), 26.

3. John Adams to Abigail Adams, July 3, 1776, in Adams, *Familiar Letters of John Adams and his Wife Abigail Adams, during the Revolution,* Charles Francis Adams, ed., (Boston: Houghton Mifflin, 1875), 193–194.

4. Charles Warren, "Fourth of July Myths," *William and Mary Quarterly,* Third Series, 2 (1945): 246. Here are the original journal entries, not included in the first printed version: "July 19. 1776. Resolved That the Declaration passed on the fourth be fairly engrossed on parchment with the title and stile of 'The Unanimous Declaration of the 13 United States of America' and that the same when engrossed be signed by every member of Congress.—Aug. 2. 1776. The declaration of Independence being engrossed & compared at the table was signed by the Members." (John H. Hazelton, *The Declaration of Independence: Its History* [New York: Dodd, Mead and Co., 1906], 204.) The original manuscript of the minutes, in the journals of the Continental Congress, was first consulted by Mellen Chamberlain in 1884. (Warren, "Fourth of July Myths," 245.)

5. Ordinary Americans were primed to celebrate on July 4 rather than July 2 because the broadside of the Declaration, which circulated widely in July 1776, bore the heading, "In CONGRESS, July 4, 1776." The record was altered to conform to this preference.

6. At least seven signers, and possibly several others, were not present on August 2: Matthew Thornton, Thomas McKean, Elbridge Gerry, Oliver Wolcott, Lewis Morris, Richard Henry Lee, and George Wythe. (Hazelton, *Declaration of Independence,* 210–219.) Thomas McKean, the last man to sign, offered convincing testimony that a single act of signing never took place. (McKean to John Adams, January, 1814, *The Works of John Adams,* Charles Francis Adams, ed., [Boston: Little, Brown and Co., 1856], 10: 87–89.) There is some question about whether George Wythe ever signed his own name. "It is unlikely that he personally signed it on his return in the fall, as some delegates did; he had probably authorized a clerk to do so for him when the document was engrossed," writes Robert Kirtland in the *American National Biography* (24: 93).

7. John A. Garraty and Mark C. Carnes, eds., *American National Biography* (New York: Oxford University Press, 1999), 4: 468; 11: 146; 13: 772; 15: 903–904; 18: 911–912; 19: 73; 21: 609; 23: 514, 721; 24: 93; Dumas Malone, ed., *Dictionary of American Biography* (New York: Scribner's, 1943), 4: 235; 17: 284; 18: 325. Even today, all these names appear as signers of the Declaration of Independence in the July 4, 1776, entry of the *Journals of the Continental Congress, 1774–1789,* available on the Internet, http://memory.loc.gov. ammem/hlawquery.html. In the case of Samuel Chase of Maryland, the notion that these men signed the Declaration on July 4, 1776, created an interesting folktale. A few days earlier, Chase had been in Maryland, attending the state convention. Because he supposedly signed the Declaration of Independence on July 4, people thought he must have engaged in a heroic ride that is still immortalized today: "In the next two days he

rode one hundred miles and arrived in Philadelphia just in time to sign the Declaration of Independence." (Margaret Horsnell's entry for Samuel Chase, in Garraty and Carnes, *American National Biography*, 4: 743.) In fact, Chase had fallen ill and didn't arrive back in Philadelphia until July 17. (James Haw, Francis F. Beirne, Rosamond R. Beirne, R. Samuel Jett, *Stormy Patriot: The Life of Samuel Chase* [Baltimore: Maryland Historical Society, 1980], 68.)

8. Wills, *Inventing America*, 341, 351. Emphasis in original.

9. *Independent Gazetteer*, July 11, 1789; cited in Len Travers, *Celebrating the Fourth: Independence Day and the Rites of Nationalism in the Early Republic* (Amherst: University of Massachusetts Press, 1997), 43.

10. Travers, *Celebrating the Fourth*, 49. These orations were generally placed in print, and some became bestsellers.

11. *Independent Gazetteer*, July 8, 1786; cited in Travers, *Celebrating the Fourth*, 56–57.

12. Sarah J. Purcell, *Sealed with Blood: War, Sacrifice, and Memory in Revolutionary America* (Philadelphia: University of Pennsylvania Press, 2002), 20.

13. See William Gordon, *The History of the Rise, Progress, and Establishment of the Independence of the United States of America*, reprint edition (Freeport, NY: Books for Libraries Press, 1969; first published in 1788). Although he did not arrive in Boston until 1770, Gordon was an ardent advocate of republican principles. In 1772 he was elected minister for the Roxbury congregation, in 1774 he preached the Thanksgiving Day sermon for the Massachusetts Provincial Congress, and the following year he was chosen as its official chaplain. His rise to prominence within patriotic circles was meteoric—too much so for John Adams. "Parson Gordon, of Roxbury, spent the evening here," Adams wrote in his diary on September 16, 1775. "I fear his indiscreet prate will do harm in this city. He is an eternal talker, and somewhat vain, and not accurate nor judicious; very zealous in the cause, and a well-meaning man, but incautious, and . . . fond of being thought a man of influence at head-quarters, and with our Council and House, and with the general officers of the army, and also with gentlemen in this city and other Colonies." (Adams, *Works of John Adams*, 2: 423–424.)

Gordon took copious notes throughout the war, always with the intent of publication. Ambitious and talkative, he placed his networking energies at the service of history: he wrote and spoke incessantly with "those in the know," then incorporated what they told him within his narrative. When Gordon finished his work in the mid-1780s, Boston printers vied for the rights to publish the first locally produced chronicle of the War for Independence. But the author chose to publish his magnum opus in England instead of America, and he drew the wrath of both jealous printers and unforgiving ideologues. "A mercenary scribbler," one critic called him. (David D. Van Tassel, *Recording America's Past: An Interpretation of the Development of Historical Sudies in America, 1607–1884* [Chicago: University of Chicago Press, 1960], 40.) Having alienated his American audience, Gordon failed to excite a British readership. His history was a flop—but it was not without influence. Later generations of writers and historians would cite William Gordon as an authoritative source. Since Gordon had lived through the Revolution and talked to all the right people, his words would be accepted as faithful and accurate representations of actual events.

14. See David Ramsay, *The History of the American Revolution* (Philadelphia: R. Aitken & Son, 1789; reprinted by Liberty Classics in 1990). Ramsay was not only a writer but also a Revolutionary activist and politician. He served as a South Carolina state legislator, the president of the state senate, and a delegate to the Continental Congress in the 1780s.

15. David Ramsay, *History of the Revolution in South Carolina* (Trenton: Isaac Collins, 1785), 1:231; cited in William Raymond Smith, *History as Argument: Three Patriot Historians of the American Revolution* (The Hague: Mouton & Co., 1966), 56.

16. See John Marshall, *The Life of George Washington* (New York: AMS Press, 1969; first published 1804–1807).

17. See Mercy Otis Warren, *History of the Rise, Progress and Termination of the American Revolution, interspersed with Biographical, Political and Moral Observations* (Boston: E. Larkin, 1805; reprinted by Liberty Classics in 1988).

18. Although Warren and Gordon focused more on "virtue," while Ramsay and Marshall wanted to strengthen the nation, the goals intermeshed. All four authors were promoting a unified sense of "America" as the embodiment of republican virtue.

19. *Columbian*, IV (March, 1789), 50, cited in Van Tassel, *Recording America's Past*, 36.

20. Van Tassel, *Recording America's Past*, 39; Harvey Wish, *The American Historian: A Social-Intellectual History of the Writing of the American Past* (New York: Oxford University Press, 1960), 41; Michael Krause and Davis D. Joyce, *The Writing of American History* (Norman: University of Oklahoma Press, 1985), 56–60; George H. Callcott, *History in the United States, 1800–1860: Its Practice and Purpose* (Baltimore: Johns Hopkins Press, 1970), 134–138.

21. Marshall did better than the others, perhaps because his title led people to believe they would be reading about the much-idolized Washington. Critics, however, took him to task for wasting two full volumes before getting to the subject promised by the title.

22. Sydney Fisher, "Legendary and Myth-making Process in Histories of the American Revolution," *American Philosophical Society Proceedings*, 51 (1912): 64.

23. Mason L. Weems, *The Life of Washington* (Cambridge: Belknap Press, 1962; reprint of ninth edition, 1809), Introduction by Marcus Cunliffe, xiv.

24. Cunliffe introduction to Weems, *Life of Washington*, xiv; Van Tassel, *Recording America's Past*, 71.

25. There is some controversy as to whether the first edition of his pamphlet was *The Life and Memorable Actions of George Washington*, printed by George Keating of Baltimore, or *A History of the Life and Death, Virtues and Exploits of General George Washington*, printed in Georgetown "for the Rev. M. L. Weems of Lodge No. 50, Dumfries." (Lewis Leary, *The Book Peddling Parson* [Chapel Hill: Algonquin Books, 1984], 84.)

26. Lester H. Cohen, *The Revolutionary Histories: Contemporary Narratives of the American Revolution* (Ithaca: Cornell University Press, 1980), 166.

27. Fisher, "Myth-making Process," 65. Fisher continued: "Reckless in statement, indifferent to facts and research, his books are full of popular heroism, religion and morality,

332
NOTES

which you at first call trash and cant and then, finding it extremely entertaining, you declare with a laugh, what a clever rogue."

28. Weems, *Life of Washington*, 109–110.

29. See David Ramsay, *The Life of George Washington* (Boston: D. Mallory and Co., 1811; first published in 1807).

30. Anonymous, *Stories of the Revolution; Comprising a Complete Anecdotal History of that Great National Event* (Philadelphia: Grigg and Elliot, 1847).

31. Fisher, "Myth-making Process," 56; John Spencer Basset, *The Middle Group of American Historians* (New York: Macmillan, 1917), 103.

32. Noah Webster, *A Collection of Essays and Fugitiv Writings* (Boston: I. Thomas and E. T. Andrews, 1790; reprint edition, Scholars' Facsimiles & Reprints, 1977), 24–5.

33. See Richard Snowden, *The American Revolution Written in the Style of Ancient History* (Philadelphia: Jones, Hoff & Derrick, 1793), 2 volumes.

34. Van Tassel, *Recording America's Past*, 90.

35. See Salma Hale, *A History of the United States from their first Settlement as Colonies, to the Close of the War with Great Britain in 1815* (New York: Collins and Hannay, 1830; first published in 1822), preface.

36. See Garry Wills, *Inventing America: Jefferson's Declaration of Independence* (New York: Doubleday, 1978), 51–52. Wills quoted one of the entries of the 1741 *Chambers Cyclopaedia*: "The REVOLUTION, used by way of eminence, denotes the great turn of affairs in England in 1688."

37. Paul Allen, *A History of the American Revolution, Comprising all the Principle Events both in the Field and the Cabinet* (Baltimore: John Hopkins, 1819), I: iv–v.

38. Benson Lossing, *The Pictorial Field-Book of the Revolution* (New York: Harper & Brothers, 1851), 1: iv–v.

39. See Peter Force and M. St. Clair Clarke, *American Archives* (Washington, DC, 1833–1853).

40. See George Bancroft, *History of the United States of America, from the Discovery of the Continent* (Boston: Little, Brown, and Company, 1879; first published 1834–1874).

41. Richard Hildreth, *The History of the United States of America* (New York: Harper & Brothers, 1880; first published in 1849), 1: introductory "advertisement."

42. John Fiske, *The American Revolution* (Boston: Houghton Mifflin, 1891), 1: vii.

43. Ann Arnold Hunter, *A Century of Service: The Story of the DAR* (Washington, DC: National Society Daughters of the American Revolution, 1991), 15–16.

44. Cited in Arthur Johnston, *Myths and Facts of the American Revolution* (Toronto: William Briggs, 1908), 27–28.

45. For a detailed chronicle and analysis of the battle over "patriotism" between progressive and conservative forces in the late-nineteenth century, see Cecelia Elizabeth O'Leary, *To Die For: The Paradox of American Patriotism* (Princeton: Princeton University Press, 1999).

46. If the choice of a leader is not immediately evident, we often invent one. Almost all American history texts, for instance, discuss a farmers' uprising they call "Shays' Rebellion," which occurred in the wake of the American Revolution. Naturally, readers as-

sume that this rebellion was led by a man named Shays, who must have been a very charismatic person to serve as the namesake for a large protest movement. It wasn't that way. Daniel Shays, an unassuming character, neither initiated the insurrection nor exerted a controlling influence over it. Shays was not even present during the early stages of the uprising. He filled an important role because of his military experience, but he in no way owned or even led the movement, as the term "Shays' Rebellion" implies. Shays himself recognized this when he said to one of his adversaries, General Rufus Putnam: "I at their head! I am not. . . . I never had any appointment but that at Springfield, nor did I ever take command of any men but those of the county of Hampshire; no, General Putnam, you are deceived, I never had half so much to do in the matter as you think." (Robert A. Feer, *Shays's Rebellion* [New York: Garland, 1988; reprint of Ph. D. dissertation, Harvard University, 1958], 212.) The term "Shays' Rebellion," first used by the authorities who opposed it, implies some sort of command by the individual over the group. It belittles the significance of the insurgents themselves, for it connotes a mass of people who simply obey their leader. Implicitly, it steers us away from their real grievances. This distortion is magnified when the rebellious farmers are labeled "Shaysites," as if they belonged to some type of cult.

47. For early formulations of this model, see John C. Miller, *Sam Adams: Pioneer in Propaganda* (Boston: Little, Brown, and Co., 1936); Philip Davidson, *Propaganda and the American Revolution* (Chapel Hill: University of North Carolina Press, 1941). Although current scholars regard the model as simplistic and misleading, it continues to serve as the basis for popular histories and textbooks.

48. This model is espoused in Linda Grant DePauw, "Politicizing the Politically Inert," in *The American Revolution: Changing Perspectives*, William M. Fowler Jr. and Wallace Coyle, eds. (Boston: Northeastern University Press, 1979), 3–25.

49. All the state standards mentioned here can be found on the Internet. According to the Georgia Standards, "key" individuals should include "men, women, and minorities." (The "minorities," in this case, seem to constitute a third gender.) The California Standards require that fifth graders learn to "identify the different roles women played during the Revolution (e.g., Abigail Adams, Martha Washington, Molly Pitcher, Phyllis Wheatley, Mercy Otis Warren)." The wording here belies an individualistic approach, for the term "roles" is equated with the lives of particular personages.

PHOTO CREDITS

INDEX

textbooks (*cont.*)
Declaration of Independence in, 122–24
early, 238–39, 242–43, 258–59
Hakim's *A History of US*, 24, 122, 156,
    237, 281n3, 283n30, 307n48, 313n24
Henry's "liberty or death" speech in, 156,
    313n24
and history education, 269–75
Indians in, 239, 240, 242–43
Jefferson in, 122–24
and lives of key individuals, 270–71,
    273–74, 333n49
Massachusetts Revolution in, 78–79, 80
Molly Pitcher story in, 29–31
Paul Revere's ride in, 23–26, 283n30
and Revolution as war of conquest,
    238–39
and Revolution in the West, 235–39, 240,
    242–43
on slaves and the Revolution, 181,
    185–86, 189
and state content standards, 271–72, 273,
    333n49
Valley Forge winter in, 85–86
on western expansion and settlement,
    238–39, 240, 242–43
Yorktown surrender in, 224
Thacher, Dr. James, 38
Thompson, D. W., 285–86n11, 287n22,
    289n44
Thomson, Charles, 3, 281n1
Thornton, Matthew, 250, 329n6
Tories
and Samuel Adams, 48–51, 54, 59, 62–63
in Congress, 138
and Revolution in the South, 197–205
Transylvania Company, 153
Treaty of Hard Labor, 241
Treaty of Paris, 239, 328n28
Trull, Captain John, 22
Trumbull, John, 3, 45–47, 117, 126, 127, 140,
    170, 210
Tucker, St. George, 148–49, 150, 198

Tudor, William, 162
Tufts, Samuel, 22
Tuscarora Indians, 229, 230

Underground Railroad, 188–89

Valley Forge, winter at, 4, 84, 85–104
and battlefield casualties, 86, 299n2
commemoration of, 103
Continental Army and, 86–92, 93, 95–97,
    98–99, 104
and cruel hand of nature, 86, 102, 104
deaths from disease, 98
desertions at, 89, 90
and Hard Winter in Morristown, 92–98,
    102, 230
historians and, 99–103, 302n50
mutinies and other resistance at, 89–91,
    92
myths of hardships of, 85–86, 89–91,
    96–104
and "patient suffering," 86, 97, 100–103,
    104, 257, 302n50
pillaging at, 89, 99
soldiers' independence and spirit at, 104
temperatures at, 92–93
textbook histories of, 85–86
true hardships of, 91–92, 95–97, 98–99
Washington and myth of, 89–91, 98–99,
    302n50
See also Morristown and "Hard Winter"
    (1779–1780)
Valley Forge National Historical Park, 103
Vanderlyn, John, 242
Vermont, 115, 186
veterans of Revolutionary War, 101–2, 257
Vietnam War, 206
Vincennes, Battle of, 236, 237
Virginia
Dunmore and Revolution in, 151–52
and early declaration of independence,
    110–11
fear of Indian insurrections in, 152–53